LONE FOX DANCING

ALSO BY RUSKIN BOND IN SPEAKING TIGER

A Book of Simple Living: Brief Notes from the Hills
Friends in Wild Places: Birds, Beasts and Other Companions
A Little Book of Happiness
A Little Book of Serenity
A Little Book of Love and Companionship

LONE FOX DANCING

My Autobiography

RUSKIN BOND

Sending my favourite friend an autobiography of my favourite author.... Lots of Love... E
Oct, 2019

SPEAKING TIGER

SPEAKING TIGER PUBLISHING PVT. LTD
4381/4, Ansari Road, Daryaganj
New Delhi 110002

First published in hardback by Speaking Tiger 2017

Copyright © Ruskin Bond 2017

ISBN: 978-93-86338-90-7
eISBN: 978-93-86338-91-4

10 9 8 7 6 5 4 3 2 1

The moral right of the author has been asserted.

Typeset in Minion Pro by SÜRYA, New Delhi
Printed at Sanat Printers, Kundli

All rights reserved.
No part of this publication may be reproduced, transmitted, or stored in a retrieval system, in any form or by any means, electronic, mechanical, photocopying, recording or otherwise, without the prior permission of the publisher.

This book is sold subject to the condition that it shall not, by way of trade or otherwise, be lent, resold, hired out, or otherwise circulated, without the publisher's prior consent, in any form of binding or cover other than that in which it is published.

'There may be no pot of gold at the end of the rainbow, but if a man believes with all his soul that there is, and spends his life in the effort to vindicate that belief, his efforts will surely bring him somewhere at last; perhaps to a brighter goal than even the rainbow's end.'

—*Aylward Edward Dingle,*
A Modern Sinbad

'From none but self expect applause.'

—*Sir Richard Burton*

'Across the boundaries of life and death
There you stand, O friend of mine.'

—*Rabindranath Tagore*

CONTENTS

DEDICATION AND ACKNOWLEDGEMENTS	ix
PROLOGUE	1

PART I

FIRST LOVES	7
AND FIRST FAREWELLS	26
ENTER GRANNY AND THE ENEMA	33
A HUT IN NEW DELHI	44
UNDER THE DEODARS	56

PART II

NIGHT, AND A HAPPY HOMECOMING	69
WINTER HOLIDAYS	77
WHEN ALL THE WARS ARE DONE	89
AT THE GREEN'S HOTEL	105
THE FISHER YEARS AND RELEASE	113
A ROOM ON THE ROOF	123
VOYAGE TO ENGLAND	135

PART III

THE LONELY ISLAND	143
THE LONDON ADVENTURE	151
DOWN TO KEW WITH VU AND GOODBYE TO ENGLAND	163
BEGINNING AGAIN	174
A RELUCTANT DELHI-WALLAH	194

PART IV

LONE FOX DANCING	217
FRIENDS AND LOVERS IN MAPLEWOOD	230
AN END AND A BEGINNING	247
A SAGA OF OLD TIN ROOFS	265
EPILOGUE: A SON OF INDIA	276

DEDICATION AND ACKNOWLEDGEMENTS

This old fox wishes to thank and dedicate this work to Rakesh and Beena, who have looked after him these many years and made it possible for him to write his many stories and books for readers of all ages.

Even a fox needs a family.

And a big thank you to Ravi Singh and his fellow Speaking Tigers for getting the fox out of his burrow and making sure he finishes this full record of his long journey—a journey that has gone on for eighty-three years, sixty-seven of these spent writing.

It is also a good time to say thank you to the friends who have helped me and my loved ones in the recent past: Vishal and Rekha Bhardwaj; Upendra Arora; Mahendra Prasad; Mayuri and Shiven. And to all my readers, young and old and ageless.

May you all prosper and be happy.

PROLOGUE

Yesterday I dreamed again that I was lost in a large city of blinding lights and traffic. I was feeling quite helpless, until a small boy took my hand and led me to the safety of these mountains that I know so well. I wanted him to stay—I was certain I knew him—but he turned and walked away, whistling, hands in the pockets of his khaki shorts, and as I called out to ask his name, I woke up.

Outside the window at the foot of my bed, it was still night, the sky tremendous with stars. I decided I would wait for the faint light of dawn to come slipping over the mountains, turning the sky light grey and blue, and when the first rays of the sun reached my bed, I would bask in the warmth and sleep for another hour.

For many months now, I've been waking up at three or four in the morning. Perhaps it is the dream; and the dream may have something to do with age, for we become like little children when we are old.

Or it could be the muted conversation of some long-departed residents of this house in the living room. I hear them from my small bedroom-cum-study, murmuring in the dark over the clink of teacups and spoons. But they are no bother to me at all. They sound like civilized, contented spirits, and if they had a good life here, they are welcome. Because on balance, I have had a good life too—in this house and others in these hills; in this land where I was born and where I have written my books and found friendship and love, and a family to call my own.

I had a lonely childhood growing up in a broken home and a boarding school in the hills. Later, companions came into my life and went away, often never to return. Or it was I who left them behind and moved on. Then, in middle age, the world embraced me for good—or I embraced it, it is hard to tell the difference—and I have been lucky ever since.

The sparrows that will come at noon to squabble on the

windowsill, the geranium in the old plastic bucket, the elegant king crows sleeping in the oak trees that grow on the surrounding slopes—they are also family. As are the trees, my brothers. I have walked among them, feeling I am a part of the forest; I have put out my hand and touched the grey bark of an old tree, and its leaves have brushed my face, as if to acknowledge me.

For the last thirty-six years, I have lived on the top floor of this windswept, somewhat shaky house on the edge of a spur in Landour. My bedroom window opens onto sky, clouds, the Doon valley and the Suswa River—silver in the setting sun—and range upon range of mountains striding away into the distance. Looking out from this perch on the hillside, I feel I am a part of the greater world; of India and the planet Earth, and the infinite worlds beyond, where all our doubles live, just as we do—with some hope and some love.

Hope, love and pig-headedness. Without these, I would not have survived into my eighties and remained in working order. I have also been lucky by temperament: the things I wanted were not out of reach; I only needed to persevere and remain optimistic. When the weather got rough, I pulled my coat tighter around me, turned up the frayed collar, and waited for the storm to pass. Then the clouds dispersed; splashes of sunshine drenched my writing table, and good, clean words flowered on the pages of my notebook.

It has never taken a lot to make me happy. And now here I am, an old man, an old writer, without regrets.

But I must correct that. I decided long ago to stop trying to grow up; and writers are only as old or as young as their readers. So here I am, a young boy, an old writer, without regrets.

∼

No life is more, or less, important or interesting than another—much of it, after all, is lived inside our heads. I have finally yielded to friends who have been persuading me to write the story of my life, but I am still not convinced it will be of any great value. I can only hope that it is, at least, a curiosity; a record of times gone by, an introduction to some interesting and unsung people, and a glimpse into one kind of writerly life.

Almost everything I have written has been drawn from my own experiences, and in that sense, fragments of my autobiography are scattered everywhere in my novels, stories, essays and poems. But there is more imagination than truth in them. An autobiography must stay closer to the truth—even though memory is unreliable, and certain things must be disguised or omitted in order to avoid hurting people, or embarrassing them unduly.

So this book is about how things happened to me—more or less. It is the story of a small man, and his friends and experiences in small places.

PART I

FIRST LOVES

Sitting in the mountains, I remember the sea: tinsel on a vast field of water, and sunny white sheets billowing in the wind.

I remember a forest of nodding flowers and patches of red, yellow, green and blue light on a wall.

And I remember a little boy who ate a lot of kofta curry and was used to having his way.

My mother always said I was the most troublesome of all her children—an angel in front of strangers, and a stubborn little devil at home. Mothers often say that of their firstborn, who are inclined to look down on the competition, but mine did so with good reason.

Evidence of my stubborn nature must have emerged when I was three or four. Baby photos show me as something of a cherub, always smiling, chubby, charming, cheeky. Visitors wanted to fondle me (or so I was told); fond aunts longed to kiss me. All that fondling and kissing probably contributed to my sensual nature, improved upon by my beautiful chocolate-coloured ayah, who smothered me with kisses and treated me as though I had been born from her own womb. No wonder I became a spoilt brat—and spent half a lifetime compensating for the privilege.

I have a good visual memory, especially of my childhood. In fact, I'm continually surprising myself by what I can remember about my early childhood in Jamnagar: the rich yellow of Polson's Butter; colourful tins of J.B. Mangharam's biscuits, with cherubs and scenes from Indian mythology painted on them; drives in our maroon and black Hillman convertible; and postage stamps from the Solomon Islands—smoking volcanos and cockatoos with big showy crests.

We had a beautiful gramophone, a black, square box-like wonder, which was probably the first love of my life apart from my ayah. It was one of those wind-up affairs, and you had to change the needle from time to time. The turntable took only one 78 rpm record, so you couldn't just relax and listen to an uninterrupted programme of music. You were kept busy all the time—changing records, changing needles and constantly winding the machine vigorously so that it wouldn't fade away in the middle of a song.

I quite enjoyed the whole process, and would work my way through two boxes of records, ranging from my father's opera favourites—arias from *La Bohème*, *Madame Butterfly* and *Tosca*—to the lighter ballads of the currently popular tenors and baritones, like Nelson Eddy. On silent nights, when the lights are out and the hills are asleep, I shut my eyes and imagine I am in the veranda of one of our Jamnagar homes, and I can hear the great Italian tenor Enrico Caruso singing *Recondita Armonia* and *Questa O Quella*...I did not understand what he was singing, but I liked the sound of those words and tried to sing along, much to my father's amusement and delight.

There was also a selection of nursery rhymes put to music, bought especially for me, and including one which began: 'Oh, what have you got for dinner, Mrs Bond?' But this was not a question we asked our Mrs Bond, my mother. She did not have to worry about dinner because we had a khansama, a cook. His name was Osman, and he took care of all our meals. I was a fan of Osman's, because he made the best mutton kofta curry in the world, and told me some very tall tales. Osman and Ayah were my first storytellers—her imagination subtler than his.

Had Osman put as much spice in his curries as he did in his stories, we would have been a household on fire. In the afternoons, when I was usually alone—even the ayah would be outside, talking to my sister's nanny, or taking a nap—I would join Osman in the kitchen as he boiled or chopped or cleaned the meats and vegetables he would later cook for dinner.

A typical story session would go something like this:

'You see this goat we have just slaughtered, baba? He reminds me of the great lion of Junagadh.'

'Where's Junagadh?'

'Two days by foot from this very house, but you can get there in your motor-gaadi in five-six hours. I worked for the Nawab of Junagadh, who took me along when he went hunting, with ten elephants, twenty dogs and a shikar party of fifty–sixty men—he was a very rich nawab, he would get himself weighed in diamonds on his birthday and give them away to his begums...But I was telling you about the great lion. It needed two full-grown goats or one bull every day. It only ate male animals. And when it could not find goats or bulls, it hunted men. Women were safe.'

'Did the lion come to hunt you?'

'No. But it took my masalchi.'

'What's a masalchi?'

'The boy who helped me prepare the meats and vegetables and washed all the dishes. We were part of the hunting party and sharing a small tent. The lion dragged him out by his soft white feet and carried him away. We found his bones in the morning. I beat my chest and cried all day, till all my tears had dried up. And I had to sleep alone the rest of the time we were in the camp. I lit a big fire outside my tent to keep the lion away—someone had told me lions are afraid of fire.'

'Did it stay away, then?'

'No, baba. Lions are not afraid of fire at all. The beast returned and walked around the fire and stuck its head in through the flap of the tent. I was still in mourning for my poor masalchi, and when I saw the lion which had eaten him up, I was very angry. I picked up the big iron tawa on which I was making rotis and hit the beast on its nose. The tawa was hotter than the fires of jahannum, and that son of Satan—'

'What's jahannum?'

'It is where bad people go after they die and are roasted in big tandoors. Little boys who keep interrupting a story go there too.'

'Sorry.'

'So I struck the lion's nose with my tawa and it let out a roar and fell backwards into the fire burning at the entrance, let out another roar, and fled into the jungle. We heard the beast roaring in agony all night!'

'Did the nawab give you a reward?
'No, baba. He was a rich badshah, but not a generous one. Not like our Jam Sahib...'

The 'Jam Sahib' was the ruler of Jamnagar State, his palace just a short walk from where we were staying. The state had a huge retinue of British and Irish advisers and professional people, from architects and accountants to pilots and mechanics. The Jam Sahib had a fleet of Rolls Royce cars—of all the princes of India, he had the largest number. There must have been about fifty, one of which, probably from the collection of his predecessor, was rumoured to have been painted a special pink to match the colour of a maharani's slippers. Rolls Royce had provided the Jam Sahib with an automobile engineer-cum-mechanic from England to look after the cars and he lived in a posh house not far from the palace.

There was a banquet every week for these foreign professionals, and for visiting dignitaries, neighbouring princes, British officials, even famous cricketers—for Jamnagar was the home of Indian cricket. We were invited, and unless there was a good reason that kept us home, we would go—my father out of a sense of duty, my mother because she was bored at home, and I because the desserts were excellent.

But what were we doing in Jamnagar in the first place?

And here I will have to bore you with a little family history.

~

I am not one of those who look up their family trees in order to discover that a great-grandmother was related to the Czar of Russia and that a great-granduncle was probably Queen Victoria's lover. I'm happy to accept that Grandfather Bond was a good soldier (he retired as drill sergeant) and that Grandfather Clerke (my mother's father) helped in the making of solid railway carriages for the Northern Railway. The former had come from England with his regiment when he was seventeen. The latter was born in a place called Dera Ismael Khan, a frontier outpost, where his father was a clerk in the office of the Commissioner, a certain Mr Durand, who drew up the Durand Line between India (the part that is now Pakistan) and Afghanistan.

A foot soldier, Grandfather Bond was always route marching from one cantonment to another, with the result that his four children were all born in different places. My own dear father was born in the hot, dusty town of Shahjahanpur, on July 24, 1896. He was baptized in the same cantonment church where, some forty years previously, the assembly of worshippers had all been massacred at the outbreak of the 1857 rebellion. My father had two brothers, who did not distinguish themselves in any way; but he was a good student, well read, and after finishing school at the Sanawar Military School, he took a teacher's training at Lovedale in the Nilgiris. He moved about the country a good deal, working at various jobs, including a stint as an assistant manager on a tea estate in Munnar, then Travancore-Cochin (now Kerala), and all the while he collected butterflies, stamps, picture postcards, the crests of Indian states, and anything else that was collectible. He used his teaching skills to land tutorial jobs in various princely states where, like E.M. Forster and J.R. Ackerley before him, he taught English, spoken and written, to the young royals before they were sent off to English public schools. He was working for the ruler of Alwar when he met my mother.

He had taken a month's holiday, and was staying at a boarding-house in Mussoorie, the popular hill-station perched on a ridge above Dehradun. It was late summer in 1933, and he was thirty-six years old. My mother was eighteen, and undergoing a nurse's training at Cottage Hospital, on the ramparts of Gun Hill, not far from her old school. They met, had a torrid affair, and very soon I was on my way.

If we are lucky, we love with both heart and body, and I like to think that my parents were lucky. Neither of them spoke of it as a courtship, however, and when I consider the short time they spent together before I was conceived, I wouldn't call it a courtship, either. The season demanded passion, and they happened to find each other; so chance had a greater role to play in my birth than it does in others.

Passionate—and often short-lived—affairs were not unusual in Mussoorie; in fact, they were expected of visitors to this hill station. Shimla, the summer capital of British India, was usually teeming with officials and empire-builders and ambitious young civil servants. As was Nainital, capital of the United Provinces. But Mussoorie was non-official. It was where people came to live their private lives, far from the reproving eyes of their senior officers. Unlike Shimla, Mussoorie was also small, tucked away in a fold of the Himalaya, ideal for discreet affairs conducted over picnic baskets set down beneath the deodars.

But discretion wasn't always required; if rules were broken and scandals erupted, the Queen of the Hills took things in its stride. As far back as 1884, a visiting reporter of the Calcutta *Statesman*, appalled by the 'immoral tone of society up here', recorded that 'ladies and gentlemen after attending church proceeded to a drinking shop and there indulged freely in pegs, not one but many', and that at a fancy bazaar 'a lady stood up on a chair and offered her kisses to gentlemen at Rs 5 each.'

Mussoorie was at its merriest in the 1930s, when another lady stood up at a charity show and auctioned a single kiss, for which a gentleman paid Rs 300—probably the price of a little cottage in those days. It was the year my parents met. My mother told me later that my father had been friendly with her older sister, Emily, whom he had known for some years in Dehradun, where he was a frequent visitor. But things hadn't worked out.

This rather complicated personal history, and the age difference between them, did not prevent my parents from becoming man and wife, although I have never come across a record of their marriage. But they certainly became Mr and Mrs Bond for my baptismal certificate; issued in Kasauli the following year, it gives everyone's names in full: father, Aubrey Alexander Bond; mother, Edith Dorothy; infant son, Owen Ruskin Bond.

I discovered later that it was my father who chose the name

Ruskin. Was it his secret wish that I should become a writer and painter like the famous Victorian John Ruskin? I never did find out. And Owen—the superfluous second name—was also his idea. Owen means 'warrior' in Welsh, so perhaps he wanted me to be both artist and soldier! Well, I did become an artist of a kind. But I am not, and never have been, a brave person. Foolhardy, yes, and certainly stubborn, but not brave. So it's just as well that nobody ever bothered with Owen; the name was soon forgotten.

I'm not very sure why my mother went to Kasauli for the delivery and not to her mother in Dehradun. Discretion seems to me the only logical explanation. In any case, it was perhaps a sensible decision because Kasauli, a quiet little hill station close to Shimla, was a good place to have a baby, and my mother's second sister was living there. Her husband, a doctor, worked in the Pasteur Institute. My father had studied for some years in the Sanawar Military School, a short distance away, and he had friends in Kasauli, including the local pastor, Reverend McKenzie. It was in his church that I was baptized. All among familiars.

Another of my father's many hobbies was photography, and I still have the pictures he took with his Rolleicord camera of the infant Ruskin a few hours old, a day old, two days old, a month old, etc., in the arms of a nurse at the Military Hospital, or at home with my mother or aunt or Mrs McKenzie, the pastor's wife. When I was a month old, we left Kasauli. There was nothing to keep us there. It was simply a good place in which to have a baby. And it was only now that my parents went to Dehra, to spend some time with my maternal grandparents.

My father had found employment with the ruler of Jamnagar, and he left a few weeks later. My mother and I stayed on in Dehradun for a few months before we joined him. I have a picture—taken, perhaps, in a Dehradun photo studio—of me in a pram, surrounded by flowers and bouquets. On the back is a little note: 'With love & a big kiss from your wee son Owen'. It is in my mother's handwriting, and addressed to my father. The affectionate tone is hard to miss; there's a note of comfortable intimacy.

I also have a picture of my mother, a portrait photograph of hers reshot by my father in an arrangement of flowers, which he later hand-painted. So that first year must have been a time of domestic bliss and love. But I was too young to experience it.

~

In Jamnagar, also known as Navanagar, my father started a small palace school for the little prince and young princesses. There were at least five of them, or maybe more; but I remember three or four quite well.

Jamnagar was a little port town in the Kathiawar peninsula on the west coast of India. Small steamers plying across the Gulf of Kutch stopped there, and sometimes large Arab dhows, which made a lovely sight with their great white sails. This part of the country was full of small, independent states, all owing allegiance to the British crown but, for the most part, running their own affairs. Jamnagar was probably the best known of these states because it was, as I have said, the home of Indian cricket.

A previous ruler, Ranjit Singhji, had played Test cricket for England, and with some distinction. His nephew, Duleep, had done the same but had given up playing due to a frail constitution. Promising young players, like Vinoo Mankad, were learning their cricket in Jamnagar. My father was no cricketer, but we dutifully attended most of the cricket matches which involved visiting teams from England or elsewhere; and I was taken along to these games as part of my parents' social obligations. Everyone who mattered would be there—the Jam Sahib (in immaculate sherwanis and churidar pyjamas, when he wasn't on the field himself) and his retinue, his family members and his European and Indian staff, visiting officials, neighbouring princes—and refreshments were constantly being passed around by bearers in smart white turbans.

I don't remember much of the cricket—I was too small to appreciate a batsman's technique or a bowler's guile—but I do remember the refreshments, offered freely at the cricket matches and the birthday parties organized for the children of the royal family, to which all those working for the Jam Sahib would be invited.

'Don't eat too much,' warned my mother, as I helped myself to gulab jamuns, jalebis, rasgullas and laddoos, all washed down with fizzy lemonade, those being the days before cola drinks came to India. But of course I always ate too much, and I would be sick when we got home and I was handed over to my ayah for further admonishment: 'Too many laddoos, too many laddoos, how much baba eats!' and she nicknamed me 'Laddoo' which gradually became 'Ladla' or Sweetheart.

I did not mind being Ayah's Sweetheart. She was a very *comfortable* sort of woman, large and loving, and at the age of four or five I could appreciate her pillow-like structure, soft and yielding and smelling of spices, and my mother's eau-de-cologne.

Eau-de-cologne was the scent of the day, there being nothing else in the shops except something called 'Evening in Paris' which (as I learnt later) was distilled in Aligarh and bottled in Bombay. In the depths of the bazaar you could also pick up little bottles of local perfume—heady stuff, distilled from roses or jasmine, guaranteed to linger on the user for weeks.

Ayah fancied a little eau-de-cologne from time to time, and I would smuggle the bottle out to her. After sprinkling it over her ample bosom and sturdy forearms, the bottle would be surreptitiously returned to my mother's dressing table. Ayah loved me for this little service. 'A friend for the sake of advantage,' as Aristotle put it!

Came the day when my mother couldn't help noticing the very low level of perfume in the bottle.

'Who's been using my eau-de-cologne?' demanded mother bear.

'I used it on the dog,' I said quickly, already a good dissembler. 'She was smelling horribly.'

Poor Beauty, our aging Alsatian, did smell a bit but not too badly. However, she was given a good bath in a Dettol solution, and sulked for weeks, not being fond of bathing.

My own baths took place in a large tin tub. I liked splashing around and flooding the bathroom, and my mother preferred to keep a distance, leaving poor Ayah to take the soaking. Sometimes my father joined me in the bathtub and we would sing sea-shanties together. Shanties were sailors' songs, sung in unison while they were at work on the old sailing ships. My favourite was 'What shall we do with the drunken sailor?' And whenever this question was sung out by my father, I'd sing back: 'Put him in a tub and wet him all over!'

These tub-baths with my father became something of a tradition, and continued for several years, until he was taken from me. He called them 'rucktions'. I don't find this word in the dictionary, so I presume he invented it. 'Creating rucktions'! He enjoyed it as much as I did. Perhaps it took him back to his own childhood. He was usually a serious, quiet sort of person, but on those occasions he would be quite boyish and noisy—and because he was parent and playmate, he was 'Daddy' to me. That was what I always called him. Not 'father' or 'Dad' or 'Papa'. My mother was 'Mum' or 'Mummy', but my father was always 'Daddy'.

Another shanty we sang was 'We're bound for the Rio Grande':

We've a jolly good ship, an' a jolly good crew:
Awa—ay, Rio!
A jolly good mate an' a good skipper too,
An' we're bound for Rio Grande!

Say goodbye to Polly, and goodbye to Sue
Awa—ay, Rio!
And you who are listenin', it's goodbye to you,
An' we're bound for Rio Grande!

I remember the words because we had them on one of our records. That, and 'Five Down Below' and the beautiful, haunting 'Shenandoah':

Oh, Shenandoah, I long to hear you—
Away, you rolling river.

Oh, Shenandoah, I long to hear you—
Away I'm bound to go...

The Jamnagar sea-front was only a twenty-minute drive from our bungalow, and some evenings we visited the little port called Rosi Bundar, which had a retired British naval officer, Mr Bourne, as port commander. My small hand in my father's, we strolled up and down the pier, and I explored with him the harbour and beach, bringing back seashells and cowries of great variety. On one occasion, I brought home a small crab, which lived in a spare bathtub for several days. Osman kept asking if he could cook it, but I wouldn't let him. I was very attached to the crab—for two or three days, I think, and then I forgot all about it. Finally, Ayah took pity on the poor creature and dropped it into a nearby well.

A small British steamer was often in port at Rosi Bundar, and my father and I would visit the captain, a good-natured Welshman who gave me chocolates, a great treat in those days, for Jamnagar was too small a place for Western confectionary shops. I was ready to go to sea with the captain, convinced that chocolates were only to be found on tramp steamers!

One day, Daddy took me for a trip in an Arab dhow. It was a fairly large ship, but it swung about tremendously, and I was quite terrified at first. We sailed down the coast for a couple of hours before being put ashore at one of the smaller ports. I was glad to be back on terra firma. I have always liked having my feet set firmly on the ground.

There was a small aerodrome at Jamnagar, and a couple of the younger royals, who were in their late twenties, liked going up in their two-seater Tiger Moths and performing stunts in the air. A smart young prince invited my mother to join him on one of these flights, and she took me along. Very reluctantly I squeezed into the cockpit beside her, and away we went! He looped the loop, and performed all sorts of aerial acrobatics in that flimsy four-winged contraption, while I screamed loud enough to frighten the gods (if they were listening). When finally we landed, I was heartily sick and quite determined never to get into a plane again.

A week later this same pilot, while showing off in a similar fashion, crashed his plane and was killed. On hitting the ground, the windshield had blown in and decapitated him.

~

We had at least three homes in Jamnagar. First there was a rambling old colonial mansion whose roof leaked every time it rained. After this—or maybe before—a wing of the old palace, which looked like a ruin from the outside but was cool and comfortable inside (though we had to share it with bats and bandicoots). Finally, we moved to the 'Tennis Bungalow', a converted sports complex, which was bright and airy and where we stayed the longest.

Jamnagar was where my habit of walking really began, because it was full of spacious palaces, lawns and gardens. By the time I was four, I was exploring much of this territory on my own. Although I was afraid of aeroplanes and sailing-ships, I was not troubled by birds, beasts or reptiles. The old walls around the palace grounds were infested with snakes of various descriptions, and I saw them often enough on the lawns or the driveway. Envious of their swift gliding movements, I tried crawling about on my belly at home but I wasn't much good at it. Curious though I was, I knew instinctively that if I did not bother them or get in their way, the snakes would keep away and allow me to pass. They did not send me into a panic, as they did Ayah, who would scream '*Saanp, saanp!*' and dash into the house, urging my father or the cook to come out and vanquish the reptile. The snakes seldom entered the house, as they had to climb a flight of steps in order to do so, and most snakes prefer not to exert themselves unduly. Unless, of course, there's a frog or a fat rat in the offing, and then they can move with great speed in order to snap up their breakfast or dinner.

My father's schoolroom and the Tennis Bungalow were located in the grounds of the old palace, which was largely uninhabited, and full of turrets, stairways and mysterious dark passages that I loved to explore. I climbed right to the top of the main tower one afternoon, and discovered a room with glass windows going right round it, and each square pane stained with a different colour. It became my favourite place for days, and I would climb up to look through different panes of glass at a red or yellow or rose-pink or indigo or parrot-green world. It was nice to be able to decide for oneself what colour the world should be! The room was always empty, and it stayed in my memory as a lonely and magical place. Some forty years later, I wrote a story about an ageing princess who had lost her mind and shut herself up in this room after she'd been prevented from marrying the palace gardener. I called it 'The Room of Many Colours'.

I never saw a palace gardener, but if there was one, he must have believed in letting nature take its course. In the old palace grounds we were surrounded by a veritable jungle of a garden. Marigolds and cosmos grew rampant in the tall grass between shady trees. I loved walking among the white, light purple and magenta cosmos flowers, always friendly, nodding to me, inviting me closer. Unlike the roses, which seemed very snobbish to me, perhaps because their thorns prevented me from getting close. An old disused well was the home of countless pigeons, their soft cooing by day contrasting with the shrill cries of the brain-fever bird at night. 'How very hot it's getting!' the bird seemed to say. And then, in a rising crescendo, 'We feel it! We FEEL it! WE FEEL IT!'

Just beyond the palace grounds was the state farm. It had ducks and geese, hens and roosters (which tried valiantly to wake me up at dawn with their loud crowing but failed). My favourite birds were the turkeys, bred mainly for Christmas and New Year banquets, for it was only the Europeans in the state who really appreciated turkey meat. 'Gobble, gobble, gobble!' went the turkeys whenever I passed them. I liked their colourful plumage and naked wattled heads. They were always waiting to be fed. The ducks and geese roamed all over the place but the turkeys had a pen to themselves, as did the pigs—pink, plump, imported all the way from England.

A middle-aged Welsh couple, Mr and Mrs Jenkins, ran the farm for His Highness the Jam Sahib. I don't think they had any children, and they seemed quite happy spending time with each other and the birds and animals, with books and magazines providing some variety. There would be stacks of *Punch*, *Country Life* and *Picture Post* lying about on their veranda. My reading skills were still rather limited, but I liked going through them for their pictures and cartoons. The lurid covers of Edgar Wallace mysteries also attracted me, but it would be a few years before I became an addict of mysteries and detective fiction.

I possessed only two books during those Jamnagar years—a big book of nursery rhymes, and a battered edition of *Alice in Wonderland*. It was by reading *Alice* (with help from my father) that I learnt to read, and my favourite characters were the Mad Hatter, the March Hare, the Dormouse, poor Bill the Lizard, the Cheshire cat, and the philosophical caterpillar smoking his hookah. I could not really identify with Alice, who seemed a superior sort of person.

All this reading happened outside the classroom, because I wasn't enrolled in a school. I did attend some of my father's classes, but more as an observer and entirely at my own whim—whenever I felt like dropping in while I did my rounds of the gardens and the rambling old palace. Among the pupils were the four Jamnagar princesses—Manha, Jhanak, Ratna and Hathi. I would spend a lot of time standing in front of their desks and watch them pore over their readers, with the result that I developed the skill of reading things upside-down. Occasionally, I still read upside-down, when I need exercise for my eyes or when a book begins to get difficult and boring.

The two eldest princesses—who must have been nine or ten—were beautiful creatures, and I had a crush on them. Except that I wasn't sure that they were girls. They were always dressed in bandgala jackets and trousers and kept their hair quite short. When my father told me they were girls, not boys, I found it all a bit confusing. I grew shy and couldn't be as familiar with them as before, and naturally my infatuation with them grew stronger.

Hathi, the youngest princess, was closer to me in age and she was my playmate in that rather informal schoolroom. The little prince, the heir to the throne, not yet in school, sometimes came over to the bungalow to play with me. The sweet-natured son of the Jam Sahib's secretary—a Bengali gentleman with a very plummy accent—was another playmate. And there was my sister Ellen, two years younger to me, whom I would push around the garden on a tricycle. She had been born with some difficulty and had suffered a forceps injury to the brain, which was to affect her development and result in her being almost an invalid for life. These companions and many others are still familiar faces in my father's photographs. How beautiful we are as small children—innocent, untouched by corruption, our faces smooth and unlined—nothing to worry about except baths and hair-cuts and running out of cream biscuits.

My biggest worry was the monthly hair-cut. I hated it. When the barber appeared on the veranda steps, I would run for cover, and Ayah would have to chase me around the house until I was trapped by my mother, wrapped up in a bedsheet, and deposited in a high chair, still struggling and kicking. The barber was a mad-looking fellow who came armed with an unusually large pair of scissors. My tantrums would only make him nervous, and I'd end up looking like one of the mop-haired urchins in a Dandy or Beano comic.

I had a number of bad habits, which included sucking my thumb. Nothing could cure me of this habit, with the result that by the time I was five or six I had buck-teeth. Over the years, the teeth have settled down a little, but I have never quite recovered from those early hair-cuts and my hair is apt to stand on end after a nap or a walk or any public appearance, rather like Stan Laurel's. Just recently I have noticed a number of young men going about with mops of healthy hair standing on end, so it appears I am finally in fashion.

Sometimes, after a particularly traumatic encounter with the barber's scissors, my father would take me to the small cinema in town, where English-language films were shown on special occasions. One of them, which I remember vividly, was *Tarzan the Ape Man*. Tarzan (champion swimmer Johnny Weissmuller dressed in a flapping mini skirt) spoke very little, but he dived off high cliffs into big rivers and swung beautifully from one tree to another with the help of conveniently placed vines and creepers. Back home, I tried swinging from my mother's curtains, only to tear two of them to shreds. I was made to stitch them together again, something I did with considerable help from my ever-loving Ayah.

And here I must pause to tell you a little more about Ayah, my guardian angel, surrogate mother, friend and beloved all rolled into one and wrapped up in a white sari. My mother, young in years and younger at heart, was often away attending the lunch and tea get-togethers that the ladies of the royal household liked to organize, or she would accompany the younger royals on picnics and excursions. My father spent more time with me, but he would be at work through much of the day. I would be left in the care of the servants—all but the ayah provided by the Jamnagar State. I had no objection to the arrangement, because the servants indulged me. Most of all, Ayah.

She was probably from one of the fishing communities of Kathiawar or from the poorer Muslim families from the north of India who worked in Christian and Anglo-Indian households. She must have been in her thirties and was unusually large and broad-limbed for an Indian woman, and shaped like a papaya, expansive at the hips and thighs. I was told she had a family of her own but I never saw them, and she never spoke of them. She was the one I spent the most time with at home—she stayed all day, washing my clothes, giving me a bath and telling me stories in Hindustani about jinns and fairies and the snake transformed into a handsome prince by the loving touch of a beautiful princess.

Ayah had large, rough hands and I liked being soaped and

scrubbed by her, enjoying the sensation of her hands moving over my back and tummy. She could also use those hands very effectively to deliver a few resounding slaps, because I really was a little devil. But her anger vanished as quickly as it came when she saw me break into tears. And then she would break down herself, and cover me with big, wet kisses and gather me into herself, pressing my face to her great warm breasts. To be hugged and kissed, and generally fussed over, is one of the joys of infancy and childhood. My mother was not a physically demonstrative person—the occasional peck on the cheek was enough emotion for her. But Ayah more than made up for it. She would kiss my navel and nuzzle my tummy and tell the other staff, 'I want to eat him up! I want to eat him up!'

Ayah taught me many things. One of these was the eating of paan. I didn't care for the taste—somewhat bitter, because of the betel nut and lime—but I was fascinated by the red juice, which Ayah would spit with great accuracy in different corners of the overgrown garden. When my parents were out, she would make me a miniature paan—I think she added a little sugar in it—and I would chew the paan and sit in the kitchen, gossiping with her and the cook. Before my parents came home, Ayah would rinse my mouth with warm water, and with her rough fingers she would scrub my teeth clean.

I was in love with Ayah—it was a child's love for a mother, but it was also a sensual, physical love. I loved the smell of her skin and her paan-scented breath and her dazzling smile. She was in love with my soft white skin and bathed and dressed me with infinite tenderness, and defended me against everyone, including my parents.

If I swallowed an orange seed, Ayah would say an orange tree would grow inside me. Being an imaginative child, this rather worried me because orange trees, I was told, had thorns on them. I did not want to worry my parents unduly, so I took my problem to Mr Jenkins, who looked serious, thought about it for a few moments, then said: 'Don't worry, it will only be a small tree.'

Still worried, I consulted Osman, who laughed and said, 'Your ayah is just a gapori, don't listen to her.'

'What's a gapori?' I asked.

'One who makes up stories—and exaggerates. Go and tell her you've swallowed a bean.'

I did, and she said, 'Oh, baba, now you'll have a bean-stalk growing inside you!'

'And there will be a giant living in it?' I asked.

She burst into laughter, seeing I'd caught her out.

'Osman says you're a gapori,' I told her. And she and Osman had a terrible fight. She chased him around the house and forgave him only when he said he meant she was a pari, a fairy, not a gapori.

Still, I think I learnt something about telling stories from Ayah, as I did from Osman, although I had no idea that I would become a gapori of sorts one day.

~

My parents quarrelled quite often. Partly it was due to the difference in age and temperament—which must have surfaced after the fire of passion had gone out. Of course, I did not understand this at the time. If they hadn't felt that the brief Mussoorie entanglement had to end in something permanent, they might have been happier people.

There were frequent dinner and marriage parties in Jamnagar—there were many small states in Kathiawar and they were always intermarrying and visiting each other. Mummy would have liked to go. But Daddy preferred his stamp collection…

And a wonderful collection it was, with postage stamps from all over the world, neatly arranged in special albums—an album each for India, Britain, Australia, Ceylon, Zanzibar, and various island nations in the Pacific. Some were recent stamps, others rare issues from the past, and Daddy went about completing sets and mounting them in the handsome albums. Registered letters would arrive from the famous firm of Stanley Gibbons, enclosing samples or purchased items, and the Gibbons stamp catalogues would occupy pride of place on the bookshelf.

Often, of an evening, I would help my father sort through cigar boxes full of loose stamps, while in the background the Italian opera star Gigli would be singing one of his famous arias. Whenever the record finished, I would rush to the gramophone to change the needle and the record.

'Put on something light, Ruskin,' my mother would say. Only then would I realize she had been in the room all along. Perhaps Daddy hadn't noticed her either.

'Put on something light.' But we did not have any fox-trots or rumbas. In my father's collection, only Strauss waltzes came close to anything light. So she taught me to waltz—very clumsily, because it wasn't her preferred style—and we would cavort around the veranda or small drawing-room, in step and in time to the entrancing, lilting *Blue Danube*, *Roses of the South* and *Tales from the Vienna Woods*.

Left alone with Ayah one day, I tried to teach her to waltz too, but she simply collapsed in hysterics on the veranda steps, squealing with laughter at having to indulge in such a barbaric rite.

'Get up, get up,' I said. 'Get up and dance with me.' But she refused and wouldn't stop laughing, and annoyed, I called her 'Ayah-papaya' and then ran like a rabbit.

Later, I put her into a rhyme, which must have been my first literary effort, inspired no doubt by Dandy comics, a big book of nursery rhymes, and Mr Jenkins' farm animals. It went something like this:

> *Gobble-gobble said the turkey,*
> *Honk-honk said the goose.*
> *Cluck-cluck said the little hen,*
> *Squeak-squeak said the mouse.*
> *Clang-clang went our motor-car,*
> *Bang-bang went the wedding band.*
> *Katar-katar went the porcupine,*
> *Tootle-tootle went the train.*

Nothing-nothing said the goldfish,
And the earthworm said the same.
Sleep tight, says Ayah-papaya,
And God protect my little baba.

Notice that most of my rhyming occurred at the beginning rather than at the end of my lines. Already, I was finding it more fun to do things in reverse. Like reading books upside-down, it's a useful skill to have, especially when life begins to get difficult and boring.

AND FIRST FAREWELLS

'Oh, Adolf
You've bitten off
Much more than you can chew,
Come on
Hold your hand out,
We're all fed up with you...'

So sang Arthur Askey, the diminutive British music-hall comedian, shortly after the outbreak of World War II in 1939. My father had bought the record on one of his visits to Bombay, and I enjoyed listening to the jingle on our gramophone. 'Big-hearted Arthur' was of course referring to Adolf Hitler, the German dictator, who had overrun most of Europe with his jack-booted army.

Six years later, Hitler was to realize that he had indeed bitten off much more than he could chew. His army in tatters, he committed suicide in his bunker in Berlin.

But when we were in Jamnagar, the end of the war was not in sight, though of course we were insulated from it. I don't remember hearing much about the war at home. It was many years later that I learnt of the horrors in Europe and East Asia, but also of the Jam Sahib's contribution to the Allied war effort through a remarkable act of humanity. As Poland was invaded by German forces, he opened his doors to refugees from that helpless country. Several hundred children and women who had fled Poland in small ships that travelled from port to port and were denied entry by the authorities everywhere—including the British governor of Bombay—were brought to Rosi Bundar by the Jam Sahib. He put them up in a special camp in Balachadi, close to his summer palace, where they stayed till the end of the war.

The Jam Sahib was one of the few enlightened rulers in pre-independent India, and when Independence came he was wise enough to accept the derecognition of princely states with good grace. One of his neighbours, the eccentric Nawab of Junagadh, fled to Pakistan, taking with him scores of his favourite dogs—he'd kept a few hundred, but had to leave most behind. Fortunately the lions of the Junagadh forests were not affected by political upheavals, and today represent the only lions in existence on the Asian continent.

My father's former employer, the Maharaja of Alwar, in Rajasthan, was another unusual ruler of that era. He kept a menagerie of beasts and would drive them all into an amphitheatre to see what they would do to each other. According to my mother, who lived very briefly in Alwar with Daddy, this maharaja modelled himself on the Roman emperor Nero and took a sadistic delight in watching various animals tear each other to pieces—a tiger mauling a buffalo, a bear wrestling with a python, a young leopard being crushed by an elephant.

This deranged king wanted a son; his wives kept presenting him with daughters. So disgusted was he at the birth of one more girl that he seized the infant and flung her out of a second-floor window. A sentry standing below saw a bundle hurtling towards him, put out his arms and caught the baby. The king was not a cricketer and did not applaud his guard's dexterity; he had the man executed. But the girl survived and lived to be ninety.

These and other tales of the Indian Nero were passed on to me many years later. At the time, I was still in my mother's womb. She and my father thought it best to avoid Alwar and head for safe and sensible Kasauli for my birth.

~

Strange things happened in some of India's princely states in those far-off days.

But not in Jamnagar.

In Jamnagar the princes played cricket or flew aeroplanes. Sanity prevailed. There were turkeys for Christmas. Caruso sang his beautiful arias. We moved around in a Hillman provided by the Jam Sahib, with a driver. And I was pampered and indulged—by the royals, the neighbours and the servants.

But there were very few children for me to play with, except when the little prince sought me out, which was rare, or when the royal children had birthday parties. But there was always Ayah to fuss over me, Osman to tell me improbable stories, the Jenkins to lend me magazines and my father to take me for walks, so that, for several years to come, I was to feel more at ease with adults than with other children. Ellen was the only other child in the house, but the gods in their casual cruelty had decided that she would remain in a kind of limbo all her life, neither child nor adult, and unable to see or walk properly. We'd kept a nanny for her, which allowed us to pretend everything was all right and get on with our lives.

'Ruskin does not play with me,' she would complain to her nanny and I would push her around on her tricycle for some minutes and then run off into the garden, or climb up to the room of coloured windows.

Through it all, my parents' quarrels became more frequent, and this broke the harmony of our life. There would be harsh words and blind, angry shouting. My mother would threaten to go away, or my father would threaten to send her away, and it was all a bit frightening. I felt helpless and insecure, and this feeling of insecurity was to become a part of my mental baggage for the rest of my life. In those early years, there was no one to turn to except Ayah, who laughed it off and said everything would be all right by morning, and she was usually right. Things would settle down soon enough and the usual routine of household life would take over. But not for very long.

Perhaps if there had been family or friends around, there might have been people to help my parents work through the problems between them. Or at least there would have been some distraction. The Jam Sahib preferred employing European people, not so much Anglo-Indians, and there were just a couple of Indians on his staff from outside the state. They were all usually older people, or professionals who preferred to keep to themselves. We had no family friends, and no one from my parents' families would come so far down. I suppose it must have been very isolating for my mother. Unlike my father, she had no experience of living in far-off and humdrum places. She had spent very little time outside Dehradun and away from her large family and circle of friends, most of whom would have been Anglo-Indian.

Jamnagar wasn't a place where a lot happened, and we rarely went out of town. The one excursion I can recall, but vaguely, was a road trip to the neighbouring state of Junagadh in our Hillman. My mother would tell me later about the ruler there—the nawab who kept hundreds of dogs, all with jewelled collars. He arranged elaborate public weddings for them, and when one of them died, he had it buried with full state honours. I don't remember anything of this trip too well; not the dogs, nor the famed mosque with corkscrew towers, nor the lions of Gir. So it may have been an early excursion, when I was a baby. But my mother remembered it; one of the few good memories she had of our time in sleepy Jamnagar.

~

My own memories are of an almost idyllic time, except for the arguments between my parents, when I would look for Ayah, or go out to roam in the garden. There, the cosmos flowers were always happy to see me, but a koel would keep wanting to know who I was. The fights at home sometimes drove me out at night as well. I would sit on the veranda steps, reluctant to go any further into the darkness, but after a while I began to enjoy the rustling sounds in the garden, and the soft hooting of the owls.

And there was of course that wonderful gramophone and its box of records. I could always turn to it when I felt lonely or unhappy or just bored. Wind it up, change the needle, place the record on the turntable—and the room would be filled with the wonderful voice of Chaliapin singing 'The Song of the Volga Boatman'; or Gigli singing 'Santa Lucia'; or dear old Gracie Fields singing 'Over the Garden Wall'. There were about fifty records in the box, and I'd played them all hundreds of times; they'd become real friends and companions.

So that when my father said he'd joined the Royal Air Force and that we'd be leaving Jamnagar, the first thing I asked was, 'Daddy, will we be taking the gramophone with us?'

'Let's see,' he said. 'We can always get another one.'

'No, I want this one,' I insisted. 'We can't leave it behind.'

And so it was agreed that the gramophone would come with us.

'And what about Ayah?' I asked 'Will she come too?'

'You're too big for an ayah now,' he said. 'And while I'm away you'll be in Dehradun with your mother and Granny—you won't be needing an ayah. And besides, your Ayah's home is here in Jamnagar. She has a husband and grown-up children. She can't leave them all behind.'

'Well, can't she bring them too?'

'Your Granny's house isn't big enough for so many people. And sometimes your cousins will be staying there too.' The cousins he referred to were the children of my mother's four older sisters, my aunts Beryl, Enid, Emily and Gwen—the former two from my grandfather's first wife. So far I hadn't seen any of them.

So what did I take with me when we left Jamnagar? The gramophone, of course, although this (fortunately for me, as it turned out) was to stay with my father in Delhi. A couple of books, including the battered old copy of *Alice*. And a pile of comic papers given to me as a parting present by Mr Jenkins.

Unlike most Indian railway stations, the Jamnagar station was a small one, minus the milling crowds that were to be a feature of future railway journeys. We had a compartment to ourselves.

Interesting food items were offered to us from the open window, but I was warned not to eat any of these mouth-watering concoctions. Only a month previously a family friend had got on to the train in Calcutta, hale and hearty, and two days later his corpse had been carried out of the compartment upon its arrival in Delhi. Cholera could take you away within twelve hours. The food served at the station restaurants was usually safe, but somewhat bland and uninteresting. But we had brought plenty of chicken and turkey sandwiches along (courtesy Mrs Jenkins) and a large basket of fruit (courtesy the palace) and a tiffin carrier full of my favourite kofta curry (courtesy Osman).

We were seen off by the palace secretary, and by Mr and Mrs Jenkins, and of course my beloved Ayah who shed copious tears and begged to be taken along.

But the guard's whistle blew, the steam engine gave a snort, and the train moved slowly out of the station. And I never saw Jamnagar or Ayah again.

~

It took almost three days to travel by train from Jamnagar to Dehradun, the lovely garden town in the shadow of the great Himalaya mountains that was to become central to my life. In those days, India was perhaps the best place to undertake a train journey—for train travel at its best is all about romance; about the great outdoors, where anything can happen.

The trains were not as crowded then as they are today, and provided no one got sick, a long journey was something of an extended picnic, with halts at quaint little stations, railway meals in abundance brought by waiters in smart uniforms, an ever-changing landscape, bridges over mighty rivers and khuds, forests and farmlands, everything sun-drenched. The air was crisp and unpolluted—and we let it rush in, for those were the days before sealed windows and air-conditioning—except when dust storms swept across the vast plains. Bottled drinks were a rarity, the occasional lemonade or 'Vimto' being the only aerated drink. We made our own orange juice or lime juice and took it with us.

As we approached Dehradun that winter of 1940–41, I woke up early one morning and looked out of the open window at dense forests of sal and sheesham; here and there a forest glade or a stream of clear water—quite different from the muddied waters of the streams and rivers we had crossed the previous day. As we passed over a largish river—my father told me it was the Song River—we saw a herd of elephants bathing. And as I turned my head to look at the gentle giants till they were out of sight, we entered the Doon valley, where fields of flowering mustard stretched away to the foothills.

When we reached Dehradun station, we were soot-covered and wilting. Coolies appeared to take our luggage, Daddy haggled with them, but not too much, and by the time we had walked out of the station, Dehra's bracing winter climate had already revived us.

We took a tonga and creaked and clip-clopped pleasantly along quiet roads. Scarlet poinsettia leaves and trailing bougainvillea adorned the garden walls, and in the compounds grew mango, litchi, guava, papaya and lemon trees that Daddy pointed out to me throughout our tonga ride. The tonga driver deposited us at the gate of my maternal grandparents' home, and delivered us—father, mother and two children aged six and four—to a future that none of us had imagined. It was the last time the family would be together.

ENTER GRANNY AND THE ENEMA

DEHRADUN WAS A SMALL TOWN SPREAD BETWEEN THE Ganga and Yamuna rivers, and nestling in a valley between the Himalayan foothills and the sub-tropical Siwalik range. Today it's a mini-city with a population exceeding ten lakhs, but seventy-five years ago the population hovered around 40,000 souls—Hindu traders and Muslim artisans from the cities of the plains; poor hill people seeking a better living; Gurkha soldiers and their families; a small but thriving Anglo-Indian community; even a few British officials who had retired in the valley. It was a popular retirement place for people from the army, railways and police—land was affordable, the roads were relatively clean and never crowded, there were trees all around, and the weather was temperate. The summer months were hot but not too oppressive. The winter months were quite pleasant, although in January a cold wind from the Tibetan plateau could get into your bones. The monsoon rains arrived with a flourish late June, celebrated Lord Krishna's birthday in August, and slipped quietly away in September.

Though it was formally known as Dehradun, as it is even today, in the 1940s and '50s everyone called it Dehra, and this intimate name suited the town well. It was small and green, somewhat laidback, easy-going; fond of gossip, but tolerant of human foibles. A place of bicycles and pony-drawn tongas—there were very few cars and hardly any buses. Some army jeeps took over the roads briefly during World War II, but after the war it was quiet again. You could walk almost anywhere, at any time of the year, night or day, without any risk of being run over.

Grandfather Clerke had built a small bungalow on Old Survey Road in 1900, the year the first train came puffing into Dehra, and had settled there in 1905. It was a typical railwayman's bungalow, very basic, tidy and compact, with verandas front and back, and a kitchen separate from the main building. The only distinctive thing about it was that instead of the customary red bricks, Grandfather had used the smooth rounded stones from a local riverbed. Through my childhood this was the only home that gave me some feeling of permanence, even if I wasn't entirely happy here.

To me, it was always 'Granny's house', because Grandfather had died the year I was born, and all those stories I was to write about him one day were made up by me or based on hearsay. I have often wished I had known him; from the stories I heard about him, he appeared to be a gently eccentric man—he would disguise himself as a vegetable vendor or a juggler and wander around in the bazaars. He was also in the habit of bringing home unusual pets—owls, frogs, chameleons and, on one occasion, a hyena, which chewed up the boots in the house and had to be released back into the forest very quickly.

After he died, Granny ran the house with her meagre pension of forty or fifty rupees and the sale of fruit from the small mango and litchi orchard at the back of the house. She also received a regular rent from a tenant, Miss Kellner, an elderly disabled lady who would become one of my early friends some three years later.

Granny lived alone, with a black pariah dog called Crazy, but her married daughters and a happily vagrant son (Uncle Ken) would come to stay in the house now and then. She wasn't a typical granny; I made her more homely in my stories. She was heavy-set, heavy-jowled, and a stern woman, not given to expressing emotion. She preferred her own company; in the evenings, even if there were others in the house, she sat by herself playing patience, a card game which does not require another player.

She didn't seem to like small boys—or it was small boys with buck teeth that she did not like. 'Little boys should speak only when spoken to,' was one of her maxims, and I was discouraged from joining in the conversation at the dining table. I was also discouraged from taking 'second helpings' of any dish, with the result that I made sure my first helping was large enough.

Her disapproval did not extend to my cousins, whom she always praised in my presence, and I think her discomfort with me may have been due to the fact that she was not sure if I was legitimate or not. Being of strict Victorian and evangelical upbringing, she would have been horrified at the thought of harbouring a bastard child in her home. My parents' marriage had been sudden and unexpected. Why had my mother married an older man? And why had they gone to Kasauli for my arrival? I did not understand any of this at the time, and I felt a little bewildered and resentful. I suppose she did love me, to the extent that she could love anyone and show it, but I was used to being the centre of attention, and now I was expected to make myself invisible. Sometimes I looked around for my mother, wanting to ask her if we could live somewhere else, but I rarely found her in the house. She was always going away somewhere, returning late at night.

Already, I was missing my father, who was posted in New Delhi, at Air Headquarters. He was over forty when he joined the Royal Air Force (RAF); he may have bluffed his age, or maybe one could enlist in one's forties during the war. He had been given the rank of Pilot Officer and was working in the Codes and Cyphers section. He must have been good at his job, because he was soon a Flying Officer. But it was to be about a year before I would see him again.

~

An old photograph of Granny's house shows a strange-looking object hanging on the veranda wall. There is no other decoration on that wall, and I can't help feeling it was placed there to terrorise me. This was an enema can with a rubber tube ending in a metal nozzle. It was Granny's remedy for a variety of children's ailments, ranging from constipation to indigestion to bad behaviour. A solution of soapy water—good old Lifebuoy soap—was poured into the can, the nozzle and the tube were then inserted into the victim's rectum, and the solution would be allowed to travel up one's lower intestine. After several minutes of this torture, the tube would be removed, and a little later the ravished victim would be rushing to the nearest bathroom to relieve the pressure.

I say 'victim' rather than patient, because I could not help feeling that my ultra-critical grandmother always singled me out for the enema cure. Even if I was suffering from diarrhoea, I would get the enema. 'This will clean you out,' Granny would say. 'Down with your knickers!' My modesty outraged, I would have to submit to the indignity of having this nozzle shoved up my backside at least once a month. My cousin Edith was exempted from this treatment, either because she was a girl or because she was never constipated.

My fear of the enema resulted in an aversion to being touched by anyone except my parents, and this aversion lasted until my prep school days in Shimla, when I was quite pleasantly cured of it in the rowdy public baths.

To escape Granny's enemas, and her stern orders to behave like 'a well-bred young gentleman', I looked for a place where I could hide, and I found it in an old banyan tree behind the house. Its large, spreading branches hung to the ground and took root again, and they were covered with thick green leaves. Here, I was very well concealed, and I would sit propped up against the bole of the tree, to read a comic, or watch the world below, on the road outside the compound wall: An English sahib in a sun helmet. A memsahib holding a colourful sun-umbrella (many European women had a horror of the Indian sun turning them so brown that they would be mistaken for an 'India-born' White). A lady in a sari with a basket of papayas balanced on her head. A man with a little hand-drum, and a monkey dressed in a red frilled dress and a baby's bonnet sitting on his shoulder.

The banyan tree was populated with little animals, birds and insects. The smaller leaves, still pink and almost translucent, would be visited by delicate butterflies, bushy-tailed squirrels, and red-headed parakeets. One day, climbing up the tree, I was startled by a giant yellow beak poised above my head. I backed away onto the closest branch, fearing an attack. I recognized the bird from my father's postage stamps, where it was strange but small, and a resident of faraway Botswana or Kenya. I hadn't expected to run into it on a friendly banyan tree in Dehra! But the hornbill, relaxing in a great hole in the tree trunk, did not move and looked at me in a rather bored way, drowsily opening and shutting its eyes. After some time, I lost my fear and climbed past it in search of a comfortable branch.

If Granny saw me when I had just emerged from my hideaway, I would be sent off for a bath. I had to learn to bathe myself. Gone were the soft hands of my Jamnagar Ayah; gone were the days of playing 'rucktions' in the bathtub with my father; or of lingering in the bath to float a paper boat or create soap bubbles. Into the hot water I went—no matter how hot!—and out again in two minutes flat. If I took any longer, Granny would walk in grim-faced, speaking not a word, and give me a good, rough scrub down. And if the soap got in my eyes, well then, it served me right for not shutting them properly.

Granny was a strong woman, and once in her grip there was no escape. In a faded old photo she appears to be a foot taller than Grandfather, who stands possessively beside her, rather like a hunter who has trapped a large tiger or gorilla and brought it back alive. I think Grandfather liked well-built women. His first wife had been a Boer from South Africa, who had trekked across the African Veldt, braving Zulu spears and British bullets (on separate occasions), finally ending up in India in a camp for Boer prisoners-of-war. Or so the story went.

This first wife had been Cousin Edith's grandmother. No wonder Edith was a tomboy—a year older than me, bigger and heavier, and always spoiling for a fight. On one occasion we had a wrestling match in the garden, flattening Granny's nasturtiums in the process. Being a boy, I was blamed for the damage, much to Edith's delight. I don't know what happened to her when she grew up. Most of our relatives left India before Independence, and I was too young to try and keep in touch with them, even if I'd wanted to. But if Cousin Edith became a lady wrestler, I wouldn't have been surprised.

There was to be no respite from stern dominating women.

'He's six years old,' said grandmother. 'Time he went to school.'

'I already know how to read and write,' I protested. 'Daddy says I know more than boys who go to school.' I didn't like Granny's home very much, but it was still familiar territory. I didn't want to go to a strange place.

But Granny felt that I needed the discipline and 'character building' that only a boarding-school could provide. My mother did not disagree. And so I was incarcerated—the right word for that experience—in a small convent school at Hampton Court in Mussoorie, the Convent of Jesus and Mary. My mother came to drop me off, and I kicked and screamed and made a terrible scene but quietened down when I realized my tantrum wasn't going to make her change her mind.

I hated that school from the first day. And I was still hating it a year and a half later, when I left. I was lonely, a misfit, unused to the company of hordes of shouting, screaming boys and girls, all of whom seemed unhappy. And the nuns were nothing like the soft and motherly Kerala nuns who are the most visible today. They were Irish and very strait-laced. Remote and unsympathetic. I suppose they made you tough, but whatever the merits of a no-nonsense upbringing, no child benefits from the absence of affection, and there was none in that school. There was no imagination, either. The nuns never told us poor children a story or sang a song that wasn't about service and suffering.

The daily chapel services seemed endless, and I felt sickened by the cloying odour of frankincense and myrrh every Sunday, when a visiting priest sermonized in Latin. Neither of my parents were overly religious. My mother had no interest in religion. My father wasn't an agnostic, but like most Church of England people, he wasn't fanatical about his faith. I was never taken to church every Sunday by my parents, or even by Granny, and the only religious tract that had come my way—a proselytizing text called *Little Henry and His Bearer*, gifted by a distant aunt—I hadn't enjoyed reading. But the nuns at the convent were determined to save our little souls. It is likely that they put me off religion. And I've never missed the comforts of organized faith. I'm an agnostic—you need something higher than religion and I prefer trees and mountains. I'm not against religion—I'm not against anything, really. To each his own. If their religious ritual makes people happy, let them have it, by all means. I'm just happy being a pagan...

But I've digressed. To return to the nuns. We had to bathe in our underwear, and do it quickly, presumably so that the nuns would not be distracted by the sight of our underdeveloped sex. I had started taking piano lessons, inspired by the songs I had heard on our gramophone. The nun who was teaching me turned out to be a perfectionist who would cane me over the knuckles whenever I hit the wrong note, and that was the end of my interest in the piano.

The food at the convent was awful—boiled stringy mutton with the cheapest available vegetable, usually pumpkin. The dormitory was overcrowded; the toilets at a distance. There were no books to read other than prayer books. How I longed for a Dandy comic! However, twice in a year we were taken to the pictures. Reverend Mother must have been a fan of Errol Flynn, because we were taken to see two films featuring that swashbuckling hero. One was called *They Died with Their Boots On*, in which he played General Custer, who goes to war against the Red Indians and gets scalped for his trouble. The other was *The Charge of the Light Brigade*, in which, as a British cavalryman, he takes on the Russian big guns and gets blown away.

My boredom and restlessness at school were relieved by the arrival of colourful picture postcards from my father, who never failed to write to me. He would send me cards from Lawson Wood's 'Gran'pop' series, featuring an ape who attended cocktail parties, went up in hot-air balloons and danced in the rain. Together with these postcards came messages from Daddy that there were books and toys waiting for me when I came home. And mid-way through that horrible year he obtained a few days' leave and came up to see me. I stayed with him in a local boarding-house; but I don't remember my mother coming up from Dehra to stay with us. He took me to the pictures (George Formby for a change; he was a funny man who played a ukulele, a sort of banjo) and bought me dozens of comics. I urged him to take me out of that wretched school and keep me with him. This he promised to do as soon as it could be arranged.

My father made a couple of visits to Dehra after these holidays, when I was back in the convent, and while I'm not sure if he stayed in Granny's house, he and my mother did meet. I think the marriage was failing and they were trying to see if it could be saved. One day I received a letter from my mother announcing the birth of my baby brother William in Dehradun.

At the convent school, I finally made friends with a boy named Buster Jones, who disliked the place as much as I did. Together we made plans to run away, and to that end we began saving up biscuits, slices of bread, rusks and other edibles that could sustain us on our flight to freedom. These bits and pieces were hoarded away in our lockers, but were soon discovered, and as punishment we were made to stand all day outside Reverend Mother's office. But we continued to make plans for our escape, although neither of us had any idea where we would go.

My father was now being posted in different war sectors, and my winter holidays were once again spent in Dehradun, under Granny's supervision. My mother was often out. She had felt stifled in Jamnagar, with its limited social life, and she was happier in Dehradun, which was more cosmopolitan and lively. There were parties and picnics and she would go to these with her friends. Sometimes, she would also take me along. There were visits to the local cinema, to see Eddie Cantor (my mother's favourite comedian) in *Roman Scandals,* and Laurel and Hardy (my favourite comedians) in *Great Guns.* There were picnics at Rajpur, and a Christmas party and a birthday party for Cousin Edith. Who would have thought there was a World War going on? Or that the country was in the throes of the Quit India movement, and that the sun would soon be setting on the British Empire?

Granny did not take much interest in parties and picnics, but

Aunt Enid (Edith's mother) was a party and picnic person, and you could not keep her away from them, especially if there were any men around. She had an eye on Mr H, a local photographer and second-hand car dealer, and something of a playboy. He didn't have the looks of a playboy, but he had the temperament. He came in a new car every other day and never seemed to have any work to do, except arranging tickets for the latest movies and finding new places to visit for a bit of fun. A man with the imagination to match his appetite for parties and games can be attractive to a certain kind of person. Aunt Enid was one such person.

But Mr H was more interested in my mother, who was both younger and prettier than Enid, and soon enough she began to go out with him. After that, I was never with her alone—picnics or the pictures, Mr H was always with us, and usually they would forget I was with them. One afternoon I left them sitting on the banks of the Eastern Canal and wandered off, finally making my way back home. I think I'd expected my mother to be alarmed and come looking for me, but she hadn't noticed. When she returned late in the evening, she had nothing to say.

There was some tension between Aunt Enid and my mother because of Mr H, but it blew over. In later years, I remember my mother saying that Enid would pursue anyone in pants, but this may just have been sisterly affection. Clement Town, on the outskirts of Dehra, had been turned into a 'Rest Camp' or recreation zone for British and American soldiers who had been on active service in Burma and the Eastern front. Aunt Enid lost no time in pursuing the soldiery, haunting the clubs and cafes where they gathered in the evenings. My mother, already engaged in her affair with Mr H, would have frequented these places to enjoy the music and spend a few hours in lively company. Enid's interests were more serious. But she was in her thirties, a little too old for the game.

A girl who lived down the road, 'Vi' or Viola Melville, had greater success, announcing her engagement to a good-looking young English corporal from the East End of London. The

Melvilles were an affluent Anglo-Indian family (not 'poor whites' like the rest of us), and the marriage was a good affair—a well-attended church ceremony followed by a grand reception at Tara Hall, the Melville family residence. I was appointed a 'page-boy' and was dressed up in my Sunday best, my duty being to fling handfuls of confetti on the young couple and the guests, something that I did with such gusto that the confetti soon ran out.

'Vi' was a pretty girl, some twelve years older than me, always friendly and full of fun. Soon after marriage she and her soldier husband left for dear old 'Blighty', and I did not expect to see her again. Strangely enough, our paths were to cross several times in the years ahead—in London, Delhi and Dehradun, again—and on the each occasion she had a different husband. She liked men, but they never seemed to come up to her expectations.

~

Over a year passed, and I was fretting for the company of my father. Picnics organized by local photographers or off-duty soldiers were not sufficient distraction from the misery of the school where I was imprisoned for all but three or four months of the year. And in any case, the picnics were not organized for me. Granny's enemas and her stern, unsmiling persona only added to my discontent.

I am probably being unfair to my grandmother, who I am sure had a heart of gold. Her own children—three daughters (my mother being the youngest), two stepdaughters (one of them being Enid), and a stepson, Ken (who lazed around doing nothing)—had pretty well done their own thing, so she couldn't have been very strict with them; though it is likely that the late Mr Clerke, my grandfather, may have been the lenient one. From all accounts he was a fairly easy-going person—although he was probably a bit helpless, saddled with six children. He was sixty-eight when he died, and by that time all his children were married, so he probably felt he had done his duty by them. For some mysterious reason (I never learnt why) Ken's marriage did not last very long.

After the winter break, I was back at school, watched over by the unsmiling nuns. But events were moving swiftly down in the Doon valley. News of wartime frolics and of the affair with Mr H had reached my father in Delhi. In the middle of the school term, much to my surprise, I was taken out of the convent by my mother, and instead of taking me home she took me straight to the Dehradun station.

'Where are we going?' I asked her.

'Your father wants you to spend some time with him,' she said.

And I was put on the night train to Delhi with a small steel trunk. Someone must have accompanied me on the journey—I was barely eight years old—but I can't remember my travelling companion. I only remember that I was met at the Old Delhi railway station by my father, and that he was in his RAF summer uniform, khaki shirt and knee-length shorts and a blue cap, already promoted to Flying Officer.

He took me to the office of the station superintendent, Fred Clark, an uncle on my mother's side, who took us to his bungalow next to the station for breakfast. It was here that I gathered from the conversation over eggs, toast and tea that my parents had separated. My mother would stay on in Dehra with my baby brother, William. I would be in the custody of my father—which pleased me, of course. And Ellen, the cross my parents had to bear, would be sent to live with our other Granny, my father's seventy-five-year-old mother, in Calcutta.

The life of a small child is dependent almost entirely on the lives of his or her parents. When a marriage breaks up, the children are often pulled in different directions and there is very little they can do about it. I had no quarrel with my mother; but I was drawn to my father instinctively. No one stood between us. No interloper, no rival for his affections. The bond formed during those early years in Jamnagar was as strong as ever—and would only grow stronger in the coming months, a brief period that was probably the happiest of my childhood.

A HUT IN NEW DELHI

TO BEGIN WITH, THERE WAS THIS LITTLE TWO-ROOM BRICK hutment in the wilderness near Humayun's Tomb. There was an entire line of them, built some distance from one another and separated by trimmed hedges; temporary and very functional abodes designed for serving officers and their families. The area is now a busy and sought-after part of Delhi, but in 1942 it was a scrub jungle where black buck and nilgai roamed freely.

Daddy went to work at nine and came back around six. On Sundays, and sometimes Saturdays, he was free. His office was in Air Headquarters in South Block which was attached to a wing of the Viceroy's palatial residence, later Rashtrapati Bhawan. His work in Codes and Cyphers was very secretive and mysterious, and if he broke any important enemy codes, he didn't tell me.

In winter he wore his navy blue RAF uniform; in summer, khaki. He always looked dapper and smart—he was a good-looking man, short and spry, with a boyish charm. I envied that uniform, and often posed in his caps and braided hats, and insisted on being photographed in them. And what's a uniform without salutes? I saw my father's juniors salute him and I saw him salute his senior officers and soon I was clicking my heels and saluting everyone in sight!

Daddy was always up early, making our breakfast, beating up the cream to make my favourite white butter. After breakfast he would be off, and I'd be left to my own devices for the rest of the day. The first couple of days, I walked across to a neighbouring hutment to lunch with an English family my father knew, but their boisterous, bullying boys took a dislike to me, and I took a dislike to them, and Daddy arranged for a khansama to come for an hour around noon and make me lunch.

There were some comics to read and a large postcard collection to go through. And there was the old gramophone, and the old records—I don't think my father had time to buy any new ones.

But I did not mind; the gramophone was a great companion, filling the room with the glorious sounds of operatic arias and duets. Daddy had told me to be careful with the records and store them flat, otherwise they could assume weird shapes in the heat and become unplayable.

That first summer in Delhi is etched clearly in my memory. I had never been in so hot a place, and I remember those scorching winds of June—the loo, the 'evil' dust-laden wind from the deserts of Baluchistan and Rajasthan which is now rarely experienced in Delhi. But it took me only a few days to get used to the heat. The bhisti, or water-carrier, came around ten or eleven, delivering fresh water from his goat-skin bag. There were no taps in the hut, so he filled the tub and a large drum and splashed water on the khus, a reed matting that hung across the front door. This had a wonderful cooling effect, which didn't last more than half an hour, but I loved the tender, refreshing fragrance of the khus and the smell of damp earth outside, where the water had spilt. It would be many years before air-conditioning came to Delhi. We had a small table-fan in the hutment, but as yet no electricity.

The cool of the rooms attracted various creatures, and I had to look out for scorpions and centipedes, which sometimes took shelter in shoes or empty mugs or the clothes' basket. One morning I opened the lid of the gramophone to find a large scorpion asleep on the turn table. I yelled for help, but there was no one around. So I shut the gramophone lid with a bang, and did not open it until my father got back in the evening. By that time the scorpion had mysteriously disappeared.

There were geckos, wall lizards, which sometimes fell on the table or on the floor with a soft thwack. At night, numerous jackals set up an endless series of wails, but they did not venture into the houses; unlike the wild cats, who came at any time of day or night, foraging for food. Sometimes they hissed and growled at me, but cats did not frighten me and I hissed and growled right back.

Despite all this wildlife in and around the hutment, I was quite happy to be on my own, a king of the castle, confident that my father would be home at six, ready to talk to me or take me out or bring out his stamp collection. Albums and boxes of stamps would be spread out on the dining-table, and by the light of a kerosene lamp we would discuss new issues, or the rarity of old ones, often referring to the prized Stanley Gibbons catalogue to see if a set was complete.

Only once did he ask me about my mother. Did she take me out sometimes? And who were her friends?

'There's a letter from Enid,' he said.

Apparently Aunt Enid, in a fit of jealousy, had written to him giving details of picnics, dance parties, the ever-present Mr H, soldiers in search of pleasure, and everyone including my mother having a good time while he, poor breadwinner, was struggling with codes and cyphers in the heat and dust of New Delhi. Not to mention the responsibility of looking after a growing boy.

Much of this was true, of course, and I couldn't really keep it from my father; nor did I wish to. Fairly or unfairly, I was on his side.

On Sundays we went on walks or little excursions in and around Delhi. Humayun's Tomb was close by; a handsome edifice that rose gracefully above the surrounding wilderness of babul and keekar trees, a testament to human enterprise, even if it had served as the burial place for many kings, queens and princes. The Purana Qila, or Old Fort, was not too far away. Here my father showed me the steps to the library and observatory that was a favourite haunt of Emperor Humayun.

'He'd been waiting to see Venus the evening he died,' he told me.

'How did he die?' I asked.

'They say he was going down the steps in a hurry and he tripped and fell to his death. He fractured his skull.'

It was an eerie, winding staircase, dark and forbidding. I could well imagine someone tumbling down those steps.

Sometimes we went further afield, to the Red Fort and its pavilions overlooking the sluggish but as yet unpolluted river.

*'If there be a paradise on earth,
It is this, it is this.'*

So said the inscription on the wall of one of the Mughal emperors' pavilions. Being tired and hungry after trudging around the ramparts of this massive citadel, I did not find it paradise enough, and was only too happy to retreat to the refreshment rooms at the Old Delhi railway station. Here we felt quite at home with Uncle Fred, the station superintendent, one of my father's few friends.

The refreshment rooms were on an upper floor of the station, free from the din of the railway platforms, the shunting of engines, the whistle of the guards, the shouts of the coolies and that cacophony of sound which was (and still is) a feature of large Indian railway stations. The food was limited fare but nevertheless acceptable to a 'growing boy'—chicken or mutton cutlets (Railway Cutlets, they were called), a mutton or vegetable curry, pillau or rice, and a flavourless blancmange or custard pudding. I ate the cutlets and curry, but left the pudding. Refrigeration was in its early days, and ice-creams were a rarity.

Back home, we kept our drinking water cool in a surahi, an earthen vessel which was kept in a shady spot. There was also a dolie, a small cupboard with a wire-mesh front in which fruit, vegetables and kitchen supplies could be stored. The legs of the dolie were kept in saucers of water to prevent ants from getting in. Even so, some of them managed to get across to feast on their favourite foods—sugar cubes, bananas, cream rolls—anything sweet and sticky. You could keep out snakes, rats, lizards and bats, but you couldn't do much about the ants. They were constantly on the march, heading resolutely in the direction of their objective. They were like a German Panzer regiment, disciplined, unwavering.

Those Panzer regiments had the upper hand in faraway Europe. The war was going badly for Britain and its allies. All of Europe was in German hands, Singapore and Malaya had fallen to the Japanese. The road to India through Burma was full of refugees—Indians, Europeans, Eurasians. British ships were being sunk,

British aircraft outnumbered. In India, demands for Independence grew stronger by the day. A sense of crisis prevailed in New Delhi.

I wasn't concerned with the war. My world was my father, and it was when he fell ill and had to be hospitalized that I had my first moments of anxiety. This was one of the earliest of his periodic bouts of malaria. He was in hospital for three or four days. The neighbours kept an eye on me during the day and the bhisti's son stayed with me at night. He was my age, or maybe a year or two older, a quiet boy, his skin burnt a dark brown, dressed in a vest of coarse cotton and khaki shorts that were too large for him. He slept in the kitchen, a silent companion. Two little boys, an outcaste and a half-orphan, giving each other company and support...It must have left an impression on me, because out of that experience grew my first story, 'The Untouchable', published some ten years later in *The Illustrated Weekly*.

Daddy returned from hospital, not fully recovered; he looked weak and was eating poorly. I think he had taken an early discharge because he wasn't sure how I would cope on my own. He stayed home for a few days, to rest and get his strength back, and unable to do anything else for him, I would play his favourite records on the gramophone to cheer him up. He was still running a slight fever, and it was strange to lie beside him through the hot afternoons on a perspiration-soaked bed, listening to Caruso sing *Che Gelida Manina*—

> *Your tiny hand is frozen,*
> *Let me warm it into life.*

I did not understand death, but I began to fear that I would lose my father somehow. To my relief, he recovered completely in a few days, and all my fears were wiped away. It was as if he had never been unwell.

After a few months, we gave up the hutment. It had been meant for family use, and I was the only indication of a family. Daddy's superiors were always wanting to know why my mother wasn't around to look after me. So he rented rooms on Atul Grove Road, a quiet cul-de-sac off Curzon Road (now Kasturba Gandhi Marg), very close to Connaught Place, which was then the commercial and professional hub of New Delhi.

~

On one side of the road were half-a-dozen bungalows occupied by officials of the telegraph department, and my father had taken the rooms on rent from one of the residents. On the other side of the road stood the offices of the department, flanked by the humbler quarters of the lower rungs of the department's employees—peons, cleaners, chowkidars and their families—and there was an open ground, well-grassed, in front of the building where the children would play in the evenings.

Among them was Joseph, the son of one of the resident officials—a dark, skinny boy from southern India, well-mannered, smiling, eager to be friends. We met quite casually. There was a letter-box, one of those red pillar-boxes, at the end of the road, and I came out of the house to post a couple of letters for my father. A boy of about my age also crossed the road to post a letter, and thrust his hand into the opening at the same time as I did. We had to hold hands in order to facilitate a smooth release.

'Pleased to meet you,' said the boy. 'I'm Joseph.'
'I'm Ruskin.'
'Which school do you go to?'
'I don't go to school,' I said.
'Lucky chap!'

It was the beginning of a gentle friendship that lasted through the long summer of 1942 and the winter that followed.

After six in the evening it was possible to run around a little, play football on the open ground, have a wrestling-match with Joseph. Wrestling with Joseph was always great fun. Being much heavier than him, I generally got the upper hand, but he would never give up—he would wriggle out from under me and lock me in some intricate arm or leg hold, and I would have to use all my superior weight to break free and sit on top of him. The children from the department's quarters would watch these bouts with great interest, cheering whenever Joseph got the better of me—for, being fair-skinned and the son of a British officer, I was identified with the colonial oppressors—but no one interfered; they knew instinctively that we were two friends engaged in an intimate trial of skill and strength.

It was the year of the Quit India movement, but it was also the third year of World War II, and New Delhi was full of uniformed British and American officers and soldiers, and they were catered to by the cinema halls, restaurants and nightclubs in and around Connaught Place. Their presence didn't seem to make any difference to the way life went on in this part of the city. Children played their games as before; the roads were full of bicycles with men in mill-made dhotis, pyjamas or knee-length khaki shorts going to work; the occasional car honked, just to be heard, because there was never anyone in its way; the reasonably-off dined at Kwality in Connaught Place and the well-off at Gaylord's, and nobody bothered if the poor had enough to eat.

The war was far away—in Burma and Malaya—but air-raids were expected, Calcutta having already received a few bombs from Japanese planes. Trenches were dug all over the capital, and our little lane was honoured with a deep trench, about fifteen feet in length, with steps cut into the sides for those who couldn't jump into it. Delhi did not experience any air-raids, but the children had a great time in the trenches; and when the monsoon rains arrived, and they filled up with water, they became extremely popular as bathing-pools, where the boys could swim and splash about with great abandon.

Connaught Place was just a ten-minute walk from Atul Grove, and my father was always quite ready to take me around this posh shopping centre, stopping at bookshops where I would sometimes buy a colourful comic paper, or at record shops where we would buy a record. We walked around in a leisurely fashion, because the circle wasn't crowded then; you could cross the road without having to look left or right. There were just a couple of buses and a few private cars. The preferred mode of transport, if you couldn't ride a bicycle, was a tonga.

At least once a week, Daddy took me to the cinema—in those war years the halls were flooded with the latest British and American movies. He would return from Air Headquarters in the evening and say, 'Let's go to the pictures,' and we'd be off to the Regal or Rivoli or Odeon or Plaza, the four cinema halls in Connaught Place. In the course of the year I must have seen some forty films, all in the company of my father. Early Disney classics—*Bambi*, *Dumbo*, *Fantasia* (an experiment with classical music); the pretty Olympic ice-skating champion Sonja Henie in *Sun Valley Serenade*; Nelson Eddy singing the song of the Volga boatmen in *Balalaika*; James Cagney belting out the title song in *Yankee Doodle Dandy*; and Carmen Miranda doing the rumba or the samba in *Down Argentine Way*.

Comedies were my favourites—the madcap adventures of Laurel and Hardy, Abbot and Costello, George Formby, Harold Lloyd, the Marx Brothers...And sometimes we'd venture further afield, to the old Ritz at Kashmere Gate, to see Sabu in the *Thief of Baghdad* or *Cobra Woman*. These Arabian Nights-type entertainments were popular in the old city.

These cinema halls still exist, although three of the four in Connaught Place have been turned into multiplexes and I gather the last remaining single-screen hall, the Regal, will soon undergo a similar transformation. But at least they survive, even if the drama is lost. The old Ritz is crumbling away; it was much older than the New Delhi cinemas, showing silent films when my father was a boy. I won't be surprised if it is pulled down one of these days, but I don't want to be told if it is.

~

Daddy's first love was of course his stamp collection. There was a trunk full of albums. He told me it was a valuable collection, and that it would be mine some day. I was encouraged to collect too, and I had my own small album, most of it filled with stamps from

Greece. I don't know why I chose Greece—I was probably attracted by the Greek gods and heroes depicted on the stamps—and my father seemed to have an unending supply of Greek stamps which he did not want.

Daddy's few friends and acquaintances were also stamp collectors. I remember accompanying him into Rankin's, a large drapery shop in the outer circle of Connaught Place, where he would have his RAF uniforms tailored. Instead of having himself measured for a uniform, he ended up sitting across from Mr Rankin at the latter's large office desk, talking about stamps, discussing irregularities in design, rare printing errors, forgeries, overprints, rarities from the Solomon Islands or Papua-New Guinea, valuable collections that had vanished, countries that had vanished!

I would sit there patiently, listening or pretending to listen to all this philatelic philosophy, but quietly watching the flow of customers as they entered and left the premises—smart ladies wearing outlandish hats (some with feathers in them), English gentleman in dress-suits (with bow-ties), American soldiers in well-pressed trousers, British soldiers in knee-length khaki shorts, maharajas in achkans and churidar pyjamas, maharanis in expensive, richly embroidered saris, Indians in European dress (those in Indian dress must have been elsewhere), and shop assistants in purple jackets. It was people who interested me more than stamps.

And stamp-collectors were people too. Like the young American lieutenant who came over to our flat one evening to look at Daddy's collection. My father had invited him to dinner, and had prepared for the occasion by investing in a bottle of red wine. I had never seen my father drink alcohol, although I had seen plenty of it at some of Mr H's parties in Dehradun.

'What's that for?' I asked, indicating the bottle.

'For our guest,' said Daddy. 'He's an American,' as though that explained it.

Our part-time khansama prepared a mulligatawny soup, pork chops and a chocolate blancmange.

The young lieutenant arrived on time and presented my astonished father with a bottle of Irish whisky.

'I don't really drink,' said Daddy. 'But if you don't care for wine, I'll open the whisky for you.'

He poured two drinks but these were soon forgotten. And there they were, three hours later, going through my father's precious albums—an album for Great Britain stamps, another for Empire stamps, another for stamps from Greece, as well as miscellaneous albums for stamps from all corners of the world. I had never before seen Daddy sell any of his stamps, but either our visitor was very persuasive, or Daddy was in need of some ready cash, because by the time our visitor left, we had sold him stamps worth about three thousand rupees—a lot of money in those days.

After that, I began to respect stamps. Especially when, the next day, Daddy bought me a dart board, a bagatelle board and a set of dominoes from a part of the proceeds. We also went to Wenger's, the popular bakery and confectionery, where I consumed a number of patties, pastries and meringues.

Daddy suffered from periodic bouts of malaria throughout that time in Delhi, and they came on without any warning; high fever, fits of shivering, sometimes delirium. A few days of rest and treatment with quinine would bring about a recovery. But on one occasion in Atul Grove the attack was so severe that he had to be confined for two weeks at the military hospital out at Palam.

I was on my own for that entire fortnight. Although I missed my father terribly, I did not feel abandoned in any way. I was sure he would soon be home. The D'Souzas, the Goan couple who had sub-let their flat to us, were very kind and had me over to tea every afternoon. Our khansama turned up every day to give me lunch and early dinner. He also kept tea or cocoa for me in a thermos flask. I made my own breakfast—there was plenty of bread, Polson's butter, and Mangaram's apple or guava jam. For company, I had the gramophone, some books and comic papers, and Joseph when he was back from school. He would stay with me all afternoon. We would play dominoes and darts or read comics, and sometimes go to sleep together on my bed.

'Won't you *ever* go to school?' Joseph would ask me.

I assured him I wouldn't.

'How will you make a living?'

'I'll help my father with his stamp collection. It's very valuable.'

I said this with complete conviction. We get used to happiness very quickly, more so when we are children. I believed that Daddy and I would always be together. I would be his best friend, his trusted assistant in stamp collection, and nothing would ever change, nothing would come between us.

All his stamp albums were kept in a large wooden trunk, and the key to the trunk was kept in an empty flower vase on the dressing table. I was so in awe of those beautifully maintained albums, that I did not dare open the trunk to look at them in my father's absence. I waited patiently for the day when he would be back with me again.

One day, kind Mr D'Souza volunteered to take me to the hospital to see Daddy, a two-hour tonga ride that ended in disappointment. No visitors, we were told; it was wartime. So we had to be content with standing on the lawns, staring up at the third floor where, we were told, my father shared the ward with other patients stricken with malaria.

'He must be somewhere up there,' said Mr D'Souza pointing to a wing of the third floor where a nurse hovered near a window. This wasn't very satisfying so we went back to our tonga and returned at a slow trot to Atul Grove. I missed my lunch, but made up for it by finishing Mr D'Souza's supply of bread.

Mr D'Souza said I could sleep in their spare room while my father was in hospital, but I insisted on staying in my own part of the house. The months spent in the hutment had given me plenty of practice in staying on my own, and I was already getting used to the idea of having a room of my own.

I wasn't afraid of being alone at night. Lights off, I would lie awake on my cot, gazing through the little window at the shadows of the two street lights and the occasional beam of a car's headlights. In the distance, dogs would bark—not at intruders, but simply out of habit. Sometimes jackals bayed or a night-bird would honk in the neem tree. The window had a protective wire netting, so I could keep it open, and moths, mosquitoes and other flying bugs would collide with the netting and fall to the ground outside. It was the start of the monsoon, and thousands of flying ants would circle the streetlights, all on a merry suicide mission; in the morning the sparrows and other insectivores would feast on the remains.

The night held no terrors for me. I was never afraid of the dark, and till today I see the night as a friend, giving me the privacy that I find so hard to find by day. Starlight, moonlight, early dawn, all have a special loveliness about them.

Of course I bolted the doors and windows. Humans were unpredictable. But, in spite of the of the war and occasional disturbances on the streets, New Delhi was a safer place in the 1940s than it is in the twenty-first century when we are told there are no mysteries left and nobody is a stranger.

Daddy returned from hospital looking wan and tired, but this time he returned very quickly to robust health, thanks largely to the acquisition of several sets of attractive postage stamps from the Pitcairn Islands and Fiji. That stamp collection kept him going!

And he had news for me.

'I've found a good school for you in Shimla,' he said. 'You'll like it there.'

'But I like it here,' I protested. 'Why do you want to send me away to school again? I can read and write. You've taught me how to do sums.'

'But I can't teach you physics and chemistry. Besides, another hot summer in Delhi won't be good for you. You've lost your pink cheeks and your eyes look yellow.'

'So do yours.'

'In my case it's due to the quinine I have to take. But seriously, it's high time you went to school again. Everyone says I spoil you. You've had over a year's holiday!'

'Another year won't make any difference. If you like, I can go to school in Delhi, along with Joseph.'

'The problem is, I may be transferred soon. This war is going on for longer than anyone thought. I may be sent to Karachi or Calcutta, or even North Africa.'

'Why can't I come with you?' I asked.

'I won't be allowed to keep you with me, son. I'll have to share digs with other officers. In Delhi, I can make my own arrangements, but not when I'm sent to other postings.'

And so it came about that I was to resume my interrupted school career.

Daddy took a fortnight's leave, Uncle Fred put us on the night train to Kalka, and we were off to Shimla, the summer capital of India.

It had all happened very suddenly, and I didn't even get a chance to say goodbye to Joseph.

But I haven't forgotten him. Some friends—their eyes, their touch, their words—cannot be erased from our memory.

―◆―

UNDER THE DEODARS

Ram Advani, the famous bookseller of Lucknow, told me once that he remembered the day my father brought me to the school office for admission. Ram was the bursar at Bishop Cotton School; a young man in his very early twenties who had landed the job because he was good at cricket. The headmaster was Canon Sinker, a High Church cleric, widely respected. There were some reservations about my admission. It was already mid-term, and how would I keep up with the rest of the class? Why had I missed school for a year, and where was my mother? My father explained the situation. Mrs Sinker, who was present, intervened. 'You must admit him, George,' she admonished her husband. 'You can see he's a bright boy. And his father's on active service.' Daddy's uniform obviously helped.

I was admitted to the preparatory school, in Chhota Shimla, some distance from the senior school; but I did not have to join immediately, as the school was having a mid-term break and my father had a few weeks' leave in hand. I'd seen the junior boys when we were walking to the school office, past the playing field. My father had pointed them out to me, saying they looked like a happy bunch and I would enjoy their company. And they did look happier than the inhibited lot at the Mussoorie convent. Some of them were chasing each other, playing a game of some kind, while others ran around with butterfly nets. A few sat quietly, reading comics. I had also enjoyed the journey to Shimla in a railcar, which had glided smoothly up and round the gradient, slipping through the 103 tunnels; and then we'd had a substantial lunch in one of Shimla's many first-rate restaurants. So I was already feeling less apprehensive about going back to school.

Shimla in the early summer of 1943 was a happening place. The Viceroy was in town, hobnobbing with various Indian leaders, all anxious to see the Viceroy and his countrymen quitting India at the earliest possible moment. But the war was still dragging on, even though America had now thrown its weight into the fray. Germany had got itself into a tight corner, with no way out, having repeated Napoleon's blunder of invading Russia and that too in mid-winter. But in the Pacific, Japanese resistance was fierce, with kamikaze pilots crashing their planes on to the decks of American aircraft carriers. And they still held most of mainland Asia.

And so Shimla's Mall Road shone with uniforms of the various services, as well as the liveried staff of the Viceregal Lodge, families on holiday, schoolboys in caps and ties, and monkeys on the slopes of Jakhoo Hill.

We stayed in a place called Craig Dhu, a hostel for officers situated on Elysium Hill, one of Shimla's seven hills. Daddy had to share a room with a British officer of a similar rank. But what was I doing there, the officer wanted to know. These were supposed to be bachelors' quarters, off limits for children. More explanations followed. The officer was sympathetic; he had a small son in Southampton whom he hadn't seen in two years. He gave me a chocolate Mars bar and we were friends.

There was sugar rationing at the time, and a shortage of eggs. Even so, Davico's, the most popular restaurant on the Mall, made some great pastries, cakes and meringues, and it wasn't far from where we were staying. There were no cars in town, only ponies and rickshaws, and we took quite a few rickshaw rides, sustained by pastries, oranges and 'curry puffs'.

Whatever happened to curry puffs? These were dainty little savouries filled with curried chicken or mutton. I suppose they are called something else now. For several years they were my favourite snack, until they suddenly disappeared, defeated by greasy samosas.

On one memorable rickshaw ride Daddy recounted Kipling's 'The Phantom Rickshaw'—an eerie little tale set in Shimla of the 1890s: a rickshaw with its occupant, a beautiful and much sought-after Englishwoman, had plunged off the road in a monsoon mist, falling into a deep ravine and killing the passenger and the rickshaw-men. Her spectre, together with those of the rickshaw-pullers, was frequently seen by one of her besotted admirers, who was eventually driven mad by the apparition.

I wasn't quite satisfied with the tale.

'They were ghosts, I suppose,' I remember saying.

'Yes,' said Daddy. 'The lady was a ghost and so were the rickshaw-pullers. Some people are said to become ghosts after violent deaths.'

'But he kept seeing the rickshaw too,' I objected. 'How could the rickshaw become a ghost? It's not a living thing.'

Daddy had to agree. He told me that his mother kept an old rocking-chair in which her mother had passed away. Sometimes, at night, the chair would rock, but only when Granny was seen to be sitting in it.

'Did you ever sit in the rocking-chair?'

'No,' said Daddy. 'I was afraid of Granny.'

'Must have been like Dehra Granny,' I said and Daddy laughed and ruffled my hair.

We went to the pictures. Shimla had three cinemas—the Regal, the Rivoli, and the Ritz. I liked the Rivoli best. It was down in a shady glade, part of the old Blessington Hotel. A small flat patch of land there was used as an ice-skating rink in the winter. Tall deodars surrounded the glade.

One afternoon we climbed to the top of Jakhoo Hill, Shimla's highest hill, to see the Hanuman temple, and on the way the monkeys stole all our pies and pastries.

Then it was time to join school.

'Well, there's only five months of the year left,' said Daddy reassuringly. 'Come November, you'll be with me in Delhi again.' And he promised me cinemas, bookshops, ice-creams and comics.

I was well spoilt by my father.

~

They were a rowdy but a friendly lot at the prep school, and I certainly had more fun there than I did at the senior school later on. Although the school had its own conventions, being modelled on English private schools—the tradition of calling other students only by their last name; the system of prefects, canings and compulsory sports—there was an air of informality about prep school. We had yet to be turned into the polished and Spartan English public school types that were being turned out every year by Bishop Cotton—the 'Eton of the East', as it was called in better days.

Nor were we half-starved convent children overseen by super-clean nuns. We were quite a scruffy lot, as I remember. We fought, we played in the dust, made a lot of noise, made friendships, got into trouble, played pranks on the teachers and had spectacular pillow wars that would result in a storm of cotton and feathers in the dormitories.

And I lost my aversion to physical intimacy—the sad affliction that was the result of Granny's enemas. Unlike in the Mussoorie convent, we didn't have to bathe in tubs and keep our underwear on—in fact, we weren't allowed to; we had to shower together in the nude, and we got used to each other's bodies, to seeing and touching each other. We were eight- to twelve-year-olds, our bodies and minds being changed by puberty, so sexual adventures were natural. But it was more inquisitive and innocent inquiry than anything else. There were no passionate affairs, and no exploitation that I can recall. It was guiltless fun that many of us outgrew and some of us accepted as part of our human experience.

The exploits of comic-book and sports heroes were much higher on our list of priorities than sex and romance. Our heroes were fighter pilots, swashbuckling pirates and buccaneers, football stars like Sir Stanley Matthews—the 'Wizard of Dribble'—and boxing champions like Joe Louis. The *Biggles* books, featuring the daredevil pilot James Bigglesworth, were a bit of a rage in those years, and when word went round that my father was in the RAF, the boys began to look at me with new respect. I made the most of it and asked my father to wear his uniform when he came to see me.

'Does he fly bombers?' the boys would ask me.

'All the time,' I'd lie and make up stories about his exploits in the skies!

But I had competition. Young Abbot claimed that he had shot a tiger with his father's 12-bore shotgun. We believed him and were all in awe of him.

I remember other boys from my first term. Bimal Mirchandani had the skinniest legs in the school and was called 'Bambi', after the little gazelle in the Disney film (he became a good wrestler when he was older). Kellnar was taking a course in body-building but was defeated by the fact that he had a very long neck and splayed feet; we called him Donald Duck. Mehta Junior was a sleepwalker who caused a sensation by sleepwalking off the dormitory roof and falling into the headmaster's flower bed without any damage to himself.

Some of the boys were unusually gifted. One of my classmates (I forget his name) was writing a novel—a detective story—on toilet paper. Due to the wartime paper shortage, he was using those little thin sheets that came in flat packets instead of toilet rolls. We were not allowed toilet rolls because the boys frequently used them to make streamers across the dormitory or in the corridors.

I had not, as yet, taken up writing—that was still two or three years distant—but my interest in acting and cinema prompted me to produce a one-act drama in which I played a demented serial-killer inspired by the film *The Brighton Strangler*, which was running at the Rivoli. The script was simple. All I had to do was strangle several victims (played by my class fellows), who would scream, choke, gurgle or beg for mercy as they perished at my hands. Alfred Hitchcock would have approved. But Mr Priestley, the prep school head, did not, and I was reprimanded and told to use my talents for something more wholesome.

Our drama teacher, Miss Khanna, decided I would make a great Humpty Dumpty in the school pantomime, and an elaborate costume was designed for me, consisting of a large egg made from cardboard into which I was fitted. All I had to do was fall off a wall at the appropriate moment, and the cardboard egg would shatter, leaving me to the mercy of 'all the king's horses and all the king's men' (my classmates, eager to lay their hands on me). I fell off the wall with precision, but the cardboard egg refused to break up, and I found myself bouncing around the stage entrapped in my costume. Naturally, this brought the house down, and I was a great hit.

All this mayhem was possible only because Mr Priestley, our headmaster, was more interested in his violin than in his wards. He might have had ambitions of becoming another Jascha Heifetz or Fritz Kreisler, the great violinists. It was impossible for us to judge the quality of his playing, but he practiced early morning, late afternoon, and sometimes late at night—in his rooms, or in his office, or in the school hall, where he was accompanied on the piano by his wife, a lady with very large breasts that the boys called 'nutcrackers'. We had of course grown used to this background music through most of the day; indeed, we welcomed it, because we knew that if the headmaster was wrapped up in one of his violin solos, we could get up to mischief of one kind or another.

School discipline was usually left in the hands of Mr Murtough, a sporting type, good at games, who also taught geography. I had learnt a fair amount of geography from Daddy's stamp collection and had no difficulty in topping the class in this subject. My one-and-half-year absence from school had not been a disadvantage. I had read more books than my classmates, and my writing skills were fairly well developed. I was promoted to a higher class, which meant that I hadn't really lost any school time.

The other male teacher I remember was Mr Oliver, a dark, brooding man, who was followed around by a pet dachshund. Mr Oliver kept to himself—he did not mix with the boys or other staff members, and it was said that he had been disappointed in love. This may have been so. Middle-aged men who have been unlucky in love often end up sharing their lives with pet dogs. Spinsters keep cats, bachelors keep dogs, or so it is said. Mr Oliver lavished his affections on his dachshund—an unfriendly dog who disliked the boys and frequently nipped us on the calves or ankles. He—Mr Oliver, not the dachshund—taught us elementary mathematics, which may also have been a cause for his depression.

We called the dachshund Hitler. In Europe, the real Hitler was still ranting, waving his arms about, threatening to take over the world as demagogues are wont to do; but he had shot his bolt and retribution was fast catching up with him. Strange, how the human race can elevate the vilest of men to positions of all-powerful tyranny and then take an equal pleasure in dragging them down into the dust. Even good men can be destroyed if they excite the envy of their fellows.

That first year in prep school passed quickly. Since I had joined the school midway through the term, it was just a five-month session for me. Now I had my father and the winter holidays to look forward to—new gramophone records, stamps, comics, milk-shakes, the cinemas—all the things that the world's more fortunate children look forward to when the end-of-term holidays approach.

And there he was, waiting for me on the platform, as the overnight train from Kalka steamed into the Old Delhi station. He was in his uniform, looking as smart as I could have wished him to be. Anyone who has grown up with a father in one of the services will know the feeling of pride that comes from seeing a parent—who might otherwise be a little on the tubby side, or shorter than the average, or balding a little—transformed by a uniform into someone of heroic proportions. A boy can visualize himself decked out as Batman or Superman, or a girl as Wonder Woman, but we know it to be make-believe. A dark blue RAF uniform and a braided cap are the real thing.

Delhi's best cinemas and music shops were of course still there, the only difference being that I was now much closer to them, Daddy having taken a flat in Scindia House, a large apartment building opposite the outer ring of Connaught Place.

Right opposite Scindia House, across the road, was the Milk Bar run by the Keventer's Dairy farms. It took me only a few minutes to cross the road and partake of a strawberry or vanilla or chocolate milkshake. My ever-indulgent father never denied me these little luxuries. In all the time I was with him, he never spoke a harsh word to me or scolded me for a misdemeanour. And I think I appreciated this, because although at times I was mischievous elsewhere, I was always on my best behaviour in his company—knowing, with the practicality of childhood, that I had only to ask him for something—a toy, a comic, a record, a particular sweet dish—and I would get it. He did spoil me, in the best possible way, and as a result I have grown old indulging other people's children.

The war wasn't yet over, but the tide was beginning to turn in favour of the Allies, and many among the British, especially those in the military and the services, were seeing signs that sooner rather than later peace would return. And it was becoming clear that the British would have to make some kind of retreat from India, the 'Jewel in the Crown'. Daddy, like the vast majority of other British and Anglo-Indian residents of India, was making preparations towards that end. As he saw it, there would be no future for us in an independent India. I was too young to have any opinion of my own about this.

In Scindia House there were no other children. But I got on famously with the other residents, especially the domestic helps—maidservants, ayahs, cooks, chowkidars, sweepers—a trait I had acquired during our Jamnagar days, when my ayah had made so much fuss over me. I was addressed as 'Baba' and was known to all as 'Bond-sahib ka bachcha'. During the day, while Daddy was at work, I would gossip with this motley crew and follow them around, learning something about their lives and their struggle to survive. Because of my innocence and curiosity, they indulged my whims—allowing me to help peel potatoes or shell peas, push the odd pram, fill buckets, water plants—or rather, over-water them—and, as a result, get in everyone's way. In India, humble working people will indulge small children, brightening up their days, and I took full advantage of this indulgence.

At this time, my principal ambition was to be a tap-dancer. This was the result of seeing too many Hollywood musicals, in particular those featuring the marvellous tap-dancer Eleanor Powell, pretty and vivacious, who danced her way through such films as *Lady Be Good*, *Ship Ahoy* and *Broadway Melody*—all showing at some time or another in New Delhi's cinemas. I would come home and go through my own tap-dance routine in the corridors of Scindia House, much to the amusement of the domestics and any residents who might be passing. I kept an exercise book in which I listed all the films I had seen, along with their casts, and I suppose this qualified as my first literary effort. There was nothing literary about it, although it did help to sharpen my memory. It also turned me into a 'list' person, and in later years I was to develop the habit (probably quite useless) of listing the books I had read, or cricket players who had represented India or other countries, or (much later) the wild flowers I had discovered growing on the hillsides.

My dear father gave me all his time, but even so, I was left to my own devices for long periods while he was away at work, and

I am surprised that I did not discover books until much later. I expect the distractions of Connaught Place were too much for me. But the winter holidays passed quickly, and early in March I was sharing a crowded compartment with a bunch of noisy boys in the Kalka-Shimla mountain train, as it chugged slowly up the steep hillsides and through those hundred and more tunnels.

~

During my second year in the prep school, there was to be no visit from my father. He and his unit were being moved about from place to place; first Karachi, then Calcutta. But he wrote to me regularly and sent me beautiful postcards, some of which I managed to keep. Besides the humorous 'Gran' pop' postcards, there were cards with famous trains or ships, or butterflies or pheasants or water-birds, or the Crown Jewels. There were also some unusual subjects, such as 'First Lady Cyclist', or 'Boy with a Dancing Bear.' I kept them all carefully. Like my father, I was becoming a collector.

And I was finally beginning to read books. Our 'library' consisted of a cupboard full of books chosen at random or left behind by departing teachers. Bound volumes of the *Boys' Own Paper* failed to excite me. Enid Blyton was far too bland for my tastes. But I discovered a set of Edgar Wallace thrillers, and proceeded to consume *The Crimson Circle, The Double* and other mysteries, to be followed by further mayhem in the *Bulldog Drummond* series of crime thrillers, and topped up with the exploits of 'Saint'—Simon Templar—Leslie Charteris's swashbuckling hero, portrayed so effectively in films by the suave George Sanders. Not many people know that the author Leslie Charteris was half-Chinese; he was always given out as a blue-blooded Englishman. In those days, authors were 'invisible' and did not lead public lives; they frequently assumed aliases. Ellery Queen was two people; John Dickson Carr was also Carter Brown; Sexton Blake was a whole series of writers.

I had gone straight into adult literature without the benefit of 'children's books', apart from *Alice,* and my beloved comic papers.

And I had begun with crime thrillers and detective stories—genres that will keep me entertained to the end of my days. It would be a year or two before I entered the world of Dickens, Stevenson and J.B. Priestley. Crime preceded the classics!

And meanwhile there was another Priestley to contend with—our venerable, violin-playing headmaster (no relation of the author's, I'm glad to say). This gentleman and his wife took little or no interest in the children, delegating all work and responsibility to their teaching staff and others. They had no children of their own and didn't particularly like us, except the few upper-class English boys, to whom they were outrageously partial. Mrs Priestley would sometimes show a little interest in us, favouring us with the flat of her hairbrush on our posteriors for misdemeanours real and imagined.

But I had no major complaints and was beginning to enjoy the school. My father wrote regularly from Calcutta, where he was now posted and living in his family home with his mother and my sister Ellen. In a long letter he wrote me on 20 August, 1944, he told me that he was recovering from yet another attack of malaria. He said he had to wear glasses for reading now, but Ellen didn't need glasses anymore and was getting better at holding a pencil and tried to draw dragons and elephants and tigers and wolves. He was looking forward to having me in Calcutta for the Christmas holidays and taking me to New Market, which he said was full of bookshops.

I was just sitting down to write him a reply, when one of my friends came up to me and said, 'Mr Murtough wants to see you. I think it's serious.'

Had I broken some silly rule? Should I have been studying instead of writing letters home? Had my stack of comic papers been discovered?

But no. Mr Murtough took me aside, led me down the path towards the school gate, asked me to sit down on a bench under the deodars, sat down beside me, and proceeded to tell me—as gently as he could, poor man—that my father was no more. God had taken him, he said. God had needed him more than I did.

PART II

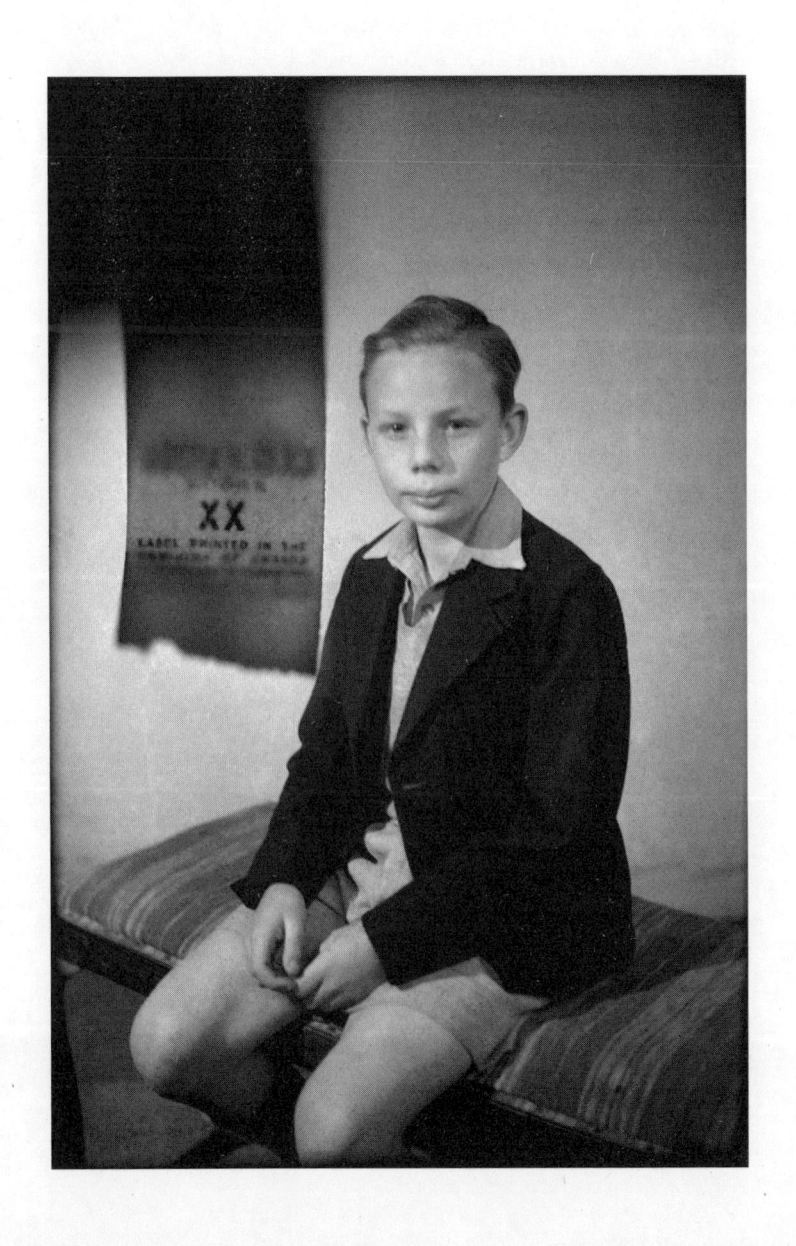

NIGHT, AND A HAPPY HOMECOMING

AND SO THE BOTTOM HAD FALLEN OUT OF MY WORLD. A great void opened up in front of me; I knew almost immediately that my life had changed forever, and that there was nothing, absolutely nothing to look forward to.

I was in the infirmary for a day, because I had broken down and then passed out after I was given the news. I have a tendency to shut out painful memories, and I have experienced no greater pain than the loss of my father. I was ten, and the only person who had loved me, and had any use for me, was gone. Time heals, but I still cannot dwell on that day when I lay in the infirmary, breathing with some difficulty. If everything begins and ends with love—and I believe it does—my world had ended. I emerged from the desolate night somehow; that is all I am willing to recall.

A week or two later, I received a letter from my mother, telling me that I would be spending the winter holidays with her in Dehra, and that I should take care of myself and concentrate on my studies. I had been wondering if I would be put in an orphanage, so this was a welcome message. It did not make me happy, because I was already distant from my mother, but it did bring some relief. She had also written to Mr Priestley, telling him this, and asking him to keep an eye on me.

One day Priestley called me to his office and suggested that I leave my father's precious letters with him for safekeeping; I could collect them a day or two before school closed. I think he had heard from some teacher or prefect that I had been reading those letters again and again, and brooding over them. I handed him all the letters, except one, Daddy's last, and a couple of postcards. Two months later, when the term ended, I went to Priestley's office and asked for the letters. He looked at me with a blank expression. What letters? Had I left some letters with him? He looked in the drawers of his desk. No letters there. He'd check with the senior master, he said. He was obviously a distracted man.

Was he worried about his job, his future in a rapidly changing world? Had he just quarrelled with his wife? Or had he broken the strings of his violin?

I stood there for some time, then turned and walked away without another word. The promises of adults had ceased to mean anything to me.

I still had one letter, and some of the 'Gran'pop' postcards. And that was all that I had from my father, apart from his everlasting love and care; for in the coming months even his stamp collection disappeared.

~

AA Bond 108485 (RAF)
c/o 231 Group
Rafpost
Calcutta 20/8/44

My dear Ruskin,

Thank you very much for your letter received a few days ago. I was pleased to hear that you were quite well and learning hard. We are all quite OK here, but I am still not strong enough to go to work after the recent attack of malaria I had. I was in hospital for a long time and that is the reason why you did not get a letter from me for several weeks.

I have now to wear glasses for reading. I do not use them for ordinary wear—but only when I read or do book work. Ellen does not wear glasses at all now.

Do you need any new warm clothes? Your warm suits must be getting too small. I am glad to hear the rains are practically over in the hills where you are. It will be nice to have sunny days in September when your holidays are on. Do the holidays begin from the 9th of Sept? What will you do? Is there to be a Scouts Camp at Taradevi? Or will you catch butterflies on sunny days on the school cricket ground? I am glad to hear you have lots of friends. Next year you will be in the top class of the Prep. School. You only have 3 ½ months more for the Xmas holidays to come round, when you will be glad to come home,

I am sure, to do more Stamp work and Library Study. The New Market is full of bookshops here. Ellen loves the market.

I wanted to write before about your writing, Ruskin, but forgot. Sometimes I get letters from you written in very small handwriting, as if you wanted to squeeze a lot of news into one sheet of letter paper. It is not good for you or for your eyes, to get into the habit of writing small. I know your handwriting is good and that you came 1st in class for handwriting, but try and form a larger style of writing and do not worry if you can't get all your news into one sheet of paper—but stick to big letters.

We have had a very wet month just passed. It is still cloudy, at night we have to use fans, but during the cold weather it is nice—not too cold like Delhi and not too warm either—but just moderate. Granny is quite well. She and Ellen send you their fond love. The last I heard, a week ago, that William and all at Dehra were well also.

We have been without a cook for the past few days. I hope we find a good one before long. There are not many. I wish I could get our Delhi cook, the old man now famous for his 'Black Puddings' which Ellen hasn't seen since we arrived in Calcutta 4 months ago.

I have still got the Records and Gramophone and most of the best books, but as they are all getting old and some not suited to you which are only for children under 8 yrs old—I will give some to William, and Ellen and you can buy some new ones when you come home for Xmas. I am re-arranging all the stamps that became loose and topsy-turvy after people came and went through the collections to buy stamps. A good many got sold, the rest got mixed up a bit and it is now taking up all my time putting the balance of the collection in order. But as I am at home all day, unable to go to work as yet, I have lots of time to finish the work of re-arranging the Collection.

Ellen loves drawing. I give her paper and a pencil and let her draw herself without any help, to get her used to holding paper and pencil. She has got expert at using her pencil now and draws some wonderful animals like camels, elephants, dragons with many heads—cobras—rain clouds shedding buckets of water—tigers with long grass around them—horses with manes and wolves and foxes with bushy hair. Sometimes you can't see much of the animals because there is too much grass covering them or too much hair on the foxes and wolves and too much mane on the horses' necks—or too much rain from the clouds. All this decoration is made up by a sort of heavy scribbling of lines, but through it all one can see some very good shapes of animals, elephants and ostriches and other things. I will send you some.

Well Ruskin, I hope this finds you well. With fond love from us all. Write again soon.

Ever your loving Daddy xxxxx

~

My father was forty-six when he died. Weakened by malaria, he had succumbed to hepatitis. This I discovered later. I did not attend his funeral, and his death was not discussed for many years at home. It wasn't callousness on anyone's part; I think they did it to protect me at first, and when I was older, I did not seek or encourage any discussion. My memories of Daddy were mine alone.

If one is present when a loved one dies, or sees him dead and laid out and later buried, one is convinced of the finality of the thing and finds it easier to adapt to the changed circumstances. But when you hear of a death, a dear parent's death, and have only the faintest idea of the manner of his dying, it is rather a lot for the imagination to cope with—especially when the imagination is a small boy's. There being no tangible evidence of my father's death, it was, for me, not a death but a vanishing. And although this enabled me to remember him as a living, smiling person, it meant that I was not wholly reconciled to his death, and subconsciously expected him to turn up and deliver me from an unpleasant situation.

It took me a lifetime to come to terms with the loss, and sometimes I still wonder if I have. You never really get over the loss of a beloved. You learn to live despite it.

Was my father a happy man? Looking back, I think he was; he had managed to live the kind of life he wanted. He studied, worked and travelled in many different parts of India, and he found the time and means to pursue his interests—collecting stamps, records and butterflies, and taking photographs. He fell in love, and he tried to start a family. If he felt he had failed at this, it wasn't something he talked about.

My mother told me later that he was very jealous, and kept her away from other men, perhaps torturing himself with imagined scenarios when she was away on her own. Who wouldn't have been jealous? She was young, pretty, vivacious—everyone looked twice at her. It was what had probably attracted him to her.

But they were incompatible. She was outgoing, he was not. Home was his favourite place. And yet he never set up home anywhere; he seemed to like moving from one place to another and changing homes frequently. When we were living in a house for any extended period, he loved moving the furniture around, changing the bedroom into the living room and vice versa, much to the irritation of my mother, who liked having things in their familiar places.

That part of my father's temperament surprises me, because he never gave the impression of being a restless man. But he never did settle down. Sometimes he spoke of making a home in Scotland, beside Loch Lomond, but of course it was only a dream. What was he searching for?

Perhaps it was an extended adolescence. Or it could have had something to do with his double inheritance. His father had joined the British Army and come to India when he was still a teenager. He had spent all his adult life here, marrying and raising his children, and through all that time there was 'home leave', when the family went to England. But England wasn't really home. Everything they had was in India, and yet this wasn't home, either.

In Shimla, when my father came to see me, and in Delhi, when I spent my holidays with him, he would say, 'When the war is over, we'll go to England. We'll put you in a school there. There won't be a job for me here.' He told me he was selling off segments of his stamp collection so that we'd have money to start life afresh there. I would go with him, and probably Ellen. He was not an advocate of Empire; I don't think he liked India less or England more—his world was mainly in his room, with his collections and his music. But as he saw it, we would always be associated with the Empire and would not be accepted in free India. He wanted comfort and security, as all of us do, for ourselves and our loved ones. He wanted the best for me, his closest companion.

After the separation from my mother, when he was alone in Delhi and his health was failing, I think he looked forward a great deal to the days that he spent with me—far more than I could have realized at the time. I was someone to come back to; someone for whom things could be planned.

My love was unconditional. And he had wanted me all to himself. It was the best kind of selfishness; it had filled my little life with so much joy.

Sometimes, well into middle age, I composed letters to my father. In my dreams, I would meet him on a busy street, after many lost years, and he would receive me with the same old warmth. We would get into a little train together, or sit in a dark hall, watching a screen lit up with bright, moving images. 'Where were you all these years?' I would ask him, and he would ruffle my hair. My father hadn't died; he was a traveller in a different dimension, and he would turn up every now and then, just to see if I was all right.

It was only in 2001, when I was sixty-seven, that I finally went looking for my father's grave. I located it in Calcutta's Bhowanipore Cemetery. 'Flight Lieutenant Aubrey Alexander Bond' had been laid to rest there by his mother, Gloriana. It must have been a small affair.

~

School closed for the three months of winter. And I was in the train, the steam-engine snorting and chugging its way through the fields and forests of the eastern Doon, bringing me to the mother I hadn't seen in almost three years.

Early morning in the Doon valley was always beautiful. I looked out of the carriage window as we passed over a small river, a tributary of the Ganga. A herd of elephants was walking into the clear waters.

The train slowed down as it took the gentle slopes of the valley. Fields of sugarcane and yellow mustard stretched away on either side. Village children ran out of their homes to wave to the passing train. Sometimes I waved back. Compartment windows were easily opened and closed in those days, you weren't shut in by immovable glazed glass. Occasionally you got soot in your eyes, for steam still ruled the rails; and at the end of a journey you were in need of a good bath, but there was no shortage of water back then, and Lifebuoy soap had already been invented.

Dehra was the end of the line. The train pulled into the little station just as the sun came up. Coolies bustled about. A few fond parents were on the platform, waiting to receive their children; for there were three or four of us from Bishop Cotton School who had homes in Dehra.

I expected to see my mother on the platform, but she wasn't there. Not a familiar face anywhere; not even an aunt. Perhaps a servant would be waiting. An elderly coolie dumped my box and bedding-roll on the platform. I asked him to wait. We both waited. I sat on my tin trunk while he chewed a paan. No one came.

'Where do you wish to go, chhota-sahib?' asked the patient coolie.

I thought about it. I was a slow thinker, but I did not have all day in which to make up my mind. My mother had written to say she was staying in a house with a lot of litchi trees, but even I knew this wasn't going to be any help at all. I remembered the way to Granny's house. Perhaps it still existed and my mother would be there.

'Can you get me a tonga?' I asked the coolie.

'Yes, come with *me, chhota-sahi*b. Plenty of tongas.' And he led me out of the station to the tonga stand, where he saw me and my luggage into a waiting tonga; accepted my rupee (leaving me with three), spat paan-juice over a film poster, and went his way.

'Old Survey Road,' I told the tonga-driver.

He cracked his whip and the pony set off at a leisurely trot.

Clip-clop through the quiet streets of Dehra. Two or three cars. More tongas. Lots of cyclists. It took the pony-cart about half an hour to get me to Granny's house. I got down near the veranda steps. And there was Granny watering the geraniums, joylessly absorbed in herself, as I remembered her from the last time I had lived in her house. Crazy, her pariah dog, was sitting on the grass some distance away. He recognized me and came bounding up to leap on me and lick my face.

Granny was surprised to see me on her steps, with my luggage in tow. She rarely smiled, and she made no attempt to do so now.

'I'm home for my holidays,' I said.

'Didn't someone meet you?' she asked, frowning a little.

'No.'

'Your mother doesn't live here any longer. They have a place in Dalanwala. Wasn't she expecting you?'

'I don't know. The school must have informed her.'

'Well, do you know where to go?'

'No.'

'Then I'd better take you there, I suppose.'

Expressionless as usual, she got into the tonga with me, and gave the tonga-driver an address in Dalanwala. Off we went again, down the Canal Road and into a maze of little lanes that all seemed to end in a dry riverbed. After several attempts we found the right lane and the right house. The front door was bolted from the inside and we had to knock on it repeatedly before it was opened by a tall and swarthy man in a pyjama and shirt who salaamed Granny deferentially.

'Where's memsahib?' Granny asked, sounding more tired than annoyed.

The servant told us she and 'sahib' were away on a shikar trip, somewhere in the forests of Motichur, hunting tigers. They weren't expecting me home so soon, it seemed; but lunch was ready any time I wanted it.

Two small children were playing on the grass. Granny took me across to them.

'These are your brothers,' she said. 'The fair one is your real brother, William. He's three now. And the other, the younger one, is Harold, your half-brother.'

They were busy playing marbles and took no notice of me.

'I'll leave you now,' said Granny. 'You can come and see me some time.'

And she got into the tonga and drove away. At least I did not have to pay the tonga fare. And I was getting used to disappointments.

I had thought I was coming home to my mother and baby brother. I didn't know she had remarried. No one had told me. I found out from the servant who the sahib was; it was Mr H.

WINTER HOLIDAYS

MY MOTHER ARRIVED THE NEXT DAY WITH MR H, WHO WAS now my stepfather, in spite of having a wife and two children in another part of the town. They hadn't been expecting me so soon. They had got the dates wrong. The tiger hunt was also something of a flop, as the tiger had failed to turn up. But there would be other tiger hunts, and I would be dragged along to some of them.

Meanwhile, I was made welcome and even given a small room of my own, which looked out on a rather neglected litchi and guava orchard. A few days later a small tin trunk arrived from Calcutta, forwarded to me by one of my father's brothers. It contained some books and records, and a postcard collection, but no stamps. Where was my father's priceless stamp collection? He had sold a few stamps, I knew, but the bulk of the collection had been with him till he died. It never did turn up, and I suspect that it was sold to dealers by impecunious relatives.

So there I was in the hamlet of Dalanwala; with two small brothers (and another on the way), and a mother and stepfather who seemed addicted to parties and tiger hunts. I made no effort to be close to them, or to my brothers; and if they made any overtures, it is likely that I rebuffed them. Daddy's death had left me more lonely and self-centred than before.

Left largely to my own devices, I got into the habit of taking long walks, usually into the fields or tea-gardens on the outskirts of Dehra. I had no friends, but I must have been wanting some, because I remember I would go down to the railway tracks near the forest, when a train was expected, and stand there, watching the carriages clatter past. One day a boy sitting at a carriage window waved and called out: 'Hey! Hello!' I kept looking at him till the train had gone, and I went to the same spot the next few days, expecting to see him again so that I could wave back, and maybe run alongside his carriage and ask his name and arrange to meet somewhere.

On one of my aimless walks I ended up at Granny's house, and asked her if there were any books lying around that I could read. I had never seen her reading a book; but there was always a chance that there would be something tucked away. Books do sometimes turn up in unexpected places. She gave me a religious tract, and told me to read it carefully.

Never despair has always been my motto, and I called on Granny's tenant next, with the same request. Miss Kellner occupied half the bungalow. She was a tiny, crippled spinster in her sixties, who had to be carried about by boys in livery and bathed by her ayah. My interaction with her till then had been limited to the occasional greeting, or a couple of sentences exchanged if we happened to be in the garden at the same time. Most of the time she was in fairly good spirits, despite her condition.

Usually she sat out in the garden, in an easy chair, in the shade of a pomelo tree.

'Do you have anything I can read, Miss Kellner?' I asked.

She was peering into a notebook. She looked up, and looked at me over her pince-nez glasses. 'Yes,' she said, and gave me a religious tract.

Apparently religious tracts were all the rage.

But hers came with a meringue and a soft nankhatai biscuit (made by a little bakery down the road), so I promised to read the tract.

Dropping in on Miss Kellner for a chat (and a snack) soon became a ritual of sorts, and I would turn up once a week, even by-passing Granny on one or two occasions. I would also play cards with her—simple games like 'Swap' or 'Beggar-my-neighbour'; the only time in my life when I had the patience for card games. It's surprising what a well-stocked larder will do when it comes to making friends with a small boy.

So there she was—my first friend after my father's death—an ageing lady with a shattered spine, twisted hands, a very large nose (which seemed to suit her) and a frail, bent-double body. I seldom saw her out of her chair, except when she was being carried into or out of the house by her helpers. She was always neatly dressed, and I believe the morning bath courtesy her ayah was a ritual she never missed. All her close relatives had over the years passed away, and she was very much on her own. But her late parents had left her some money, which she seemed to manage quite well, employing the ayah, a cook and four boys whose job it was to carry her into the garden and back. When she needed to go out of the house, the boys carried her in a sedan chair, and when she went into town or to visit her friends for bridge parties, they took her around in her private sky-blue rickshaw. She was feather-light, and she kept the boys well fed, so the rickshaw flew down the road, and I think I once saw her clap her small hands in delight.

In spite of her infirmities, Miss Kellner had a healthy complexion and a good appetite. There was a story going around that she bathed in rosewater. I couldn't be so familiar as to ask her if this was true, but I decided to question her ayah on the subject. From my Jamnagar days, I usually got on well with ayahs, and they were fountains of gossip and esoteric knowledge.

'Tell me, ayah-ji, does Miss Kellner really bathe in rosewater?' I asked quite innocently one day.

'None of your business,' snapped her loyal ayah. 'And what do you bathe in, inquisitive boy?'

'Donkey's milk,' I said mischievously, and allowed her to chase me around a pomelo tree.

I couldn't ask Miss Kellner about her disability, either. It was my mother who told me that when Miss Kellner was a baby, some fond uncle had been tossing her high in the air and catching her, when he was distracted by something and dropped her. The fall broke her spine, and her limbs, which never set properly. She had been an invalid ever since.

But mentally she was very alert. She would do her hisaab—accounts—in a large notebook, and though her hands were crooked, she would correspond with friends or distant relatives (I never found out who they were or where). She had a front room filled with all kinds of bric-a-brac she had collected over the years, and she would get her staff to dust and polish it every once in a while.

Soon enough, her ayah grew a little fond of me too. After we had talked for some time and played card games, Miss Kellner would say, 'You must be hungry', and I'd immediately say 'Yes', and she'd call the ayah, who knew exactly what was needed and would come with the meringues, patties and nankhatais.

I was the only child who would sit and talk to Miss Kellner. There were other younger people in the area, including my cousins who came to visit Granny, but I think they were intimidated by her, or unwilling to be around an old and deformed person confined to her chair. Despite my mischievous nature, I was not a very outgoing person, and in those days I was confused and at a loose end; it was our shared loneliness that brought us together. It wasn't just the meringues she gave me! I found her interesting, and oddly comforting. She had time for me, as I had time for her. In fact, she looked forward to my visits, which was not something I experienced anymore. At home, in my mother's house or Granny's, I felt I was usually on sufferance after my father died. This was, of course, not an entirely fair judgement. They did not dislike me, and I certainly didn't make it easier for them to love me, expecting them to put aside their life and the rest of the family for me, as I thought my father had done. But this sort of understanding comes with age; a ten-year-old is not so forgiving.

I continued to spend time with Miss Kellner during my holidays for the next five or six years, and sometimes she wrote me cards when I was back at school in Shimla. My Granny thought a lot of her, but I don't remember seeing them together. Granny kept a great deal to herself. But she valued and respected Miss Kellner; I learnt later that she had made it a condition in her will that after she died, my aunt Emily, who inherited the house, would continue to keep Miss Kellner there. (And when my aunt and her family sold the house and moved to Jersey, they took an undertaking from the new owners that they would not evict Miss Kellner, who lived there till she died in the early 1950s.)

There was another friend I made in Granny's garden. Granny kept a gardener, Dukhi, a quiet man, who could have been forty, or sixty—I don't think anyone knew. He spent almost the entire day on his haunches, weeding the flower beds with the little spade, or khurpi, that he carried around. Dandelions, daisies, thistles, and other 'weeds' received no mercy from that relentless khurpi. Even some common marigolds flew from his spade.

'Don't throw those away,' I protested one day. 'They're so pretty!'

'Your grandmother doesn't like them,' said Dhuki.

In their place came petunias, poppies, sweet-peas, larkspur, snapdragons.

I liked the snapdragons. They came in many colours. And

the sweet-peas gave out a heady fragrance. I think Granny grew most of her flowers for the sake of their fragrance. She could be unsmiling most of the time, but at least the garden was a friendly place.

~

That winter I began reading a lot. My visits to Miss Kellner finally resulted in the acquisition of some fascinating literature. A friend or relative of hers in England would mail her copies of the *Daily Mirror*, a lively tabloid for the working classes, sets of seven bound in bright yellow folders just in case you wished to preserve them—which I did. When Miss Kellner had no further use for her *Daily Mirrors* she would pass them on to me—and I would feast on the latest society scandals and sensational murders, all of which were given priority over the war news. There was also an entire page devoted to comic strips, and another to films, which was fine—but nothing about books! Didn't people in England read books? It was to be years before I saw the *Manchester Guardian* or *News Chronicle*, so the *Daily Mirror* was (for some time at least) to be my sole guide to the cultural preferences of Britain.

More substantial literature I found in Tara Hall, the large, friendly house close to Dilaram Bazaar that belonged to the Melvilles (an old Anglo-Indian family of Dehra whose daughter 'Vi' had married the English corporal). People were always dropping in for tea or badminton practice at their place and the gramophone on their veranda would be playing popular records. One of them, Mrs Chill, was a kind-hearted person who had taken an interest in me. She had lost her husband to cholera just after their marriage, and had never remarried. But I always found her cheerful and good-natured, sending me presents on Christmas (the kindest people are often those who have come through testing personal tragedies). One day I asked Mrs Chill if she had any books I could read.

An entire shelf of books was put at my disposal. But almost all the books were by her favourite author, P.C. Wren, who had written romantic sagas about life in the French Foreign Legion—*Beau Geste, Beau Sabreur*, etc. The novels seemed rather unreal to me, though I got through one called *The Snake and the Sword*, which was set in India, and told the story of an otherwise brave Army officer who had an incurable fear and horror of snakes. I would have thought someone who hated snakes could easily avoid them, but the book's hero encountered them everywhere—in his bedclothes, in his bathroom, on parade, wherever he went. He finally got over his obsessive fear by actually killing a snake with his sword—having taken over 300 pages to get around to this final act of liberation.

Years later I discovered that P.C. Wren served in the Indian educational service and had co-authored an English grammar book which was used in schools throughout India and was still in use well into the 1970s—long after *Beau Geste* had been forgotten. Wren had never served in the Foreign Legion, but it's wonderful what a lively imagination can achieve.

I was still going through Mrs Chill's collection, beginning to despair at the number of P.C Wrens there, when I chanced upon a small treasure of novels on a memorable trip into the jungle between Dehradun and Hardwar. It was Mr H who insisted I join him and my mother and some of their friends for a shikar expedition. They usually went alone, but perhaps they were concerned about the time I was spending roaming around Dehra like a vagrant. I went reluctantly; I hated guns and shikar seemed a barbaric way to relieve boredom. But in the end I was glad I went. I refused to go out hunting with them, and spent most of my time in the forest rest-house, where I found a shelf full of books and discovered P.G. Wodehouse's *Love Among the Chickens*, M.R. James's *Ghost Stories of an Antiquary*, Agatha Christie's *Death on the Nile* and *Murder at the Vicarage*, A.A. Milne's *The Red House Mystery*, and *Sketches by Boz*, a collection of Dickens's short pieces—all solid English fare, for a change.

As for the shikar itself, nobody shot anything, the resident tiger having failed to put in an appearance; but while the hunters were away, I saw a leopard slinking across the clearing in front of the rest-house. Nobody believed me, but the incident made me a leopard fan as well as a Wodehouse fan.

A word about Mr H, my stepfather. He was never unkind to me in any way; most of the time he hardly noticed me, caught up as he was in his frenzied living. His attitude to me was one of benign neglect, but most of the time he seemed unaware even of his own children, from his first wife and from my mother.

He hailed from Amritsar and his marriage to a Punjabi lady had brought him a dowry consisting of a photography studio in Dehradun, where his family had shifted when he was young. It was never clear to me why he had agreed to that marriage, because the lady he married and soon abandoned, and whom I came to know well in later years, was very traditional, with no interest in the Western and city lifestyle he favoured. Perhaps it was the dowry. As he was more interested in automobiles, he sold half the studio, leaving the other half to his wife, and bought a car dealership and motor workshop. This was when he met my mother. It was the era of the jeep, and their mutual interest in shikar resulted in many a jeep-ride into the surrounding forests, where big game still abounded. When not on expeditions into the jungle, they liked to go to parties.

Like my mother, Mr H wasn't very good with money. He was irregular with his payments and casual about keeping accounts. Repair jobs were seldom finished on time. If a customer left a nice car with him for servicing, he would drive around in it for several weeks on the pretext of 'testing' it, before handing it back to the irate owner (this was how he appeared in a new car every day when he was courting my mother). But he was popular with his workmen and mechanics, as he was happy to sit and drink with them, or take them along on his shikar trips. Everyone had a good time, except his customers.

Naturally the car business suffered, and Mr H was soon in debt. Rents went unpaid, and we were frequently on the move.

Every time I came home for the winter holidays, I would find that they had shifted to a new address. It was with some help from the RAF that my mother was able to pay my school fees, and later, William's. My sister Ellen was still in Calcutta with Daddy's mother, now into her eighties, but it wouldn't be long before she, too, had to join us in Dehra. The RAF sent an allowance for Ellen's maintenance, but it only went so far. My mother didn't turn away from the responsibility, but she also didn't make things easy for herself or her children.

She lived life in a slightly haphazard fashion. Of all her sisters, with the exception of the eldest, Enid, she was the unconventional one. The others never did anything risky, and had found and kept conventional husbands, all well-settled professionals. Even Aunt Enid ensured her marriage survived and her husband did not stray, even as she herself made a habit of straying.

My mother wasn't interested in being a good girl; she liked to drink and swear a bit. The ladies of the Dehra Benevolent Society did not approve. Nor did they approve of her going to church without a hat—this was considered the height of irreverence in those days, and there were remonstrances and anguished letters of protest from other members of the congregation. As a result, she stopped going to church.

The life choices my mother made got her nowhere socially. The snootier Anglo-Indians and domiciled Europeans cut her off for having left a decent member of the community to engage in a public affair with, and then marry, an Indian—and a non-Christian, too—who even lacked the redeeming attribute of wealth or professional status. That their disapproval made no difference to her probably infuriated them even more.

While the ladies and gents of the Dehra Benevolent Society were in church, my mother and Mr H would be in one of Dehra's cinema halls, watching both English and Hindustani films with equal pleasure. I remember going to my first Indian films with them: *Tansen*, starring K.L. Saigal (Mr H's favourite singer-actor) and Khursheed Bano, that winter of 1944; and later, *Jugnu*, with

Noor Jehan and Dilip Kimar, and *Nadiya ke Paar*, with Dilip Kumar and Kamini Kaushal (who was to become my favourite).

But these 'family excursions' were rare events. Usually my mother and Mr H would leave the younger children in the care of the cook and ayah, and me to my own devices, and disappear into the surrounding jungles. Back in town, they would go out almost every night. The old Ford convertible we owned would bring them back at two or three in the morning. My old insecurity resurfaced, and I would lie awake wondering what I would do if they had an accident of some kind and died. Would I be expected to look after my brothers and sister? How would I do it? Where would the money come from?

No such anxieties seemed to plague my mother and stepfather. They remained committed to enjoying life instead of paying their bills in time. I returned from Miss Kellner's one afternoon to find our boxes, bedding, furniture, pots and pans piled up on the driveway. The rent hadn't been paid for months and the landlord had secured an eviction order.

Granny had to take us all in, her privacy and peace of mind shattered once again by her unconventional daughter. We stayed in her house for the remainder of my holidays.

~

Dehra in 1944–45 was a lively place. The town had been designated a rest and recreation centre for Allied troops a couple of years ago, and it was still awash with soldiers on a break from active duty in Burma and the Far East. There was some hostility between the British and American soldiers because the latter were better paid and had more money to throw around. To avoid bar fights and street brawls, the Americans were allowed into town three days a week, and the British three days a week. One day of the week was reserved for the Italian prisoners of war, a better-looking and more charming lot, but poor. They tried to earn some pocket money by selling postage stamps and wooden toys.

Restaurants and nightclubs had sprung up in and around

Astley Hall, and every evening they would be filled to capacity with roistering soldiers panting for pleasure before they returned to the warfront. Many of the younger Anglo-Indians became regulars at these watering holes and dance halls, looking for a bit of fun and maybe some romance. For the girls, it was as if the world had come to worship at their feet.

Some nights, there would be laughter and whistling in the streets and some drunken soldier would be heard weeping and swearing, looking for a girl called Gracie or Lara—a resident of Dehra, or perhaps of Brighton or Tennessee.

One of the more popular cafes, which also functioned as a nightclub, was the Casino, owned by a magician named Gogia Pasha, a Punjabi gentleman whose real name escapes me. We called him 'Gali-gali', because he would preface all his tricks with 'gali, gali, gali', producing rabbits and roosters from his pockets and eggs from his ears, or sawing a lady in half. And he kept up a rapid-fire commentary as he went along, making jokes and engaging the audience. After his magic show, a live band would start playing and the dancing would begin, and the air would be full of romantic possibilities.

The songs were from popular Hollywood films and by the American big bands. Everyone was in love with Rita Hayworth in those days, and songs and dances from her hit films like *Gilda* ('Put the blame on Mame, boys') were in great demand. There were also Ella Fitzgerald and Doris Day songs, and songs by Bing Crosby and Frank Sinatra. Delhi and Bombay had the bigger bands, of course—Rudy Cotton with his saxophone was king—but the scene was livelier in Dehradun, because it was a small place, a fun-and-games hothouse that would soon return to its pre-war slumber.

The reader might wonder how I know so much about what went on in those nightclubs when I was just ten. Well, there was this pretty Anglo-Indian girl, eighteen or nineteen years old, who would fuss over me whenever my mother took me to the store below the Casino where she worked. Her name was Irene, and both she and her sister Rhoda were regulars at the Casino, where the soldiers vied for their attention. Rhoda was even more beautiful, but Irene was my favourite. On a couple of occasions, she took me with her to the nightclub, and it was a magical new world for me, the hall full of smoke and music and laughter. I had a crush on Irene. But to her I was like a kid brother, a besotted boy whose company and attention she enjoyed. She could kiss me on the forehead or ask me to press her back, or adjust her dress in a corner while I stood guard, and think nothing of it.

Irene made that New Year's Eve memorable. She invited me to the dance party at the Casino, and my mother and Mr H encouraged me to go. I accompanied Irene into the club, where a four-piece live band was playing the latest Glen Miller hits—'In the Mood' and 'Chattanooga Choo Choo' and others that I forget. The tobacco smoke and beer and whisky fumes were headier than ever before. Irene gave me a quarter glass of rum which I downed like a seasoned drinker, and then I led her to the dance floor to much applause and cheering. We did a foxtrot, and the crowd roared and whistled in approval. But as soon as the song was over, a smart soldier stole Irene from me and I retreated into a corner to sulk and glower at them. Someone—the soldier or Irene—had a plate of fish fingers and a glass of the raspberry-flavoured drink Vimto sent to me. But I continued to sulk.

But when the lights were turned off and the hall exploded into 'Auld Lang Syne', Irene came to me, calling my name, and she gathered me in her perfumed arms and kissed me full on the lips!

It was my first rum and my first kiss and I was quite intoxicated.

And the magic time wasn't over yet. Two days later, it snowed in Dehra. I was out walking when it began. It came down quite suddenly, and soon the litchi and guava trees were covered with a soft mantle of snow. I vividly remember running in and telling my mother, 'It's snowing outside, Mum!' and she said, 'I don't want any of your silly jokes right now, Ruskin,' because she had just given birth to my second half-brother, Hansel, and was in bed. So I ran out and came back with some litchi leaves which were covered with snow, and her face lit up with a delighted smile.

Later Miss Kellner told me it had snowed in Dehradun once before, forty years earlier, when she came to Dehradun.

'Now maybe it's a sign that I should go,' she said.

'Don't go,' I said. 'Wait for the next snowfall.'

This pleased her, and we played Snap. The ayah brought us ginger biscuits, and I polished them all off and asked for more.

WHEN ALL THE WARS ARE DONE

IT WAS MARCH AND TIME TO HEAD BACK TO SCHOOL. I WAS PUT on a train to Ambala, from where I was to catch the train coming from Delhi going to Kalka. I was a big boy, almost eleven, and I could do this alone. In Ambala there would be many other boys going to BCS after the holidays. Trains usually kept to their schedule in those days, but this one didn't, and when I reached Ambala station I had missed the train from Delhi. So there I was on the platform, with my trunk and bedding, and I didn't know what to do. It would soon be night.

I walked around on the platform for a while, and then I left my luggage in the waiting room and walked out of the station and kept walking, with no plan, except to keep moving till something happened to resolve the situation. After some time, I saw a police post, and I walked over to the post and told the policeman I'd missed my train and I wanted to inform my parents. Fortunately, my mother and stepfather had a telephone in the house. I gave the policemen their names and the number and they put me through and I told my mother I was stuck at Ambala station.

Gosh, she said. Was I really? Well, not to worry, I should just stay there and someone would be with me soon to sort things out. I went back to the station and went to sleep on the bench—

Ambala was a busy enough station and there were a few other people, sitting or lying on the benches and on the floor. It was morning by the time help arrived—someone from my stepfather's workshop, who got my ticket made and put me on the next train to Kalka. A few other boys had arrived with a parent or guardian and I joined the group.

In Kalka, as was the practice, there were a couple of teachers to escort batches of students to the school. The small narrow-gauge train took all day to get us up the mountains to Shimla. The rhododendron trees were flaunting their scarlet blossoms, but there was snow on the ground, and when we approached Shimla we found the tracks blocked by snow. We spent a cold and uncomfortable night, all crowded together and sitting upright, until dawn broke, when we got off the train and began the long trudge to school, about three miles distant. The luggage came a day later. I don't remember if there were hot baths at the end of the long trek through the snow; probably not.

We were a hardy lot, I suppose. Unlike the posh boarding schools of today, BCS had no heating, and there were no fireplaces for us in the dormitories, and not enough hot water in the winter. However, the school was developed enough to have installed a flush system—almost all homes and most establishments in India, even big hotels, used some version of thunder boxes at the time (many did so well into the 1960s). But going to the toilet at BCS was still an adventure. There was a long line of potties, and there was a flush but you didn't have chains to pull, the water came down automatically every ten minutes. And usually, because of the large population of boys using the potties or because they were poorly maintained, they would overflow. So as soon as you heard a rumble approaching, you knew the water was coming down and you leapt up and ran before a wave rose under you!

Not posh, then, but infinitely more comfortable than the lives that millions in India lived, and which we were almost completely insulated from in schools like Bishop Cotton's. None of us had experienced hunger. There were wartime shortages, but we weren't deprived of much. Omelettes were made from 'egg powder'—a mysterious thing, which I later discovered was dehydrated egg and that the Chinese had been making it centuries earlier. Deadly-looking sausages were also made up of several mysterious ingredients and were known to soldiers as 'sweet mysteries of life'—named after the Nelson Eddy–Jeanette Macdonald love duet 'Ah! Sweet Mystery of Life', featured in the film *Naughty Marietta*. The Keventer's farm at Taradevi supplied us with butter, but refined sugar was hard to come by, and our tea was sweetened with raw gur or shakkar, which was probably healthier. The school tuck-shop was a popular destination if you had any pocket money in hand. The fare was limited to buns, samosas, pakoras and jalebis, which was fine with most of us. (The fast-food era had yet to dawn; the nearest to it being the packets of chewing-gum which American soldiers dispensed freely until they were sent home at the end of the war.)

This was probably the norm for most boarding schools of the time. Bishop Cotton's was, after all, one of the most prestigious. Apart from English and Anglo-Indian boys—some of them fairly privileged—the Indian, Nepali and Tibetan boys were from royal families or landed gentry. There were very few from families of professionals. Although royalty didn't mean we had too many future kings and dewans with us. A lot of these boys lived in the shadow of royalty, and they would do so all their lives.

There were the Patiala boys, for instance—the sons of the late Maharaja of Patiala, Bhupinder Singh, from women he slept with but did not marry. There were a great number of them. But he looked after all the women and their children. Several of the boys were sent to BCS and the girls to the nearby Auckland House; other progeny went to boarding schools in Dehradun and Mussoorie. In my time, there were about twenty Patiala brothers in BCS. He used to give them all English names, in addition to their Sikh names: Hemender was also Maurice, Devinder was Cecil, another boy was Dennis—it was a quaint fancy of the

Maharaja's. I remember we had a funny situation once, when the football team from Colonel Brown's school in Dehradun came to play a match against us: half their team were my friend and teammate Hemender's brothers—all the sons of the Maharaja of Patiala from different women!

I was by then a regular member of the football team. My affair with the game—alas, cut short very soon after school—had begun in my second or third year in BCS. All games were compulsory, which I neither understood nor appreciated, but I was surprised how quickly I took to football, and how much I liked it (I ended up as captain of the school team!). I was happy with hockey, too, but not so happy with cricket, which bored me.

But the two sports I disliked were boxing and swimming. I figured out soon enough that I could get myself disqualified in a boxing match by butting my opponent in the head or midriff, and so end the torture. There was no clever way out of swimming, however, and I had to overcome my fear of water and struggle to contain my panic as I thrashed about noisily in the pool, trying to come to grips with the freestyle and the butterfly and back stroke. Finally, it was a kind and wise teacher, Mr Jones, who taught me the breast stroke, saying it was more suited to my temperament.

Like sports, church-going was also compulsory, although unlike at the Mussoorie convent, no one was fanatical about it. For the boys—many of them not Christian, anyway—it was like going to the library or PT class. Some of them even enjoyed it, especially the choir, where again not all the boys were Christian. I remember we had two or three Sikh boys in the church choir, and they'd sing beautifully, looking very sweet in their cassocks and turbans—a lovely advertisement for mixing up religions and cultures and making the world a far more interesting and colourful place.

But I couldn't sing. Our music teacher, Mrs Knight, put me in the school choir because, she said, I looked like a choir boy, all pink and shining in a cassock and surplice. But she forbade me from actually singing.

'You will open your mouth with the others, Bond,' she said, 'but you are *not* to allow any sound to issue forth!'

She reminded me of the strict nuns at the Mussoorie convent, and I feared for my pink knuckles.

But there were some good teachers. A little odd, but nice. Like kind Mr Jones, who smoked a cigar and had a pet pigeon which was often perched on his head. He didn't bring it to class, but he would walk around outside with the pigeon on his head—and he had a bald head, so it was a very amusing sight. In his bachelor quarters, the pigeon was completely at home in the middle of untidy piles of books and papers and clothes, all reeking of cigar smoke.

Mr Jones was a rare teacher who got on well with the younger boys. Without exception, we all liked him, one reason being that he never punished us. He was a lone crusader against the custom of caning boys for their misdemeanours, for which he was ridiculed as an eccentric by the other masters and lost his seniority.

In Mr Jones I found a sympathetic soul. He was a Welshman, retired from the army, who taught us divinity. He seemed to sense I had no interest in religion, but that did not upset or disappoint him, and such were his gentle ways that he actually got me to read the complete Bible! It was the King James version, and though it did not make me a good Christian, or even a bad one, I was affected deeply by the classical simplicity of its style.

He was a Dickens fan, and when I told him I'd read *Sketches by Boz*, he gave me access to his set of the *Complete Works of Charles Dickens*, handsome illustrated editions all, and I was lost for days in the life sagas of David Copperfield, Nicholas Nickleby and Oliver Twist. If I had to choose a moment when I began to think seriously about becoming a writer, it would have to be this period.

Being a socialist, Mr Jones had an aversion to P.G. Wodehouse, whose comic novels I greatly enjoyed. According to him, Wodehouse glamourized upper-class English life, which was true. But he did not try to dissuade me from reading about Bertie

Wooster and Jeeves and all the rest. In a few years, I would discover that the world Wodehouse described, and so many of his readers across the world were charmed by, did not really exist.

Nevertheless, I continued to read and enjoy Wodehouse, but with Mr Jones's encouragement, I began to spend as much time as I could in the school library—the Anderson Library. It was very well stocked, and it became something of a haven for me for the rest of my school years.

~

The callous and classist headmaster, Priestley, was still around. But the war was coming to an end, and he and several English expatriate teachers and students would soon be leaving. Indian Independence was also just around the corner, and many Anglo-Indian families were emigrating to England and Australia. With Independence would come Partition, and I would lose a couple of dear friends to arbitrarily drawn borders and the hate and violence that often come in the wake of such political upheavals.

In that last year at prep. school, my friends included Azhar Khan, who came from Lahore; Cyrus Satralkar, from Bombay; and Brian Adams, an Anglo-Indian boy from New Delhi. We called ourselves 'The Four Feathers', the feathers—of a falcon, a peacock, a parakeet and a woodpecker—signifying that we were companions in adventure, comrades-in-arms. Our occasional escapades were confined to breaking bounds when opportunity arose, or sharing our food parcels, or going into town together on Sunday afternoons to watch movies. Satralkar received the largest number of food parcels from home, and he became the most valued member of the group.

But it was Azhar who became my closest friend. He was a quiet, precocious boy, the ideal companion on long walks or scrambles down the hillsides. While I was losing much of my shyness, and was not as much of a loner as before, he was an introvert and took no part in the form's feverish attempts to imitate the Marx Brothers at the circus. He showed no resentment at the prevailing anarchy in the classroom, nor did he make a move to participate in it. Once he caught me looking at him, and he smiled ruefully, tolerantly. Did I sense another adult in the class? Someone who was a little older than his years?

Even before we began talking to each other, Azhar and I developed an understanding of sorts, and we'd nod to each other when we met in the classroom corridors or in the dining hall. We were not in the same house. The house system practiced its own form of apartheid, whereby a member of, say, Curzon House was not expected to fraternize with someone belonging to Rivaz or Lefroy. But these barriers vanished when Azhar and I found ourselves selected for the school hockey team—Azhar as a full-back, I as goalkeeper. A good understanding is needed between goalkeeper and full-back, and we were on the same wavelength. I anticipated his moves, he was familiar with mine.

It wasn't until we were away from the confines of school, classroom and dining hall that our friendship flourished. The hockey team travelled to Sanawar, on the next mountain range, where we were to play a couple of matches against our traditional rivals, the Lawrence School, which was then still a military school (my father's old school, in fact). Azhar and I were thrown together a good deal during the visit to Sanawar, and in our more leisurely moments, strolling undisturbed around a school where we were guests and not pupils, we exchanged life histories. Azhar was from the North-West Frontier Province, and he had lost his father too, shot in some family dispute. A wealthy uncle was seeing to his education, as the RAF was seeing to mine.

I had already started writing my first book. It was called *Nine Months*, but had nothing to do with a pregnancy; it referred merely to the length of the school term, the beginning of March to the end of November, and it detailed my friendships and escapades at school and lampooned a few of our teachers. I had filled three slim exercise books with this premature literary project, and I allowed Azhar to go through them. He was my first reader and critic. 'They're very interesting. But you'll get into trouble if someone finds them.' And he read out an offending verse, chuckling in obvious delight:

Olly, Olly, Olly, with his balls on a trolley,
And his arse all painted green!

This bit was about our melancholic mathematics master, Mr Oliver. I had no quarrel with Mr Oliver, but I hated maths.

We returned to Shimla, having won our matches against Sanawar, and were school heroes for a couple of days. And then my housemaster discovered my literary opus and took it away and read it. I was given six of the best with a Malacca cane, and my manuscript was torn up. Azhar knew better than to say 'I told you so' when I showed him the purple welts on my bottom. Instead, he repeated the more scurrilous bits he remembered from the notebooks and laughed, till I began to laugh too.

'Will you go away when the British leave India?' Azhar asked me one day.

'I don't think so,' I said. 'My stepfather is Indian.'

'Everyone is saying they're going to divide the country. I think I'll have to go away.'

'Oh, it won't happen,' I said glibly. 'How can they cut up such a big country?'

'Gandhi will stop them,' he said.

But even as we dismissed the possibility, Jinnah, Nehru and Mountbatten and all those who mattered were preparing their instruments for major surgery.

Before their decision impinged on our life, we found a little freedom of our own—in an underground tunnel that we discovered in a corner of the school grounds. It was really part of an old, disused drainage system, and when Azhar and I began exploring it, we had no idea just how far it extended. After crawling along on our bellies for some twenty feet, we found ourselves in complete darkness. It was a bit frightening, but moving backwards would have been quite impossible, so we continued writhing forward, until we saw a glimmer of light at the end of the tunnel. Dusty, a little bruised and very scruffy, we emerged at last on to a grassy knoll, a little way outside the school boundary. We'd found a way to escape school!

The tunnel became our beautiful secret. We would sit and chat in it, or crawl through it just for the thrill of stealing out of the school to walk in the wilderness. Or to lie on the grass, our heads touching, reading comics or watching the kites and eagles wheeling in the sky. In those quiet moments, I became aware of the beauty and solace of nature more keenly than I had been till then: the scent of pine needles, the soothing calls of the Himalayan bulbuls, the feel of grass on bare feet, and the low music of the cicadas.

Lord Mountbatten, viceroy and governor-general-to-be, came for our Founder's Day that year and gave away the prizes. I had won a prize for something or the other, and mounted the rostrum to receive my book from this towering, handsome man. Bishop Cotton's was the 'Eton of the East'. Viceroys and governors had graced its functions. Many of its boys had gone on to eminence in the civil services and armed forces. There was one 'old boy', of course, about whom they maintained a stolid silence—General Dyer, who had ordered the massacre at Jallianwala Bagh in Amritsar in 1919.

Now Great Britain wanted to do the right thing. Mountbatten spoke of the momentous events that were happening all around us—World War II had just come to an end, the United Nations held out the promise of a world living in peace and harmony, and India, an equal partner with Britain, would be among the great nations...

He mentioned Independence, without, as far as I can recall, actually using the word. He said nothing about dividing the country.

A few weeks later, Bengal and Punjab provinces, with their large Muslim populations, were bisected. Everyone was in a hurry—Jinnah and company were in a hurry to get a country of their own; Nehru, Patel and others were in a hurry to run a free, if truncated, India; and Britain was in a hurry to get out. Riots flared up across northern India, and there was a great exodus of people crossing the newly drawn frontiers of Pakistan and India. Homes were destroyed, thousands lost their lives.

The common room radio and the occasional newspaper kept us abreast of events, but in our tunnel Azhar and I felt immune from all that was happening, worlds away from all the pillage, murder and revenge. Outside the tunnel, there was fresh untrodden grass, sprinkled with clover and daisies, the only sounds the hammering of a woodpecker, and the distant insistent call of the Himalayan barbet. Who could touch us there?

'And when all wars are done,' I said, 'a butterfly will still be beautiful.'

'Did you read that somewhere?' Azhar asked.

'No, it just came into my head.'

'It's good. Already you're a writer.'

Though it felt good to hear him say that, I made light of it. 'No, I want to play hockey for India or football for Arsenal. Only winning teams!'

'You'll lose sometimes, you know, even if you get into those teams,' said wise old Azhar. 'You can't win forever. Better to be a writer.'

When the monsoon rains arrived in June, the tunnel was flooded, the drain choked with rubble, and Azhar and I had to suspend our little adventures. But now the town was out of bounds, too. One Sunday, we were allowed out to the cinema, to see Lawrence Olivier's *Hamlet*, a forbidding film which did nothing to raise our spirits on a wet and gloomy afternoon, and we had barely returned, when communal riots broke out in Shimla's Lower Bazaar as well.

One morning after chapel, the headmaster announced that the Muslim boys—those who had their homes in what was now Pakistan—would have to be evacuated. They would be sent to their homes across the border with an armed convoy.

It was time for Azhar to leave, along with some fifty other boys from Lahore, Rawalpindi and Peshawar. The rest of us—Hindus, Christians, Buddhists, Sikhs and Parsis—helped them load their luggage into the waiting British Army trucks that would take them to Lahore. A couple of boys broke down and wept, including our departing school captain, a Pathan who had been known for his unemotional demeanour. Azhar waved to me and I waved back. We had vowed to meet again some day. We both kept our composure; either our experiences had hardened us, or we truly believed that we would be together again.

The headmaster announced a couple of days later that all the boys had reached Pakistan and were safe. But their journey hadn't been without incident. Though we weren't informed officially, we learned that the amiable Muslim baker who ran the school canteen, bringing up our favourite buns and pakoras from his home in Chhota Shimla, had been killed. He and two of the school's Muslim bearers who were travelling with the boys had strayed into an off-limits area when the convoy made a halt in Kalka. They were set upon by a mob, and while the bearers managed to escape, the baker hadn't been able to outrun the mob armed with sickles and knives.

As in the rest of Punjab on both sides of the border, chaos and violence reigned in Shimla. There weren't enough soldiers to stop the rioting—the British were abandoning the country, and the local administration had collapsed. Our school was under threat; the authorities had equipped some of the teachers and senior boys with rifles, and we were forbidden from stepping outside. We remained confined to the school till the end of the term, the only exception being the morning of August 15, 1947, when we were marched up to town to witness the Indian flag being raised for the first time. Shimla was still the summer capital of India, so it was quite an event.

It was raining that morning. We were in our raincoats and gum-boots, while a sea of umbrellas covered the Mall. What did I feel as I saw the Union Jack being lowered and the Indian Tricolour replacing it? My father had seldom spoken about India or Britain or our place in either country, except to say, occasionally, that we would be going away once the war was over. I was still a boy, and I don't think I had strong feelings about the issue, one way or the other. I remember being more interested in the colours and design of the Indian flag than in the speeches that were being made from the rostrum. (Two years later, as a school prefect, it became my duty to raise the Indian flag on the school flat. It seemed quite natural to be doing so; and it seemed quite natural and thrilling to be a member of the NCC, the National Cadet Corps.)

What I did feel strongly about was the senseless division of the country that had separated me from my friends. Towards the end of the school year, just as I was getting ready to leave for Dehradun for the three-month winter holidays, I received a letter from Azhar. He told me something about his new school and how he missed my company and our games and our tunnel to freedom. I replied and gave him my home address, but I did not hear from him again. We were always shifting houses in Dehradun, so if a letter did come, it might easily have been lost. And there were many new borders in any case. Even without those borders, the land, though divided, was still a big one, and we were very small.

Eighteen years later, I did get some news, but in an entirely different context. India and Pakistan were at war and in a bombing raid over Ambala, a Pakistani plane was shot down. An old school friend wrote to say he had heard the pilot's name was Azhar, but he couldn't be sure if it was the Azhar we knew.

~

The war had come to the borders of India and changed our world forever. But as a boy I barely understood the consequences. Later, I would read and hear about the horror of that global war—the concentration camps and Hitler's extermination of the Jews; Japanese atrocities in China and Southeast Asia; and finally, America dropping the atomic bomb on Hiroshima and Nagasaki, wiping out hundreds of thousands of civilians.

As with over-ambitious conquerors before them, the aggressive had over-reached themselves, and brought about their own defeat. But Europe had been left in a shambles. Britain's colonial Empire was no longer sustainable, which, at least, was a positive outcome—if anything positive can result from war—and Independence had come to India a little earlier than expected. But the rejoicing had been marred by tragedy.

Partition was a messy, nasty business. It resulted in a chaotic exchange of populations, inevitable conflicts, and murder and mayhem on a massive scale. Even small towns like Dehra and tranquil hill stations such as Shimla and Mussoorie were not spared during those months of communal passion.

While the Muslim boys of BCS had been evacuated safely, others were not so fortunate. Domestic servants, small shopkeepers, labourers, humble workers were slaughtered in the streets. This happened all over northern India, and in what had become Pakistan. In Dehra, my mother told me, the little canal was jammed with dead bodies. Only the rich could afford to get away. Others survived by taking sanctuary in refugee camps. My stepfather, a Hindu, was one of the few who went out of their way to assist people in those months of savagery. He helped many of his Muslim friends and employees to escape across the border—driving them through hostile territory till he got them to some frontier crossing, where they would disappear under cover of darkness. He risked his life doing this, and he did it more than once.

By the time I came home from school, things had settled down to some extent. In India, periods of great turmoil are often followed by uneasy calm—a sudden cessation of violent events, the need to recover from the shock of what has happened, and to look around to see who is missing.

Dehra Granny was missing, but it wasn't the Partition violence that had taken her. She had died a few months after Independence. She had been visiting a friend in Ranchi when she died, probably of a heart attack, and she was buried there. Typically, I hadn't been informed.

That winter I was soon back on my walkabouts, browsing in the local bookshops, or visiting the cinemas when I had pocket money. Three of the several cinema halls were still showing English, or rather, American films, and one of them, the Hollywood on Chakrata Road, was new, showing all the latest Warner Brothers and MGM releases.

I must have been a familiar figure on the quiet roads and lanes of Dehra—a solitary youth, fair-haired, more pink than white, hands in his pockets, head lowered as though searching for something on the pavements. It was a habit I'd acquired in Jamnagar, looking for seashells on the beach. Of course, there were no seashells in Dehra, although sometimes I'd stop to pick up a coloured pebble. I had a small collection of coloured pebbles.

No one took much notice of me on my walks. Occasionally an urchin would call out '*lal bandar!*'—red monkey!—but I was used to that. On one occasion some college boys on cycles crowded me off the sidewalk and into a ditch before riding on, shouting obscenities; but this was an isolated incident, something that college boys did even to their own.

Up in Shimla I had school friends, English-speaking boys, but in Dehra I was very much a loner—until one day, while crossing the maidan (the old parade ground) a football came bouncing towards me, and being a decent football player, I gave the ball a good kick and sent it back into play. An informal game was in progress, the players being Hindi-speaking, or rather Hindustani-speaking boys from Paltan Bazaar and other market areas, and one of them called out: 'Good kick! *Aap khelega*?' I accepted the invitation and joined in the game, and soon I was a regular fixture in that little group, playing football in the evenings and sometimes joining them at the chaat or gol-guppa stall near the clock tower.

And suddenly, my world had expanded a little.

~

Dehra was well served with cinemas, but I was a lonely picture-goer. I would trudge off on my own to the Orient or Odeon or

Hollywood, to indulge in a few hours of escapism. There were books, of course, providing another and a better form of escape, but books had to be read at home, and sometimes I wanted to get away from the house and pursue a solitary other-life in the anonymous privacy of a darkened cinema hall.

The little Odeon cinema opposite the old Parade Ground—now gone—was my preferred hall. It was probably the most popular meeting place for English cinema buffs in the 1940s and '50s. You could get a good idea of the popularity of a film by looking at the number of bicycles ranged outside. The Odeon was a twenty-minute walk from the Old Survey Road, where we lived at the time, and after the evening show I would walk home across the deserted parade ground, the starry night adding to my dreams of a starry world, where tap-dancers, singing cowboys, swordsmen and glamourous women in sarongs reigned supreme in the firmament.

During the intervals (five-minute breaks between the shorts and the main feature), the projectionist or his assistant would play a couple of gramophone records for the benefit of the audience. Unfortunately, the Odeon management had only two or three records, and the audience would grow restless listening to the same tunes at every show. I must have been compelled to listen to Bing Crosby singing 'Don't Fence Me In' about a hundred times, and felt thoroughly fenced in.

I had a good collection of gramophone records at home, passed on to me by relatives and neighbours who had started leaving India a couple of years before Independence, and were still leaving. I decided it would be a good idea to give some of them to the cinema's management so that we could be provided with a little more variety during the intervals. I made a selection of about twenty records—mostly dance music of the period—and presented them to the manager, Mr Mann, an Indian Christian, who wasn't very communicative but had a kind face.

He was surprised, but pleased, and in return, he presented me with a free pass which permitted me to see all the pictures I liked without having to buy a ticket! Any day, any show, for as long as Mr Mann was the manager.

This unexpected bonanza lasted for almost two years, with the result that during my school holidays I saw a film every second day. Two days was the average run for most films. Except *Gone With the Wind*, which ran for a week, to my great chagrin. I found it very boring and I left in the middle. But there were many that I enjoyed—usually the films based on famous or familiar books. Dickens was a natural for the screen; *David Copperfield, Oliver Twist, Great Expectations, A Tale of two Cities, A Christmas Carol* (Scrooge), all made successful films. Daphne du Maurier's novels also transferred well to the screen. As did Somerset Maugham's works: *Of Human Bondage, The Razor's Edge* and several others.

Those films made that winter, and the two that followed, memorable for me, and I had Mr Mann to thank. I believe he did me the favour because he was sympathetic towards me—maybe he had seen me roaming the streets of Dehra with no fixed address, almost always alone. A local man, he was aware of my circumstances. My giving him the records gave him an excuse to help me. He could see that I was fond of movies and couldn't always afford the price of the ticket.

Sometime after I went to England, the little cinema closed down, and when I returned, preparations were being made to demolish the entire building. Mr Mann had moved to some other place, where, I like to think, other cinema buffs received the same kindness that I had.

~

January, 1948. I was watching a film—in the Hollywood, for a change, the cinema on Chakrata Road. After the film had been running for about ten minutes, the show was stopped, the lights came on and the manager came up front to announce that news had just been received that Mahatma Gandhi had been assassinated, shot dead at his morning prayer meeting. The film would have to be discontinued, and the cinema would be closed for a week.

I walked back home across the vast maidan, shocked and

confused by the news, and dejected that there would be no films to see for a week. I was thirteen, so my lack of sensitivity could perhaps be excused. But I remember clearly passing little groups of people who looked stunned and grief-stricken, talking in hushed tones and wondering what turn the country would take now. The assassin was a Hindu, and there was undisguised relief that the tragedy would not result in more communal riots. At home, my mother and stepfather and the household helps looked bewildered, even bereaved.

But it was my sister Ellen who took it to heart more than anyone else in the family. In the days that followed, she did not draw dragons, elephants and tigers. She would spend hours drawing pictures of Gandhi. Her eyesight was poor, and some of the portraits took strange shapes, but we could recognize Gandhi's round-rimmed glasses, sandals and walking stick. Nobody had thought she noticed or understood a lot of the things around her, much less in the world outside. Somehow, the Mahatma had touched her.

We never knew what went on in Ellen's mind, which would remain that of a five-year-old all her life.

AT THE GREEN'S HOTEL

THE WINTER BREAK OF 1947–48 WAS OVER TOO SOON, AND I WAS back in boarding school, getting bored with cricket nets and early morning PT and sermons on Sundays. Three of the Four Feathers gang were in different parts of the world—Pakistan, England and New Zealand—and I missed them, Azhar most of all.

The lone Feather did not enjoy being at BCS anymore. I wrote to my mother asking if I could shift to a school in Dehra, and she said she'd try, but I thought better of it. The school library and my love of books helped me get through that year.

Then it was December, and I was glad of the three-month winter break.

I came home to find my mother managing an old hotel, the Green's, situated a little way off the main Rajpur Road. Dehra was having a slump, and my stepfather's business ventures continued to fail, and this time my mother had taken matters into her own hands and moved out. Mr H, I gathered, had been reconciled to his first wife and moved in with her, albeit temporarily.

The Green's was a large single-storey bungalow-type hotel with about twenty rooms. It was a rather rundown place, which had been bought over by a Sikh family who owned a large shop nearby called Perfection House. They had employed my mother as the manager and she'd been given a little cottage behind the hotel, where she was staying with my brothers—William, and half-brothers Harold and Hansel—and Ellen. The effects of the damage Ellen had suffered at birth had become severe. She was epileptic, unable to do very much on her own, and needed constant care and attention. My mother could not run the hotel and look after her and three growing boys at the same time, so she had employed a widowed lady, Mrs Kennedy, to work as a full-time nanny for Ellen. The hotel salary being modest, it was almost hand-to-mouth, despite the RAF allowance for Ellen.

It was very cramped in the cottage, and as the hotel seldom had any guests, my mother arranged for me to stay in one of the smaller empty rooms through my holidays. The room was separated from a larger one by a locked door with a cupboard in front of it, but that did not prevent the sound of loud arguments waking me up late at night. On the other side of the door were an Anglo-Indian mother and son duo, who had fallen on hard times and were always at each other's throats. It was depressing listening to the despair and nastiness, but there was nothing to do but to put up with it—I had been allowed use of the room because it was the smallest in the hotel; the owners wouldn't agree to my being given a bigger room for free.

But the owners' son, Jasbir, was a very friendly boy, and we would spend a lot of time playing badminton together. We'd made a badminton court on the rather neglected garden of the hotel and soon it became popular and other boys and some girls began coming to play. It didn't do very much for the hotel's earnings, as they bought nothing there except the occasional lemonade, but at least the place became a little livelier.

There were no long-term residents at the hotel, only some people in transit—medical salesmen, tourists on their way to Mussoorie, and, rarely, parents of students enrolled in one of the town's smaller boarding schools. There was a very basic breakfast service, and no functioning restaurant. There was a bar, however, a bit dark and dank, attached to a billiards room, which was patronized by a few non-resident regulars. The marker who ran the billiards room was an entertaining man of indeterminate age who had been with the hotel for fifteen or twenty years, and recalled a time when there was a bandstand in the garden and a dance floor in the veranda. The hotel was abuzz with activity then, with Europeans and well-to-do Indians—zamindars, members of royal families and successful professionals—coming to stay or to dine. If that was true, the decline in the hotel's fortunes had been very swift and dramatic. In the late 1940s and early '50s, that could be said about Dehradun itself. All but a few of the British and Anglo-Indian families had left, and the Partition had resulted in an exodus of the old Muslim families. The Sikh and Punjabi refugees had only just started arriving, and were struggling to establish themselves, having lost their properties in Pakistan.

So there wasn't much work at the Green's Hotel. Every morning, at about ten, I would go to my mother's office, supposedly to help her with the accounts and some paperwork, but there wasn't a lot to do, and I went really for the coffee and pakoras that were brought to her, and to read the newspaper. That done, I would go to the cottage to chat with Mrs Kennedy.

Mrs Kennedy was Irish, with tales to tell, and I was happy to listen to her. She had seen better days, as had many of the poorer Anglo-Indians and Europeans who had been affected by the sudden departure of the British. People like Mrs Kennedy, who had worked for more prosperous white employers, suddenly found themselves stranded. Her husband had been a travelling salesman of sorts, selling termite-control chemicals, but he had died in a train accident, and there were no pensions for the widows of pesticide salesmen. Mrs Kennedy would, in due course, be repatriated to England or Ireland, but in the meantime she had to make a living, and looking after my sister did not require any great skills—just patience and sympathy. Mrs Kennedy had a bit of both.

She told me that her husband had been a wonderful singer, rather like the great Irish tenor John McCormack, and he was often in demand at parties, marriages, even funerals. Mrs Kennedy liked to sing too—she had a passable contralto voice—and gave us sentimental renditions of 'Danny Boy', 'Sweet Rosie O'Grady' and 'When Irish Eyes Are Smiling'.

And she had a good appetite, two helpings of any dish being her norm. As my brothers also had voracious appetites, my mother had to make sure there was plenty of dal, rice, and potatoes in the larder. Mrs Kennedy, being Irish, liked her potatoes, especially in a stew, and she was proud of the fact that potatoes had been introduced to India a century or so before by her namesake, Captain Kennedy, in the Shimla Hills, and by a fellow Irishman, Captain Young, on the Mussoorie ranges. Now, of course, everyone ate potatoes—in curries, with other vegetables, and as potato chips to go with fried fish, or as an adjunct to almost anything.

'What would we do without potatoes?' she wanted to know.

'Eat turnips,' I said. 'We always had turnips in India.'

'You'd soon get tired of turnips. Only good for pickles!'

Mrs Kennedy chided me for my fickle appetite. I wasn't in the same gourmand class as her or my brothers.

'You'll never marry,' she said.

'Why's that?'

'You can't stick to any one thing,' she said. 'Sometimes you want fried egg, soft-centred, sometimes scrambled, sometimes half-boiled. And something different with each toast—mango chutney on one, marmalade on another, mustard on a third! You'll never marry.'

'What's the connection?' I asked.

'You won't settle on anyone—wives, mistresses, sweethearts, jobs, whatever—you'll be wanting something different every day!'

'In that case,' I said, 'pass the guava jelly.'

Maybe she was right. Or was it just Irish folklore? I think my craving for variety in what I ate stemmed from the fact that the diet in school was plain and rather monotonous. And maybe I was wise not to marry or find a partner for life—I really can't say. As for sweethearts, I did not have the looks to attract them. And yet, there were loves; some unrequited, some mutual and intense—a few of these I have put in my stories and I will recall them in these pages, and a few will not be spoken of, for some passions are private, and the world is no poorer not knowing of them.

But as a young man I did go through a number of jobs, and as a writer I must have been published by some thirty or forty publishers over the years. I haven't slept with any of them, so I don't think they would qualify as wives, mistresses or sweethearts. But two or three have been good friends.

Mrs Kennedy loved to talk, and I enjoyed all of it because she had a lovely sing-song voice and an accent that I liked. But Ellen took a strong dislike to her, as indeed she did to anyone who was put in charge of her. She hated bananas, and if Mrs Kennedy tried to get her to eat one, saying, 'Bananas are good for you, dear,' bananas would fly about the room and everyone present would have to duck for cover.

Anything that was 'good for her' was immediately resented and cast aside. So I tried a different tack. 'Brain cutlets,' I informed her one day as this delicacy arrived on the dining table. 'Bad for you. You're not supposed to eat them.' She immediately devoured three brain cutlets and asked for more. To her dying day she loved brain cutlets, which my stepsister Premila, who took charge of her in later years, had a tough time arranging in Ludhiana, where she settled after her retirement, taking Ellen with her.

Mrs Kennedy, however, decided to leave us the day she received a grapefruit in her eye. Ellen was actually aiming at me—I had been teasing her—but her vision being poor, the grapefruit, thrown with considerable force, struck Mrs Kennedy instead.

She went to work as a dormitory matron in a local convent school, and was later repatriated to Ireland.

~

Dehra was emptying of British and Anglo-Indian families, as indeed were many other towns and cities across India. The Bowens, the Shepherds, the Clarks, the Clerkes, the Whites, the Browns, the Greshams, the Greens—they had all left, or were preparing to leave. Some would stay, including my mother. She was the only one remaining of her large family. All her sisters, even her happy-go-lucky half-brother, Ken, had chosen to emigrate.

The exodus had begun in the final years of World War II. For some, the choice was a hard one. They had no prospects in England, and often no relatives there. And they had no prospects in India, unless they were very well qualified. For many of them, 'assisted passages' to England were the order of the day: for a couple of years after Independence, 'poor whites' and down-and-out Anglo-Indians could go to the British High Commission and ask to be sent to Britain, and they were given the fare to make the journey—an assisted passage. They were usually people who felt stranded—people without an occupation, or women and the elderly without any support.

I suppose I qualified as a 'poor white' with an uncertain future. But there were many whose circumstances were much worse than mine. One such was Mrs Deeds.

Mrs Deeds, a woman in her late thirties, and her seventeen-year-old son, Howard, were the two occupants of the room next to mine at the Green's Hotel. They were waiting, with all their possessions, for an assisted passage. God knows where they had come from, or why they were in Dehra, where they had no friends or relatives. They were the flotsam of Empire, jettisoned by the very people who had brought them into existence. Mrs Deeds was an intelligent, good-looking woman, but an alcoholic. Over a few conversations, my mother gathered that she had been deserted by her husband, who had also sold their house and left her with nothing. She had no other family, or at least no one who would help her. She had worked in a store somewhere for a few years and brought up her son, but now there was no job, either.

When she was hitting the bottle, her son ridiculed her, and they had the most terrible fights, of which I could hear every word. He was a self-righteous young man who blamed her for the situation they were in. He was always in need of pocket money, and she would accuse him of stealing and selling her meagre personal belongings. He would retaliate by calling her a lying drunk, and on a couple of occasions he accused her of sleeping with any man who would buy her some drinks. Her feeling of guilt was compounded by her son's attacks on her, and as a result she hit the bottle with renewed vigour. When she was broke, she would cadge a drink from my mother. When he was broke, he would borrow a rupee from me.

To no one's surprise, Mrs Deeds could not pay her bills, and the mother and son had to leave the hotel. They took up residence in the second-class waiting room at the Dehradun railway station. An indulgent stationmaster allowed them to stay there for several weeks; then they moved into a cheap, seedy little hotel outside the station.

Mrs Deeds was always expecting a money order from someone who'd bought a little property she had inherited in Nainital. It never came. She'd sold her wedding ring and her watch to pay for drink and the rent. Howard loafed around, talking big—when they got to England or Australia or wherever they were going, he'd find a job to his liking. It did not occur to him to look for one in Dehra.

Late one evening, after Mrs Deeds had been drinking at a small liquor shop near the clock tower, she set out to cross the maidan to see someone at the club who had promised her some help. She was set upon by a gang of three or four young men who beat her badly and then raped her. Although she cried out for help, no one came to her assistance. The maidan had always been a safe place; but times were changing.

My mother went to see her and gave her what help she could. Then the remittance for their passage to England arrived from the High Commission, and Mrs Deeds and her son went their way, and presumably started a new life somewhere.

But not all stories were tragic, or about going away. Quite a contrast to Mrs Deeds was my mother's friend Doreen. Everyone called her the Jungle Princess, because she had grown up in a jungle, and because she was dusky and very attractive. Her parents had land at the edge of the forest outside Herbertpur, a small township between Dehradun and Paonta Sahib, originally settled by an Anglo-Indian family in the nineteenth century. After her parents died, Doreen—whose husband had also deserted her—took over the land and farmed it on her own, as none of her siblings were interested and had all gone away.

She had a young daughter, who grew up on the land, both surviving quite successfully out in the wilderness with assistance from a couple of loyal farmhands. By Independence, theirs was the only family in the area. Doreen's income came from her mango and guava orchards, and she seemed quite happy living in this isolated rural area near the Jamuna (the Yamuna River; but for old-timers like me it will always be the Jamuna). Occasionally she came into Dehradun, a bus ride of a couple of hours, when she would visit my mother, a childhood friend, and stay overnight.

One winter, I went with my mother to spend a few days at Doreen's farm. She possessed two or three guns, and could handle them very well. I saw her bring down a couple of pheasants with her twelve-bore spread shot. It was said that she had also killed a cattle-lifting tiger which had been troubling a nearby village.

When I last saw her, some forty years ago, Doreen was in her seventies and still managing the farm. Shortly afterwards, she sold her land and went to live elsewhere with her daughter, who by then had a family of her own.

THE FISHER YEARS AND RELEASE

MY LAST TWO YEARS AT SCHOOL, 1949 AND 1950, WERE FAIRLY tempestuous. I was in and out of hospital, first with dysentery and then with jaundice. My face, never much to admire, was disfigured by a severe form of acne. And I was constantly at odds with the new headmaster, Mr Fisher, and out of favour with his wife, who was a great one for favourites. Sometimes, briefly, I would be in the grip of anger and a feeling of hopelessness that I did not understand—and one day I found I had smashed the windowpanes of the school library for no good reason. Perhaps this was part of the mood swings teenagers experience, and might have been aggravated by the Fishers, or my dispiriting illnesses, or the continuing sadness of the separation from Azhar and other friends which I could not articulate.

The jaundice came on insidiously, my urine going from pale ale to dark amber, and laid me low just as I finished taking part in the school play—*Tonnes of Money*, or a similar farce. I was despatched to the Ripon Hospital, the local government hospital, where I spent two nights in the general ward, in some agony from abdominal pains. Then I was shifted to a small private ward, a tiny room, but all my own, and I was here for nearly three weeks, making a slow recovery. The treatment consisted of rest, plenty of barley water and Dr Beecham's Liver Pills which were supposed to increase the flow of bile to the liver. I spent a lot of time on the bed-pan.

A kindly matron discovered a cache of old books and

magazines in a storeroom, and soon my bedside table was taken up by old numbers of *Punch*, as well as the novels of such authors as A.A. Milne, Barry Pain, Stacy Aumonier, W.W. Jacobs, and other popular storytellers from the 1920s. Stacy Aumonier, an actor, was also a first-class short story writer. Jacobs wrote stories about comical seafarers. A.A. Milne was of course the popular author of the Winnie-the-Pooh books, but I knew him better as the author of a detective novel, *The Red House Mystery* (still readable today), and plays such as *Mr Pym Passes By*, which had been put on by Shimla's Gaiety Theatre the previous year.

A visit from Kasper Kirschner did something to cheer me up in hospital. He was a German boy who, with his parents and younger brother, had spent the war in various prison camps. Interned first by the Dutch in Indonesia and later by the British in India, they were fellow prisoners in Dehra with Heinrich Harrer, who escaped to Tibet and later wrote about his experiences there in *Seven Years in Tibet*. After the war, Kasper's father, an enterprising man, worked at first in the Nahan Iron foundries, then became the manager of the Keventer's Dairy Farm at Taradevi, outside Shimla. Kasper and his brother Andreas joined my school in 1948 and soon proved themselves to be brilliant scholars. Kasper's best subject was science, but he took an interest in literature, and we were soon discussing the rival merits of Dickens and Thackeray, Maugham and Hugh Walpole, Agatha Christie and Arthur Conan Doyle. It was amazing how quickly he had mastered the English language in the few years since leaving Indonesia.

He was a solid, restraining influence on me during those last years at school; reasonable when I was rebellious, mature where I was raw. In the years to come we would stay in touch, correspond, even meet occasionally—in London in 1953, and then here, in Landour, in the early 1980s, when he and his wife came to see me at Ivy Cottage in the course of a hiking expedition.

I digress from my incarceration in the Ripon Hospital, if only to explain why Kasper's visit meant something to me. He was my only visitor. As I was on a strict diet, he could not bring me any of the delicious cookies that his mother used to make, but he brought me his favourite book, R.D. Blackmore's *Lorna Doone*. A romantic streak obviously lurked beneath his solid, unexcitable nature.

Both he and his brother Andreas were fine swimmers, having learnt to swim in the sea off the Sumatra coast. But he was an awkward footballer, using his knees instead of his feet. Still, he made it to the school football team, and I still have the group photo of 1950, in which he stands just behind me, easily the tallest in the team…

I had been in the BCS football team since 1948, mostly as the goalkeeper (I've always preferred walking to running), and in 1950 I was made captain of the team—an achievement of which I remain shamelessly proud.

Only the other day someone asked me about the team photograph from that year, which I still display in my living room. And I surprised myself by remembering, almost seventy years later, the names of all the players. Besides Kasper Kirschner, there were Boga, an Irani boy; Lama, from Nepal; Plunkett, an Anglo-Indian boy who later went to England and joined Scotland Yard; a Sikh boy, Jogi, always smiling, and his brother Nepinder; Shakabpa, a Tibetan boy, whose father was the Dalai Lama's finance minister; Hemender, one of the sons of the late Maharaja of Patiala; Kruschandel, an Austrian boy, whose father was running Shimla's Clarks hotel; and Hilton, an English boy.

We played quite a few games with rival schools, most of which we won, and though we lost to all the professional Shimla teams who would come to play in our field, we rarely disgraced ourselves. Football was the one game in which I really excelled, and so I was naturally resentful when, after a game in which we lost narrowly to a visiting team, Mrs Fisher criticized me for letting in a goal and called me a 'doodhwala' (milkman). I'm not sure why she thought that was an insult—or why I took it as one. I retaliated by calling her a 'doodhwali' (milkmaid), and I was summoned to her husband's office and given the mandatory caning—this time four strokes of the cane instead of the usual three!

The reader must not take my exchange with Mrs Fisher as proof of my command over Hindi. I was terrible at it. Hindi was only introduced into our school in 1948. Our first Hindi teacher didn't last very long, and he was replaced by a new teacher, a promising young Hindi playwright named Mohan Rakesh. He became quite famous later on. I'm told one of his most successful plays was *Aadhe Adhoore*, about marital discord and general dissatisfaction with life. Perhaps it reflected his own experience—he married and divorced a few times, living a somewhat tortured life. But that happened later; in school, he was a popular teacher, though he gave up on me soon enough—but not before I had surprised him on one occasion. He asked me to translate an English poem into Hindi and I chose the opening lines of Tennyson's 'Charge of the Light Brigade':

Half a league, half a league,
Half a league forward,
All in the valley of Death
Rode the six hundred.

And my translation went roughly like this:

Aadha meel, Aadha meel
Aaadhe meel aage
Chhe sau aadmi ghoda pe bhaage

I'd skipped one line and I knew my grammar was probably wrong, but he was delighted with it!

Some sixty years later, I was in Dehradun interacting with some readers and signing books, and a lady came up to me and scolded me for my poor Hindi. 'Mr Bond,' she said, 'you've lived in India all your life and yet your Hindi is so bad.' I said, 'Well, ma'am, it was your husband who taught me!' She was one of Mohan Rakesh's ex-wives whom I had recognized.

I didn't put Mohan Rakesh into any of my stories, but I did write one about his predecessor. I called it 'Masterji', and it became quite popular. There was some exaggeration in it, but not very much. He wasn't fooling everyone by teaching us spoken Punjabi, as in that story, but his Hindi wasn't much better than ours. And the part about him being up to no good and getting arrested is not so dramatic an invention, either, when I compare it to how some of the BCS boys ended up in later life. Though their stories are rather grim—it was almost traditional for Bishop Cotton boys to get murdered or have accidents.

There was this Sikh boy who grew up to be a senior police officer. He married and had children, but he used to play around with other women, and one morning he was fished out of the Chandigarh lake. The official verdict was death by drowning, but later an autopsy revealed there was poison in his system. It was widely believed his feisty wife had had him poisoned and then dumped in the lake to make it look like drowning. She was under investigation for many years, but in the end she escaped conviction.

Hemender, one of the by-products of amorous and over-sexed royalty, got into a brawl in Calcutta and was killed. A couple of his older half-brothers had already died in suspicious hunting and car accidents.

Among other Old Cottonians who came to tragic ends were the Sikand boys, whose family owned a big motor company in Delhi (my stepfather would later work for them). One of them, Kishen, whom I remember as a very pleasant-mannered boy, began a love affair at the age of forty with the estranged wife of an army colonel. On his next birthday, Kishen received a beautifully wrapped-up present from the colonel, and when he opened the parcel, it blew up in his face and killed him.

I don't know what it was about those years at BCS. I suppose I should count myself lucky for being one of the few survivors.

~

My feud with the Fishers came in the way of any serious study. On one occasion I answered an exam paper with the words 'Exams are rubbish', which earned me not one but two zeros. Another day, at lunch time, Fisher asked me, as the senior-most boy in my house, if the food was satisfactory, and I replied, quite bluntly, that it was not. In those days, in boarding schools, you did not complain about the food. There followed the mandatory caning, and I was forced to apologise in front of the rest of the house—the alternative being immediate expulsion from the school.

Anyway, Kasper, the only schoolmate from that period who became a close friend, was always a calming influence. At the end of 1950, school days over, we went our different ways—he to college and university in Germany, I to the small back room in Green's Hotel, Dehradun.

Three years later, in the summer of 1953 (I think it was the time of the present Queen's coronation), Kasper and Andreas turned up in their hiking clothes, on a walking tour of Britain. I wanted to put them up in my small attic room on Glenmore Road (the first of many habitations in London), but my landlady, who was Jewish, grew alarmed at the prospect. 'Are they Germans?' she asked anxiously, memories of the Nazi regime haunting her. Kasper and Andreas were both very blond and Germanic, and my landlady was not convinced that they had grown up with me in India.

Very enterprisingly, the boys walked down the road to the Belsize Police Station, declared that they were short of funds and had nowhere to stay, and were allowed to spend the night in an empty cell, where they were classified as 'vagrants'. Next morning, they were given a jail breakfast and sent on their way; a pleasant example of Anglo-German fellowship seven years after the conclusion of hostilities.

But I have made too big a jump, and must return to dear old BCS and my friends and familiars in its hallowed halls. There was the Irwin Hall, where we staged plays and held important school functions. Long, boring speeches were made there. As a prefect, I was supposed to see that small boys did not drop off to sleep in the middle of the Governor's speech. It must have been torture for those little fellows. I fell asleep myself, on more than one occasion, only to be given a poke in the ribs by Fisher, forever on his rounds.

The jaundice had left me weak, and so had the treatment for my acne: female hormones administered from a little bottle of pills called Stilboestrol. Whenever someone says, 'This is the latest in medical science,' I am immediately suspicious. It usually results in side-effects and other abnormalities. After a month of Stilboestrol, my breasts swelled up, and my muscles became flabby. Was I undergoing a sex-change? When the doctor saw what was happening, he switched me over to male hormones—testosterone—with the result that my testicles became enlarged and hair started growing from my ears. Through all this, the acne persisted. Kasper proved a better doctor. He made me strip to the waist twice a day (my back was covered with pus-filled pimples) and scrubbed me down with good old Lifebuoy soap. By the end of that final year, the acne had disappeared. But not the effects of those hormones.

I took it philosophically, and resigned myself to coming last in the school marathon (also mandatory). At least by coming last I could stop, unobserved, at Kwality's on the Shimla Mall and help myself to an ice-cream while the other boys carried on, huffing and puffing to their medals and consolations. Every cloud has a silver lining.

For Shimla's boarding school inmates, the Mall Road was our enchanted mile—brimming with restaurants, shops and cinemas. How we looked forward to our ten-day summer and autumn breaks, when we couldn't go home but would be allowed into town. We lost no time in getting to the Mall for snacks and then tramping up to the Ridge to take in the last pictures. Sometimes we'd arrive wet or perspiring, but the changeable weather did not prevent us from enjoying the film. Packaged chips and colas hadn't yet reached us, but roasted peanuts or bhuttas (corn on the cob), would keep us going. They were cheap, too. The cinema ticket was just over a rupee. If you had five rupees in your pocket you could enjoy a pleasant few hours in the town.

Shimla had three cinemas, one of them owned by the family of Virbhadra Singh, who was to become chief minister of Himachal

Pradesh. Virbhadra was my junior in BCS and he would oblige us—we would pressure him to—with free passes. I have to admit I was grateful for those passes, as I rarely had pocket money in those days.

Back in school, the library became my retreat and harbour. A kind teacher had put me in charge of the library. I had the keys, and would go there at odd hours, ostensibly to catalogue the books but, in reality, to pore over them and become familiar with both the illustrious and the neglected. Over a year and a half, I read Dickens, Stevenson, Jack London, H.G. Wells, J.B. Priestley, the Brontës, Maugham and Ben Travers; the complete plays of J.M. Barrie and Bernard Shaw; and the essays—a form that I have always liked—of A.G. Gardiner, Belloc, Chesterton and many others. And then, of course, there were the humorous writers—Mark Twain, Thurber, Wodehouse, Stephen Leacock, Jerome K. Jerome, Barry Pain, Damon Runyon—and George and Weedon Grossmith, whose *The Diary of a Nobody* remains my favourite humorous book.

My own life being rather dull, it was good to lose myself in the worlds conjured up by these writers.

The best place in school after the library was the common room. Every house had a junior and a senior common room. These came up in my final two years in school. Here you could relax in comfortable chairs—there were books to read, and there was a radio, and we were encouraged to listen to the news and the cricket or football commentaries. I remember it was All India Radio that was on most of the time, because this was after Independence. But even before Independence, AIR was popular in the school. Our school had a very good choir in the early 1940s, and I remember its recital of Handel's *Messiah* was broadcast on AIR.

But the boys were more interested in dance music. I became a radio buff later, when I had finished with school and come home, and then I would listen to BBC's talk shows and comedy programmes. But I enjoyed the radio broadcasts in the common room, too. It was the era of the big bands, the swing jazz bands—

Benny Goodman, Gloria Parker and others were popular—and ballroom dancing was all the rage. We boys would practice the dance steps with each other, there being no girls to dance with.

Dances with girls happened once or twice a year at the most, when the senior boys were taken to Auckland House for socials, so that we would know there was another sex too—in the real world, outside films and comics—and there were possibilities we could have beyond each other. We could chat with the Auckland House girls, and dance with them—which was a big thing to look forward to. I danced with a girl called Indu in 1949-50, a princess from Jazdan, a tiny princely state in Kathiawar. Perhaps we had even met as infants at one of the Jam Sahib's parties in Jamnagar and fate had brought us together again—who is to tell? And we met again as oldies over half a century later—she dropped in one day, grey-haired, still slim (I was not) and smart and very charming, and we spent a pleasant evening indulging in a bit of nostalgia.

I remember writing Indu a letter after our first dance. It was intercepted by her headmistress or some other teacher and it was sent to my nemesis, Fisher, and of course I got into trouble—I always did with him. We had a karmic misconnection, Fisher and I!

But one result of that episode was that I became popular, and was sought after by some of the boys who wanted me to write similar letters for them. Some years later, when I was in Dehradun after school, I wrote many love letters for the boys and young men there. They didn't care for my stories, but they would come to me to get their love letters and job applications written!

In my final year in BCS, we staged a one-act play called *Borrowed Blooms*, a farce by some English humourist whose name I forget. I played the part of a drunk, which I enjoyed, except that the bottle contained tea without sugar or milk, to look like whisky. This tepid liquid was all I had to put me in high spirits. Anyway, I did it quite convincingly and was given the best actor's award that year. My schoolmates were convinced I was a secret drinker, to have delivered such a realistic performance. I wish I was. There was no liquor to be found inside the school, not even in the masters' quarters.

Though it was considered glamorous to drink, we were so far out of town, drinks weren't available. I remember fondly the time when one of the younger teachers got married, and he invited some of the senior school prefects to his reception in a restaurant on the Mall. We all tucked into the beer and the wine which was being passed around, till someone noticed and put a stop to it. Walking back that afternoon, the sky was bluer than before, the leaves and the grass greener and the birdsong sweeter. I was light-headed, and in the mood for love, but there was no one to love!

~

One day, on being summoned to Mr Fisher's study for some silly instructions he liked to give the prefects, I noticed that his bookshelf was lined with the works of Guy de Maupassant, that French genius who contracted syphilis, went mad, and then cut his own throat. So Mr Fisher was a Maupassant fan. And Maupassant was a ladies' man, mistresses abounding, women of the streets in and out of his apartment. An admirable quality in a writer of tragic fiction, but it made me wonder…Did Fisher model himself on this man-about-town, this Casanova of the Paris boulevards?

The answer came the following year, when I was no longer in school, no longer in India. But the old school grapevine brought me the startling news that the Fishers had, like naughty children, been expelled, dismissed at short notice.

Like a good Maupassant hero, the respectable Mr Fisher had been enjoying a long-standing affair with the junior school housekeeper, an attractive widow in her thirties. Not to be outdone, the plump and cuddlesome Mrs Fisher had taken up with one of the senior boys, who felt his education would not be complete without a little intimate education from the headmaster's wife. While Fisher was busy on a midnight round of the junior school, one of his head prefects was slipping into bed with his buxom lady. The perfect Maupassant story.

However, the Board of Governors had not, as far as I know, read Maupassant or even Zola for that matter, and when the whole affair blew up, the Fishers had to leave. Unlike Maupassant, Fisher did not cut his own throat, nor did his good wife take to the streets. Instead, they emigrated to Australia.

A ROOM ON THE ROOF

IN SPITE OF MY AVERSION TO EXAMS AND EXAMINERS, I OBTAINED my Senior Cambridge School Certificate—the equivalent, I suppose, to today's Class X Board exam. And that was the end of my academic career. I received the rest of my education in old libraries and second-hand bookshops.

Aunt Emily, who had sold the Dehra house and moved to the Channel Islands with her husband—Dr Heppolette, a successful gynaecologist—and her children, had expressed a willingness to put me up, should I decide to leave India for the United Kingdom. My mother thought it would be a good idea.

'Have you decided what you want to do with yourself?' she had asked me, on my return from school.

'Well, I'd like to be a writer,' I'd said.

'Don't be silly. You can't make a living as a writer. Go and join the army.'

The army was the only alternative to joining Dehradun's DAV College, an admirable institution, but it would involve sitting for more exams! We did not, in those far-off days, have the considerable variety of career choices that young people have today. Most of the boys I knew were going into the army. Those who did not like the idea of army life were training to become lawyers. Very few studied to become doctors or engineers, the chances of success there being low. For those who had some public school education and spoke English well, the easy option was to join the tea estates as managers—the tea companies weren't fussy about degrees.

My mother was being pragmatic, for once, when she told me I should join the army—by which she meant the British Army. As my father had died in service, the RAF would have paid for my passage to England and for my stay there, provided I joined the RAF or the British Army or Navy. My mother pressed me to, saying my future would be secured that way, but I was not interested in a career in the armed forces. However, I wasn't averse to the idea of going to Britain. It seemed to me the natural thing to do if I hoped to be a writer—that was where all the writers I admired had made their careers.

But I was in no hurry. After ten years of boarding-school (two in Mussoorie and eight in Shimla) I was determined to have at least ten months of relative freedom.

The Green's Hotel was sold that winter, and we moved (for the fifth time in five years) to a flat in the old Station Canteen building behind the Orient cinema; here we were joined again by my stepfather, who seemed to come and go at unpredictable intervals. My mother had been given a little money after the sale of Granny's house, so we were not too badly off.

I was sixteen, stubborn, hoping for adventure, and with ambitions to see my name in print—on the cover of a book, most of all. I was young enough to be scornful of money, and while fame would have been nice, it wasn't my primary concern. The romance of being a writer was what attracted me.

But I was—have always been—by nature a lazy person. Disciplined, but lazy, because beauty interested me more than anything else—a beautiful person, beautiful in mind or body; a delicate flower; birds and birdsong; sunlight and moonlight on trees and tin roofs.

And there was enough beauty and romance, or at least the possibility of it, in Dehra in 1950–51. Hands in my pockets, I wandered about town—to gaze at girls in sunny balconies and young wrestlers under the peepal tree; feast my eyes on colourful film posters; look at the trains arriving and departing at the station; study a hoopoe looking for insects on a lawn; watch the dhobis washing clothes on the canal banks; listen to the cool sizzle of rain on twilit roads and then take shelter in a little food stall in the bazaar and eat hot pakoras and wash them down with steaming tea.

And yet I did write occasionally—my early stories, some of which soon appeared in a couple of magazines. These stories were written in a room that I had all to myself, a room on the roof that I acquired because I quarrelled with my mother.

~

We had a radiogram in the house, which I would listen to a lot—talks, commentaries, and my favourite comedy shows on the BBC, especially *Much-Binding-in-the-Marsh*, set in a fictional RAF station. One evening my mother asked me not to listen to the radio all the time, because Mr H (whom I still resented) wanted to listen to something and never got a chance. I got very upset, and I said, 'All right, you can have it. I don't want to stay here any longer,' and I put some books and clothes in a bag and marched off into the sunset! I was very touchy in those days.

I reached the maidan, and I realized I couldn't spend the night in the open—it was late January and Dehra was reeling under a cold wave. Off I went again, this time to the railway station, but all the benches were occupied by other vagrants, bundled up in blankets that smelled mightily even from a distance. I hadn't brought a blanket, and I didn't want to share one of theirs, so I landed up at Bhim's—an enterprising fourteen-year-old who had become my friend on the football field the previous year. His father was an eye surgeon and they had a bungalow on Rajpur Road, where I had gone a couple of times.

I spent the night in Bhim's small bedroom, and in the morning I said, 'Bhim, I'm not going home.'

'You don't have to worry about finding a place to stay,' he said. 'You can stay here. But what will you do for money?'

'Well, I've got these school prizes, I'll sell them.' I'd got a few prizes for essay writing and acting in school—expensive volumes of the collected Shakespeare, biographies of Dickens and others, and some medals.

'The medals are useless,' said Bhim. 'But I'll sell the books for you for a commission. There's a shop opposite St Joseph's Academy which buys second-hand books.' And he went and got me forty or fifty rupees for the lot, and I was okay for a couple of days.

On the third day, I was passing Geoffrey Davis's gate and he stopped me for a chat and I told him I'd left home. Geoffrey had been with me at BCS; he knew me as a reserved but headstrong boy and he didn't seem surprised by my decision—he managed to look admiring, sympathetic and amused all at the same time. When he met me later that day, he said, 'My aunt asked me to give you this,' and slipped me ten rupees.

Geoffrey's aunt was Charlie Wilson's widow. Charlie had inherited a lot of property from his father, 'Pahari' Wilson, the legendary Englishman 'gone native' who had been the Raja of Tehri's contractor and had raided the forests for timber, amassing a large fortune. Charlie had squandered almost all of it, but his widow was still well off. Geoffrey's parents, who weren't well-to-do, lived in her house.

With Mrs Wilson's grant I managed another day. And then I went to the Cambrian Hall School and asked for a job. It was run by the Mainwarings, who'd taught at BCS. They asked me why, and I told them, and Mr Mainwaring, a good man, sat me down and had a chat with me.

'Don't be upset, Ruskin. You've only got one mother, she means well. Go home, as if nothing has happened, and everything will be all right.'

I took his advice—it was already the fourth day and things were getting difficult!

My mother was in the veranda as I entered.

'Is lunch ready?' I said to the air.
'It's on the table,' she said to the air.
And that was the end of it!

But my little rebellion worked to my benefit. Perhaps my mother and stepfather were worried, because to appease me they got me a separate room a couple of months later—a barsati on the roof of the building. Until then I'd been sharing a room with my brother and half-brothers, a noisy trio who left me a bundle of frayed nerves. I did not resent them, but I hadn't learned to love them. They were seven, nine and ten years younger than me, and we had spent very little time together. We were all relieved when I was given the barsati.

So I had a room of my own. I got myself a second-hand typewriter, joined a 'Typing and Shorthand Institute' around the corner from our building, and that was the beginning of my writing life.

There is supposed to be something very romantic about being a writer, and some of us set out to write as if we are on the road to romance. Very often, for those who persist, it is the road to drudgery; we end up as hacks or literary critics. I was fortunate in that I ventured into the literary world with a certain wide-eyed innocence, and managed to maintain that innocence for most of my life.

I had a typewriter, a table and a chair and a clay surahi for my drinking water—and I discovered that's all you really need. Sixty-five years later I still need the table and chair (or bedside), but I have dispensed with the typewriter, it makes for too much clutter, and I now write with a ball-point or roller-ball. I like the physical connection, or rapport, between pen and paper, and pen, hand and mind. I like using words to make poems and stories and vignettes of prose, and that is probably why I never gave up writing, even in the worst of times.

Of course I did not expect to make a lot of money when I started out. My mother, and later my aunt, both thought my desire to be a writer was a passing whim, and that I would sooner or later settle into a job or profession with a 'future'. I came dangerously close a few times, but survived without any lasting damage.

My first efforts on that typewriter were little more than exercises in story-writing, but I sent them all over the place and they came back with rejection slips attached. But there was a little magazine down south (published from Madras) which was prepared to publish almost anything I sent them, even paying me the handsome sum of five rupees per story or article.

Well, I could do a lot with five rupees in 1951. See four movies if I wanted. Or buy three magazines and a paperback book. Or give a chaat party for the young friends I was beginning to acquire. I did not scorn those five-rupee money orders.

The magazine itself—called *My Magazine of India*—survived on advertisements for lucky gemstones, aphrodisiacs, digestive powders, astrological predictions, watches and perfumes, all available by post. You paid for them when the parcel arrived. I never did order any of these attractive items, but I am sure a lot of people did, because the magazine was still around when I returned from England four years later. The pages without ads they would fill up with pulp fiction. For me it was a good magazine—all my rejects from other magazines and papers would go here and they would all be accepted. I even contributed to its finances, though unwittingly. One day, along came a money order for two rupees eight annas for a story, instead of the standard five rupees, and I wrote them a very strong letter asking why they had reduced my fee. They replied promptly, saying they hadn't cut down my rate, they had only deducted one year's subscription to the magazine!

None of the stories I sent them have survived, which is fortunate, because they were terrible. They were based on characters from the mystery movies I had seen—Raymond Chandler's Philip Marlowe or Earl Biggers's Charlie Chan of the Honolulu police. In my stories the detective was myself, chasing killers and hoodlums in Delhi and Shimla after dark, but I usually lost interest in the chase midway and the story lost its way, but no one at *My Magazine* noticed or bothered.

I also wrote a couple of stories of a more personal nature, and one was picked up by a magazine called *Caravan*, and another—'The Untouchable'—by the prestigious *Illustrated Weekly of India*, which sent me a cheque for the magnificent sum of fifty rupees. I had arrived! (Or so I thought.)

All the time I was keeping a diary, or journal, in school exercise books, recording some of the events of my daily life, including my friendships and the comings and goings of the people who lived in and around the Station Canteen building.

~

My tiny barsati opened on to the flat concrete roof of the building. There was no other construction on the roof, and a flight of stone steps ran up to it on the outside of the building, so it was quite private. I lived more or less independent of my family—I saw them two or three times a day when I went down for my meals. My steps were steep and people seldom came up to see me, the exceptions being the boys of the neighbourhood—Somi, Haripal, Krishan and Ranbir being the friendliest of them.

But they came later. In the beginning, there was only the woman who came to sweep the room, and several visitors who were not of the human kind.

There was a banyan tree just opposite. Squirrels were busy in it all afternoon, sparrows, crows and other birds in the morning and evening, and flying foxes at night. This was the first time I'd had a room with a view all to myself, and I think this was when I really began responding to the sights, smells, colours and everyday theatre of the world around me.

A broad path ran beside the building which wasn't very busy, but the activity on it was always interesting: a 'boxwallah', with a tin trunk on his head, selling everything from bread and biscuits from the bakeries to hair oil, safety pins and elastic for pyjamas; an ayah with a baby in a pram; the rent-collector, with the teeth and nostrils of a horse; the postman on his brand new Atlas bicycle; the fruit-seller calling his wares in high-pitched, rather eccentric cries; a line of schoolgirls with red ribbons in their pigtails.

When it rained, there was greater activity. At the first

rumblings, women would rush outside to bring in the washing—and if there was a strong breeze, to chase a few garments across the compound. When the rain came, it came with a vengeance, making a muddy river of the path. A cyclist would come riding furiously down the path; an elderly gentleman would be having difficulty with a large umbrella; naked children would be frisking about in the downpour.

I had a window and two doors. One door was at the top of a flight of twenty-two steps by which I entered the room (by an odd coincidence, my present abode, Ivy Cottage, also has twenty-two steps leading up to the front door). Another door opened on to the flat cemented roof of the building. It was hot by the end of April, and as I had no fan I kept the doors and windows open day and night to let in whatever breeze might be coming down from the hills. Sometimes it was a hot wind from Delhi, but occasionally the wind came off the Tibetan plateau and the distant snows to provide a little relief from the soaring temperatures.

Open doors and windows meant easy access for birds and other small creatures. A pair of noisy mynahs—one of them bald after a fight—were frequently in and out of the room, paying no attention to me as I sat at my desk or lay supine on my bed in vest and shorts. Sparrows were resting in the little skylight, and I dared not open it, for fear of knocking down their rather precarious abode. A chameleon circled the room in search of lost friends, and sometimes raised its head to look in from the threshold.

Two or three lizards were always to be found clinging to the walls or ceiling, on the prowl for moths or mosquitoes. Occasionally one of these lizards would lose its foothold and land with a plop on desk, bed, floor, or my person. The sweeper-woman told me that it was usually lucky for a lizard to fall on some part of my body.

'Lucky for the lizard or for me?' I asked.

'For you, of course.' And she elaborated by telling me that if the lizard fell on my tummy, I'd become fat and greedy; if it fell on my feet, I'd travel; if it fell on my exposed back, I'd have many friends. And so on…

She was a good lady who came from one of the slums to sweep the rooms of the tenants. She made about thirty rupees a month, with which she fed a small family. She liked to gossip, and finding me a good listener, would keep me updated on events in the locality. Such as: Mr Lal had got drunk and fallen down his stairs, breaking an arm. Mrs Saigal was down with typhoid. Someone's son had been caught cheating in his exams. Another boy had been caught shoplifting. An incoming train had run over an elephant. My stepfather's first wife was suing him. The circus was coming to town. The Prime Minister (Mr Nehru) was passing through, on his way to Mussoorie. And she had a pain in her lower back which wouldn't go away. I gave her a strip of Aspirin tablets (Aspro was the commercial name), and after that I became her medical adviser, listening to all her complaints and handing out Aspirin or Anacin, Oriental Balm, and occasional doses of Eno's fruit salts.

As I have mentioned, I would leave the front door open, even at night. But late one night, I was woken from deep sleep by a hideous howling right next to my bed. Switching on the light, I found a jackal right beside me, baying at the moon or the stars or some lost love on the rooftops. I gave a shout and it ran away, down the steps and across the road, hotly pursued by all the dogs in the area barking furiously. I expect the poor jackal had received a bigger fright than I had; but after that, I kept the front door closed at night.

But during the day the door was always open, and through it, one morning, came a light-eyed Sikh boy of about twelve, as yet unbearded, wearing khaki shorts and chappals, looking at me as if I were an exotic and endangered bird. Then he laughed, and it was like a shower of rain on a hot summer day.

This was Somi, whom I'd met briefly at his brother Haripal's house.

I don't remember how I met Haripal. Perhaps it was Bhim who introduced me to Ranbir, who introduced me to Haripal—H.P. Sauce to his friends. Haripal had pen friends in Germany, Mexico and Japan, and he said I was his first British friend. I told him I wasn't British, I had been born in India, where my family and I had always lived. He nodded: Yes, I couldn't be British, I didn't speak like one; in fact, my English wasn't very good. So I was his first Anglo-Indian friend, he said. Even back then I didn't care very much for the term Anglo-Indian, but I didn't feel strongly enough about it to object.

Haripal was fifteen, studying in the tenth standard, after which he wanted to join the army or navy—which did not impress me, because I had a low opinion of regimentation of any kind. I told him I wanted to be a writer—which did not impress him, because that was not a career, and in any case, that sort of thing was possible only in England or America, and I was in India.

He took me home for lunch one day, and it was there I met his mother, who made me welcome, and his brothers Somi and Chhotu and his cousins Dipi and Daljit. Their home was on the outskirts of the town, where civilization began to merge with the jungle. It was the first of the few large families I would attach myself to over the years, and they were all kind enough to put up with me, letting me come and go as I pleased. The arrangement suited me; I found it easier to be a visitor rather than a resident, a habit that I would lose only in my forties.

After that first visit, when he came wanting help with English lessons—which were soon forgotten—Somi would turn up at odd hours. Soon, we were laying out a roof garden. Somi played truant from school and we spent two days carrying up mud in a bucket from a nearby field. By the evening of the second day, we had laid out a neat little flowerbed. Somi and Chhotu buried some pumpkin seeds in it, though I would have preferred flowers, and we had a little argument about this and later made up by going out to eat chaat.

Many were the afternoons we spent lazing around and chatting in that room. When it was evening and time for them to go home, I would have to carry them piggyback down the stairs. Somi enjoyed this even more than Chhotu, laughing in delight and urging me to go faster, faster—I was his favourite tattu, his donkey, and at the foot of the stairs, when I deposited him on the ground so he could get on his bicycle and pedal off home, he would declare I was his 'best favourite friend' and that he loved me dearly.

It was cycling Somi enjoyed most of all. I wasn't much of a bicycle rider; I was always falling off, and once went sailing into a buffalo cart and fractured my arm. But it was fun being with Somi and his brothers, and I would hire an old bicycle from a cycle-hire shop and accompany them on rides in the hot sun—sometimes to the sulphur springs, or to Premnagar (where the Military Academy was situated), or into the tea gardens along the Hardwar road, or across the dry riverbed at Lachiwala and into the forest. We would spend hours sitting by the canal and discuss our hopes and dreams.

Everyone wanted to go away. Dehra was too small for our ambitions, and at that age we all wanted to conquer the world. My dream—to be a writer—could only be realized in England, where, I believed, the doors of the literary world would open for me.

After the long cycle rides, we would end up in my room, tired and thirsty, and my five-rupee money order from *My Magazine of India* would be splurged on ices and cold drinks. Those money orders helped me make a bit of an event of my seventeenth birthday—for the first time in my life, I celebrated with a party. Six boys, some crows and a dog (Chhotu's pet) feasted on samosas, ice-cream (homemade, from blancmange powder), lemonade and Indian sweets and English confectionery, served in plates and tumblers borrowed from the neighbours. Chhotu and Somi got the most to eat because one was the youngest and the other the most loving and good-looking of the gang.

Krishan and Ranbir, my neighbours, were also part of the gang but much as we all loved them, they were far from good-looking. Krishan, a couple of years younger than me, had beetling eyebrows and a frequently dripping nose; Ranbir possessed hardly any forehead, so that he looked a bit like a Neanderthal man.

Ranbir was a sturdy boy, but his athleticism did not compare with his sister's. Raj, older than him by three or four years, was a champion badminton player who could vanquish the best of us on the open-air court that we had laid out on a small patch of wasteland. She could also vanquish most boys with sidelong glances from her dark and fiery eyes. I don't think she meant to, but that was the effect she had. I used to love watching her play, because she was one of the most unusual-looking girls I had known. She had lovely loose limbs, the legs of a long-distance runner, supple arms, strong wrists, sturdy shoulders—some attributes of the male but feminine all the same.

It was a pleasure to play with her and be beaten by her. She played barefoot, and on one occasion a large thorn pierced her heel and went some way into her flesh. She subsided onto the grass and tried removing the thorn but it broke off in her hands. I am not the most resourceful of people, but I surprised myself by coming to the aid of the damsel in dress. Taking her slender foot in my hands, I got to grips with the thorn and removed it quite deftly. Everyone clapped, and Raj showed her gratitude by allowing me to take a few points off her in the next game. She enjoyed my company, perhaps because for the most part I treated her as I did any of my male friends. It must have been liberating for her, and it allowed her to come up to the roof with Ranbir one evening and hold my hand while we talked about nothing in particular, and on her way down she stuck her tongue out at me and bit me lightly on the cheek.

I was fond of Raj without being in love with her. It was different with Krishan's mother. She must have been fifteen or sixteen years older than me, a very beautiful person, both by nature and by physicality. Gracious, dignified, but at the same time radiating a tremendous amount of sexual energy, she looked like the actress Kamini Kaushal. I adored her, as one adores a goddess; and she took my puppy love in her stride, neither encouraging it nor rejecting it. I was her young son's friend, and that was enough for her. I could come and go as I pleased. We played carom in the evenings, while her alcoholic husband slumbered in the veranda. He'd lost his job as a PWD engineer and was drinking himself into the next world. Sometimes I was asked to type out his appeals and petitions to the authorities, but they had no effect. I forget what his misdemeanour was, exactly; something to do with unaccounted money lying around in his Mussoorie residence—a common enough practice, in the fine old traditions of the Public Works Department, but Mr Lal hadn't been clever enough to get away with it.

All these good friends and neighbours went into my journals, although at the time I had no idea that some of them would later be fictionalized and turn up in my first book, *The Room on the Roof*. The 'room' in my novel was certainly the real one, the room I shared with the wall lizards and the mynah birds. And Somi and Krishan and Ranbir went into the book unchanged. But the plot (if you can call it that), the incidents, the sequence of events, the running away, the relationship with Meena, the going away and the return, were all part of the 'novelization' of my journal.

I suppose most writers, to a greater or lesser extent, base their fictional characters upon real people. Mine come very close to the reality. It is my own response to them that varies. The most fictional of all my characters is myself.

VOYAGE TO ENGLAND

AND YOUNG RUSKIN, STILL ONLY SEVENTEEN, WAS NOW LEAVING for England.

My passage was booked on the P & O liner *S.S. Strathnaver*, one of several smart passenger liners that plied between Bombay and London; or rather, Sydney and London, because it began its voyage in Australia. My ticket arrived. It cost Rs 450, which included meals on the ship. The voyage would last just over a fortnight. The ticket and some clothes and a few other belongings for my early days in England were bought with some money that Dehra Granny had left me in her will. She did not have much, but she had thought of me. She hadn't told me, and up until now my mother hadn't either, and now that stern old Granny wasn't around for me to thank her.

As the day for my departure approached, I began to panic at the thought of leaving, and an old feeling of loneliness returned. Leaving my family wasn't the hardest part; it was the friends I had made that enchanted summer I would miss the most. But I was clumsy at expressing my feelings, as were most of the other boys—except Somi, always frank and spontaneous in his affection.

'I will be sad, Ruskin,' he said simply.

'I'll come back,' I said.

'You won't. You will forget us.'

A week later he was ill with pneumonia. I didn't think I could leave, but Haripal, always pragmatic, told me not to worry. Somi would get well soon enough, but I would lose my only chance to do what I'd always wanted to do. My staying wouldn't help.

And Somi willed himself to health, as if he was determined to send me off without guilt or worry. His mother took me aside the last time I went to their home. 'Do you need anything, son?' she asked. 'You belong to this family, you must tell me if there's anything you need.'

She took my face in her hands and I broke down. 'Be brave,' she whispered, and kissed my forehead.

It was early November when I left Dehra. My mother and Mr H came to the station to see me off. A far cry from that day some six years earlier, when they had failed to meet me—a ten-year-old schoolboy—arriving in Dehra after my father's passing. But time heals many wounds, and I was now more or less reconciled to the circumstances of my life. And they had high hopes for me.

My friends were also at the station to see me off. Somi and his brothers, Krishan and Ranbir. So it was quite a jolly affair in the end. No tears, no regrets. Everyone admired me for going off on my own, while still a minor.

'You're going to be a great writer,' pronounced Krishan. 'Best in the world!' And I was naïve enough to believe him. Krishan, whose favourite reading was the Beano comic paper.

How I loved those loving boys, now being left behind in a small town called Dehradun, unheard of outside India, while I set off for the land of Dickens and Buckingham Palace!

The train set off for Bombay, and as I looked out of the window and saw them standing there on the platform, waving and cheering, I knew I was saying goodbye to my own boyhood and to theirs, and that if I ever saw them again we would all be grown men, the days of innocence far behind us.

Somi ran beside the carriage, shouting goodbye, and laughing as he ran, tears streaming down his face.

I wouldn't see these friends again till we were almost old men—except Dipi and Krishan, who remained in Dehra for some years, and Ranbir, who disappeared into India's vastness, and Daljit, who died young.

Haripal—H.P.S. Ahluwalia—did join the army, and became one of the first Indians to climb Mount Everest. Some months later, in the 1965 war, he received gunshot wounds which resulted in his being confined to a wheelchair for the rest of his life. Never one to give up, he set up the Indian Spinal Injuries Centre in New Delhi, which he still heads.

Somi studied engineering and moved to America, from where he has made a few trips to India and met me on a couple of occasions—a silver-bearded father of married children. But he remains fixed in my memory as an eternal innocent, a boy in shorts, his turban slightly askew, riding his bicycle down an empty road.

Daljit joined the air force after finishing school, and lost his life soon after in a training flight.

Krishan was to reappear at different periods of my life—in Dehra, Delhi and Mussoorie—our easy friendship undiminished, till I lost him too. He was in his forties, a successful engineer in Bombay, when he died trying to save a child from drowning in Goa.

~

I spent two days and nights in a seedy, unsanitary hotel on Bombay's Lamington Road, and then boarded my ship, feeling quite unwell. It was a day or two before I could eat anything. But for that, it was a smooth voyage—an eighteen-day voyage from the time we left Bombay to the time we docked in South London, including three stops on the way—Aden, Port Said and Marseilles.

There was a first class and a second, or tourist, class. I was in the tourist class, where you shared the cabin with one other passenger, but I was lucky to have the cabin to myself till Port Said. The P&O liners would start in Australia those days, stop in Bombay and then continue to England. So there were a lot of Australian passengers on the voyage, including a team of professional all-in wrestlers from Australia—'all-in' being the term for 'anything goes'. They would practice and wrestle on the decks most of the time, throwing each other about, and sometimes drinking a lot of beer and getting out of hand. There was also an Australian lady, very slim and elegant, who was a classical pianist, going to England to give a concert, and she'd practice in the salon where there was a piano, while rowdy wrestling sessions were going on outside. King Kong moves to Beethoven's *Moonlight Sonata*—it was sublime comedy.

Equally entertaining was a Parsi man from Bombay, hoping to make a fortune when he got to England. Everyone was showing him their palms. He read mine too, looking very pessimistic, and said I would have a difficult time till middle age, and then I would die in my fifties. That kind of thing wasn't going to make him a fortune, but one never knew. Later, when I was in London, I didn't see him, but I saw a lot of other astrologers and palmists there, all of them from India.

At Port Said, a down-and-out Englishman who had been stranded in Egypt for some years, and was being sent back to England, was put in the second berth in my cabin. He was a sorry kind of character, broke and always trying to scrounge a drink off me. I had barely enough for myself, so I didn't enjoy his company very much! Luckily, there was enough going on to distract me. There were film shows in the evenings, and fancy-dress balls—I attended one sitting in a pram, dressed in a bathing costume and sucking on a pacifier. I thought I was quite amusing, but they didn't give me a prize.

Like most P&O liners which took that route, our ship passed the volcanic island of Stromboli, north of Sicily. As evening settled over the volcano, the captain called us to the deck, and we saw a spectacular fountain of lava-rays and fire rising from the summit hundreds of metres into the darkening sky. We were at a distance, so we only witnessed nature's beauty and not its destructive force.

When we stopped at Marseilles, I went ashore and bought postcards with French stamps to send home. And then we were on the last stretch, to the Tilbury docks.

Towards the end of the voyage I wrote a little poem, which has managed to survive these many, many years. I write from memory:

I boarded the big ship bound for the West,
The clean white liner.
In a cold grey fog we docked
In London's great river.
But I saw only a cow at rest
And a boy who sang to himself
In the shade of an old Sal tree,
And his song would be mine forever.

PART III

THE LONELY ISLAND

I SPENT A LITTLE OVER A YEAR IN JERSEY, THE LARGEST OF THE Channel Islands. This would be followed by two and a half years in London. I would be caught between East and West, and would have to make up my mind about where I belonged. The link with Britain was tenuous, after all; based on heredity rather than upbringing.

I had come to England with a dream of sorts, and I was to return to India with another kind of dream; but in between there were to be four years of dreary office work, dank and cheerless bed-sitting rooms, shabby lodging houses, cheap snack bars, hospital wards, and the struggle to write my first book and find a publisher for it. I discovered that the world could be a lonely place for someone like me. And I found that becoming a writer wasn't just a matter of putting pen to paper—although that was certainly the first step!

~

Jersey was a beautiful island—wide bays, pretty inlets, a busy little port, a quaint capital (St Helier), and farms famous for tomatoes and Jersey cows. But I knew no one outside my aunt's family, and my relatives showed no great interest in my literary ambitions.

Within a week of my arrival I was down with jaundice again. I must have picked it up in that seedy little hotel in Bombay, and the virus had been lurking in my system throughout that long sea voyage. Certainly no one in Jersey suffered from jaundice or any tropical disease. But with the right diet and rest I recovered quickly, and immediately set about looking for a job. I did not want to be a burden on my aunt any longer than was absolutely necessary.

I did not waste time with job applications or employment agencies. I simply set out down the high street of St Helier, knocked on doors, waited outside offices, walked up to anyone who appeared to be in charge and enquired politely: 'Excuse me, sir, I'm looking for a job. Do you have a vacancy?' Usually there was no vacancy, but people were surprised at my direct approach and occasionally someone would ask me what I could do. 'I can type,' I'd say. 'I know a little shorthand. I can attend to correspondence. I can make out a bill.' And then in desperation: 'I can make tea.'

The office manager of a large grocery chain, Les Riches, looked me up and down and asked me if could do any accounting. 'Not very good in maths,' I said honestly 'But I can add and subtract!' He gave me a job as a junior clerk on three pounds a week, which wasn't bad for those times. I gave one pound a week to my aunt, and spent the rest on books, films and stationery. And I bought myself a new pair of shoes, because my aunt would say, 'A man is always judged by his shoes, Ruskin, your shoes look very shabby.'

I had never paid much attention to my appearance, and my trousers were usually unpressed, my shirt sleeves frayed, my ties ragged (you had to wear a tie to work in those days), but I made an effort to smarten myself up, both to please my aunt and to impress the girls who worked at Les Riches. I worked with some twenty other clerks, a mixed bunch, in a large, gloomy office above the store. It was winter—dark when I walked to work at eight in the morning, dark when I walked back from work at six in the evening. Saturday afternoons we were free, and of course Sunday was a holiday. My fellow clerks, most of them senior to me, were a friendly lot, who talked about football, films, the weather and the Royal Family. When King George VI died, we observed a minute's silence. He'd been a popular king, very brave and unselfish during the war, in spite of poor health. I remember my father used to think highly of him.

I would always miss my father, but now I was missing India and my friends in Dehra. During that last year, I had made many attachments—Somi and his brothers; Krishan and his mother; Ranbir and his sister Raj; and I missed our games and picnics and little expeditions into the foothills. And the bazaar with its sweet shops and chaat shops, and the little railway station, and the lonely mango groves, and the bulbuls and mynahs and other small birds who would visit my room on the roof. Here in Jersey, there were only seagulls! And it was an insular place. There was little here to remind me of India or the East, not one brown face to be seen in the streets or on the beaches. I'm sure it became a different sort of place in a decade or two, but in the 1950s it had nothing to offer by way of companionship or good cheer to a rather sensitive boy who had left home and friends in search of a 'better future'.

Occasionally, after an early supper, I would walk along the deserted seafront. If the tide was in and the wind approaching gale-force, the waves would climb the sea wall and drench me with their cold salt spray. My aunt thought I was quite mad to take this solitary walk; but the fierce wind and the crashing waves gave me a sense of freedom, and some solace. Not since the year following my father's death had I been such a loner.

The attic room I'd been given had no view, so one of my favourite occupations, gazing out of windows, came to a stop. But perhaps this was helpful, in that it made me concentrate on the sheet of paper in my typewriter. At night, I would take out my Dehra journal and put some of the entries into story form. Perhaps they would make a book of sorts. And I was writing stories and sending them to English magazines, but they came back with polite rejection slips.

I discovered the St Helier library, and lapped up the collected plays and poems of Rabindranath Tagore; a couple of novels by Mulk Raj Anand and R.K. Narayan; a charming childhood memoir by Sudhin Ghose set in the Santhal Parganas (*And Gazelles Leaping*); and the novels of Rumer Godden. These books—particularly Tagore's poems—kept me in touch with the soul of India.

One of Rumer Godden's novels, *The River*, had recently been filmed by Jean Renoir, the great French director, and it ran for a week in one of St Helier's cinemas. I saw it several times—

enchanted by its lyrical intensity, its glorious colour, and the way in which it captured the atmosphere of a corner of India that resonated in my heart. I read all Rumer Godden's 'Indian' novels—*Black Narcissus* (also a beautiful film), *The River*, and *Breakfast With the Nikolides* (possibly her best)—and resolved to capture, or recapture, my own corner of India in the novel that was slowly taking shape.

By now I had left Les Riches, and taken a job as an assistant in the newly-opened office of Thomas Cook, the travel agency. Thomas Cook had sent a representative, Mrs Manning, over to Jersey to look after their expanding travel business (hotel bookings mostly) on the island. Mrs Manning needed an assistant who was polite and who could speak good English, and I seemed to fit the bill.

One of my faults is that I am over-polite, too willing to please, and as a result I am bullied and over-ridden by strong, masterful types—particularly women. Mrs Manning was the strong, masterful type, who soon had me doing everything in the office, from making tea to answering the phone to making hotel bookings to starting a filing system to typing the office correspondence and then to going out to post it while she chain-smoked and spoke non-stop but distractedly on the phone. Sometimes she was absent for hours, for she was having a passionate affair with a smooth-talking, good-looking man who made a living from selling used fire extinguishers. He was a conman, really, and a smart one. He bought up old fire extinguishers, put them in working order, gave them a fresh coat of paint, and then drove around the island selling them as new. My boss, Mrs Manning (I never did learn who Mr Manning might have been) accompanied him on his drives around the island, which must have been fun—Jersey's climate and scenery was just right for middle-aged lovers.

Left in charge of the affairs of a famous travel agency, I did my best to cope with an ever-increasing volume of work; but inevitably there was some confusion and several mix-ups. An elderly couple had wanted a room with twin beds—why had I given them a double-bed? And there were the honeymooners who wanted a double-bed and who'd been given separate beds. Some hotels still had a colour bar—the rest of Britain had, largely, begun to acknowledge and address its centuries-old racism, but not Jersey—and I was given a dressing-down for booking a group of Samba dancers from Brazil into a hotel meant for all-white customers.

Coming under fire, Mrs Manning fired me. A few weeks later she was recalled to London; maybe she took her fire-extinguisher lover with her. I never found out because by that time I had another job, this time in Jersey's Public Health Department.

The idea of being dependent on others never appealed to me, and I was never without a job for long.

In the offices of the Public Health Department, close to the St Helier docks, I was in the company of several senior clerks, engineers and secretaries, and got on famously with everyone. Of the year I was with them, I have only fond memories.

I was the youngest, and everyone called me Russ—or, when they learned of my writerly ambitions, Pushkin! I remember their names—Mr Bromley, the gentlest of them all; a human chimney called Bliault (a French name—the Channel islands being originally French; most people spoke a French patois); Mr Cummings, who had been in the navy during the war; and our chief, Mr Gothard, a very nice, soft-spoken man. There was also an engineer, McLintock, a Roman Catholic, and as Catholics don't believe in birth control, he had twelve children. I don't know how he was managing on his salary, bringing up so many children. He was a nice man too, except that he would keep telling me I should 'look up the Catholic faith.' He was trying to convert me. Although a Protestant, I wasn't into religion at all, and I let him carry on, showing no interest whatsoever, till he got the message and stopped.

I ended up spending a lot of time with Mr Bromley, a quiet, gentle man in his early fifties. A widower, he lived alone in lodgings close to my aunt's house, and we would walk back together every other evening. He was a Yorkshireman who had settled in Jersey for health reasons. Yorkshire, he said, was too damp, which wasn't good for him, and he'd been told by the doctors to go to a sunnier place. He did not tell me the nature of his illness; but he often spoke about his son, who had been killed in the war, and about the North Country, which was his home. He sensed that we were, in a way, both exiles, our real homes far from this small, rather impersonal island.

Mr Bromley had read widely, and he rather admired my naïve but determined attempt to write a book. I think it was he who had given me the name Pushkin, and would ask every now and then how my book was coming along.

One evening I stopped in front of a shop which had a little portable typewriter on display that I'd been admiring for some days, and I said, 'How I wish I could buy that.' My old typewriter was in bad shape, a couple of the keys had jammed and I had to ink the letters by hand after I had finished typing.

'Is it very expensive?' Mr Bromley asked.

'It's nineteen pounds. I only have six pounds saved up, so maybe in a few months.' And I began to walk.

Mr Bromley stopped and said, 'I tell you what, lad. Give me your six pounds, and I'll add thirteen pounds to it, and we'll buy the machine. Then you can pay me back out of your wages—a pound or two every month. How would that suit you?'

Something about Mr Bromley's demeanour, and the rapport we had developed, made me accept his offer without hesitation. We bought the typewriter and I walked home feeling a little more confident about my writerly efforts. It took me several months to repay the loan—I kept sending some money every month even after I moved to London—but Mr Bromley was always patient.

~

While in the Public Health Department, I was persuaded by my senior colleagues to sit for the Jersey Civil Service exam, which was open to everyone regardless of qualifications. There were papers in General Knowledge, Elementary Maths, History and English Literature, as well as an Intelligence Test. As the reader knows, I had an aversion to exams, but Mr Bromley and the others prevailed upon me to take the exam, which I did, along with some 200 other candidates.

To my surprise (and to the astonishment of my aunt and uncle) I stood fourth in the island, with special mention of my excellent English Literature paper.

This meant that I was now eligible for a permanent post in the Public Health Department, or in any other department of the local government. There was an interview for those who had cleared the exam, and one of the men who was interviewing me said they would give me a promotion if I moved to the medical service department, where they needed people. I said I was happy in the Public Health Department; I was used to the work and the people, so I'd rather stay there. The interviewer looked a little surprised, then said, 'Well, there's something to be said for loyalty.'

I suppose it was loyalty of a kind. Mr Bromley and the others had been good to me, and if it was going to be Jersey and a routine job, I'd rather be among people with whom I was comfortable.

But the real reason was different. Yes, I could have settled down in Jersey and grown old there, on a comfortable salary and the prospect of a pension. Everyone would have approved—my aunt and uncle; my mother back in India; my well-meaning colleagues. But I wasn't looking for permanency or the unexciting life of a government servant. I didn't refuse the permanent job, but in my heart I knew I wasn't going to stay.

Encouraging noises were coming from a publisher in London, who had read the first draft of my novel. Her name was Diana Athill, a partner and editor in the firm of Andre Deutsch Ltd., an up-and-coming publisher. She was enthusiastic about the book, but she felt it needed some re-working, and she had suggestions to make. And I have always been open to suggestions.

London beckoned. That was where writers and publishers flocked together. That was where Dickens had lived, and

Thackeray, and Galsworthy, and dear old Hugh Walpole, a brave man, and a friend to young writers. That was where Barrie was commemorated with a statue of Peter Pan in Kensington Gardens. That was where Bertie Wooster and Jeeves and the members of the Drones Club indulged in the festive spirit. Or so I imagined...

But the real impetus or catalyst to my leaving Jersey was a falling-out with my relatives, specifically my uncle.

A Christian from Pondicherry, Dr Heppolette was upright, honest and hardworking (and he'd been a well-known doctor in Lahore), but he was set in his thinking and his prejudice against the country of his birth. He did not think much of India or of Indians, and frequently expressed the gloomiest of forebodings on the future of the country, just five years into Independence. He was also very vocal about his disapproval of my mother and the life choices she had made, ending up with an 'Indian'. Both he and my aunt had led a privileged existence in British India, and had left because of the loss of privilege. There were many like them. I felt that his attitude was unfair, and said so; but because I was living with them as a 'poor relation', even though I was paying my way, I did my best to avoid heated arguments or any unpleasantness. Instead, I put down my thoughts and feelings in the diary I was keeping. Unfortunately—or fortunately, I suppose, now that I look back—it fell into the hands of my uncle, who couldn't resist reading it, and we had an almighty row. Among other things, I was accused of ingratitude, and that by itself convinced me that I ought to move on.

Whenever I was unhappy or disturbed, I used to go for a walk along a lonely stretch of seafront, and that was what I did now, although it was late evening. There was a storm brewing and the waves were crashing in and there was nobody else on the seafront. The tide was high, and a wave smashed itself against the sea wall, sending the salt spray on to my head and face. I almost lost my balance, but I stood my ground, and then I stood defiant, taking another stinging spray on my body, and then another, as the wind howled around me, testing and daring me. It was an exhilarating sensation, guaranteed to make me feel brave and indomitable—I would survive. With the help of the natural elements around me, I resolved, there and then, that I would leave Jersey the next day.

And this is exactly what I did.

Suitcase in one hand and portable typewriter in the other, I made my way down to the docks and bought a ticket on the first small steamer leaving for Plymouth. I hadn't even bothered to give notice to my employers, and as a result I lost the previous week's salary. But I had about twenty pounds saved up, and in 1952 that would have kept me from starvation for about a month.

It was March, and the Channel was foggy, and the sea choppy. But I felt quite confident in myself and in the future. I suddenly realized that for the first time in my life I was really and truly on my own. No parents to back me, no relatives to fall back on. Alone. All by myself in a wilderness of wind and water. The way I wanted it. Eighteen, and in control of my own destiny. For that man is strongest who stands alone.

THE LONDON ADVENTURE

I DIDN'T SEE MUCH OF LONDON FOR THE FIRST COUPLE OF DAYS, the fog was so thick and all-pervading. I spent two or three nights in a student's hostel; it was cheap, but very noisy. I had the address of an old BCS boy, Shyam Kishan, who was in London for 'higher studies'. He had a room in Belsize Park, and he insisted that I stay with him. He had been my senior in school, not a very close friend, but now he treated me like a brother. But I knew I had to fend for myself, and at the first opportunity I made my way to the nearest employment exchange and asked for a job.

I must have looked rather shabby. My trousers, as usual, were unpressed, my coat—the only one I possessed—a bit worn at the cuffs, my shoes unpolished. I had no overcoat, and I was feeling cold.

'And what can you do?' asked the clerk, looking at me doubtfully.

It was no use telling him that I'd written a book. They weren't looking for an unemployed author.

'I can type,' I said. 'I can write letters. I can make out bills. I can do accounts.'

'Quite an all-rounder,' he remarked, laughing. 'Anything else?'

'I can play football.'

'Can't help you there. You'll have to join a football club. But there's this factory in Swindon that makes football boots. Would you like to work in a boot factory?'

'No, sir.'

'All right, so here's a desk job for you,' he said, taking a card out of his index cabinet. 'Photax, Photographic Accessories. They need an accounts clerk who knows some book-keeping. Starting on five pounds a week. That suit you?'

Five pounds a week sounded like a fortune. In Jersey I'd been getting three pounds.

'Sounds all right.'

'Here you are, then.' And he gave me the address of Photax Ltd, who were to employ me in their office off Tottenham Court Road for the next two years.

~

Shyam, whom we knew in school as 'Jackson', which was the name of the high-end garments shop his father owned in Jodhpur, insisted that I could stay with him as long as I liked. But I didn't want to impose on his goodness and hospitality. I went out and found a room for myself.

I moved around a fair amount during my stay in London, and that restlessness must say something about my state of mind at the time. First, there was a small attic room on Glenmore Road in north London, not far from the Belsize Road tube station and within a short distance of the Everyman Theatre, a small cinema which showed revivals of old films, and where I often spent a lonely evening. But the Glenmore Road room was cold and miserable, and it had a view of the overcast sky and the roofs of other houses—an endless vista of grey tiles and blackened chimneys, without so much as a proverbial cat to relieve the monotony. So I moved to a more pleasant abode on Haverstock Hill, where I lived for some months; then, for short spells, to lodgings on Belsize Avenue, Tooting, in south London, and Swiss Cottage in north London again.

Most of my landladies were Jewish. The first, whom I remember best, lived on the ground floor, two floors below my attic room. The only telephone in the building was outside her room, and occasionally when there was a phone for me, she would shout to call me down. But she could never pronounce my name right! 'Rooskin!' she would shout. 'Roo-oo-skin. Call for you.' And I would climb down the stairs, in no great hurry, because in those early months there were hardly any people I would have wanted to spend time with. I usually came back to my damp and sparsely furnished room to make myself a cheese sandwich—occasionally with ham—and then sit at my typewriter to work on my Dehra journal. Alone, till one day I noticed a roommate—a little mouse peeping out at me from behind the books I had piled up on the floor (I had no bookshelf). I threw him some crumbs and a bit of cheese from my half-eaten sandwich, and soon he was making a meal of them. After that, he would present himself before me every evening, and I was happier for the company.

My worldly possessions had increased, not only by the typewriter bought in Jersey, but also by a record player which I had bought second-hand from a Thai student, a friend of Shyam's. I had become an ardent fan of the Black singer Eartha Kitt, and had bought many of her records; but they were no good without a player until the Thai boy came to my rescue. Then the sensual, throaty voice of Eartha—singing 'Uska Dara' and 'I Want To

Be Evil'—reverberated through the lodging house, bringing complaints from the landlady and the gentleman on the first floor. I had to keep the volume low, which wasn't much fun. I was also fond of the clarinet (turi) playing of an Indian musician, Master Ebrahim, who did versions of popular Hindi film songs which transported me back to the streets and bazaars of small-town India.

On weekends I would explore the city, usually on foot, that being the best way to get to know a place. My conception of what London would be like was based on my early reading of Dickens and P.G. Wodehouse. Well, the London of Dickens was long gone, and the London (and England) of Wodehouse had never existed. There was more of the real world in *Alice in Wonderland* than in the world of Jeeves and Bertie Wooster. I would have gained a better idea of the city from the stories of Arthur Morrison (*Tales of Mean Streets*) and Patrick Hamilton (*Hangover Square*); but I came to these writers much later.

London was still recovering from the war, and in the East End and dockland there were still bombed-out buildings and empty sites where there had once been offices or residences. Sugar was still rationed, and I soon got used to the strong, sugarless office tea. Meals in the cheaper restaurants were on the skimpy side, and when I had finished my 'meat and two veg' in the nearest ABC café, I was still very hungry!

Still I tramped around the city whenever I could—searching the Thames dockland and the Mile End Road for traces of *Bleak House* or *Our Mutual Friend*. Dutifully I wandered through Kensington Gardens and paid homage to the statue of Peter Pan, took up my position on a corner of Baker Street and looked across at the entrance of the house where Sherlock Holmes and Dr Watson had met so many mysterious clients…

In the evenings, I usually took the tube train home after work from Tottenham Court Station to Belsize Park. Sometimes I walked. One evening I started walking through the maze of streets and I saw a little roadside restaurant and decided to have dinner there, having tired of cheese and ham sandwiches. I'd never been there before. I walked in, sat down, had a nice, good meal, and when it was time to pay the bill I found I didn't have my wallet on me! It was getting towards winter and I'd kept it in my overcoat, which I'd left hanging in the office. I fiddled with the cutlery for a while, then decided to come clean. I went up to the manager and said, 'I've had my dinner, sir, and it was very nice. But I don't have any money with me. I'm sorry, I've left my coat in the office with my wallet in it.' I told him where I worked, not far from the restaurant, on Goodge Street, but the office would be closed now. He looked me up and down, assessing me to see if I was telling the truth or pulling a fast one, and then he said, 'All right. You can come by tomorrow and pay the bill.' Which was what I did, first thing the next morning.

I would go to the restaurant once in a while after that in the evenings. During the day, a fellow clerk at Photax, Ken Murrel, would share his marmite sandwiches with me, made by his mother, or we would go out together to a snack bar during the lunch break. Ken was always very helpful; working class himself, he could tell that I was having a harder time. We exchanged a few letters soon after I returned to India, and then there was a period of some forty years when we didn't correspond. About ten years ago, I received a letter from a man, who wrote to say he had my address from his father—Ken Murrel. Ken had been suffering from Alzheimer's and barely recognized anyone. One day his son told him he was going on company work to a town in India called Dehradun, and Ken's eyes lit up and he said, 'That's where Ruskin went, you know. He's my friend.' It was very touching to read that. Ken's son came up to meet me from Dehradun, and I shared my memories of working with his father when we were both young, just nineteen or twenty.

But I did not make many English friends. If they were a reserved race, I was even more reserved. Always shy, I waited for others to take the initiative. In India, people will take the initiative, they lose no time in getting to know you. Not so in England. They were too polite to look at you. And in that respect, I was more English than the English.

The gentleman who lived on the floor below me on Glenmore Road occasionally went so far as to greet me with the observation, 'Beastly weather, isn't it?'

And I would respond by saying, 'Oh, perfectly beastly,' and pass on.

It was all very polite and insular, and rather dull. Things changed when I bumped into a Gujarati boy, Praveen, who came to live on the basement floor. He gave me a winning smile, and I remember saying, 'Oh, to be in Bombay now that winter's here,' and immediately we were friends.

He was eighteen, and studying at one of the polytechnics with a view to getting into the London School of Economics. At that time, most of the Indians in London were students, the great immigration rush was still a long way off, and racial antagonisms were directed more at the recently arrived West Indians than at Asians.

Praveen took me on the rounds of the coffee bars, and introduced me to other students, among them a Vietnamese, called Thanh. He would become the subject of one of my stories, as would a distant cousin of his, a girl named Vu, and both relationships would end in some disillusionment, but more of that later.

Praveen liked gangster films and wanted me to accompany him to anything which featured Humphrey Bogart, James Cagney, George Raft and other tough guys. He wanted to be a tough guy himself, and often struck a Bogart-like pose, cigarette dangling from the side of his mouth. There was nothing tough about Praveen, who was really rather delicate, but his affectations were charming and comic and it was fun being with him.

∼

From the room in Haverstock Hill, my second abode in London, it was a short walk to Hampstead Heath, the large park in London with its ancient woodlands and chain of ponds, and on one occasion I walked from Primrose Hill down to Regents' Park. There was no shortage of greenery and parkland in London, and I wrote a story called *The Green City* which was never published, in fact lost by a future publisher.

Not much was being published, not even by the 'little' magazines to whom I submitted the odd poem. This prompted me to write the following verse:

> Who'll buy my poems?
> I sang out to the silent stones.
> And came the dread reply
> In deep sepulchral tones:
> We'll buy your eyes
> We'll buy your heart and bones
> We'll buy your rags
> And settle all your loans
> But please don't send us any poems,
> We will not buy your rotten poems!

Needless to say, no one published it. Even *Punch* did not find it funny.

However, I had better luck with radio.

Dear old BBC. I was finally repaid for all my years of loyalty in listening to *ITMA*, *Much-Binding-in-the-Marsh*, and *Waterlogged Spa*, not to mention the endless cricket commentaries, by having a story accepted and broadcast on the Third Programme, which was aimed at highbrows and super-intellectuals, which I definitely was not, but the producer, a nice lady named Prudence Smith, assured me I could pass for one. The story was called 'The Rainbow,' and I was invited to read it live, a daunting prospect; but I did it with aplomb after some rehearsals with the producer!

I no longer have the script; but it was to become one of the early chapters of *The Room on the Roof*—the episode in which Rusty plays Holi with the local boys and begins his discovery of India.

My employers at Photax were impressed (there was no one else to impress) and gave me leave to give two more talks, these on the more popular Light Programme—one of them about growing up in India (called 'My Two Countries'), and another about life in the bazaars of an Indian city. The producer of this programme was a kind man called P.H. Newby, a well-known novelist and travel writer. Over the years, and even after my return to India, the BBC was to provide a home for many of my short stories.

A small digression at this point, to describe a brief encounter that shows how different the life of a writer was fifty or sixty years ago, before the advent of television and the internet, when only film or sports stars and popular singers, or the occasional fashion model, were celebrities. Even newspapers did not write about them so much as they did about their books (book covers were photographed more than the authors).

I was outside one of the BBC studios, waiting to give my talk, when a man came out of the studio, greeted my producer, passed the time of day with him and me and then left. I don't remember what we talked about—could even have been something as mundane as the weather. Anyway, after he left, the producer asked me, 'You didn't know who that was?' and I said no. 'That's Graham Greene,' he said.

Greene was then at the height of his fame. He'd even done the screenplay recently for *The Third Man*, which was running in the West End. He was a nice-looking man, but understated, and not immediately recognizable. He wasn't a public face. And you could have said that about most authors at the time. Except for those who sought out publicity—someone like Hemingway, who liked being in the public eye and would do things like crashing his plane somewhere in Africa in order to get into the newspaper headlines.

But let me return to my BBC stories. Another to be impressed by this little achievement was Diana Athill, of Andre Deutsch, who had been corresponding with me in regard to *The Room on the Roof*, which she had first read as a journal and suggested that I rework it as a novel. It was now in its second or third draft—what started out as a journal became a first-person fictional narrative, and finally ended up in the third person. Diana would send me feedback—her own, and from the firm's 'readers'—which was sometimes useful, and sometimes contradictory and confusing. But I did benefit from much of it, especially Diana's suggestions, which were about the story; she did not tamper with my language or style.

To give the reader some idea of how the novel evolved, and what a good editor's engagement with a young writer's work can be like, let me reproduce one of Diana's letters to me. (In the draft of *The Room on the Roof* that Diana is responding to in this letter, Kishen had become Kamini—purely a literary sex change—but reverted to Kishen in the final draft.)

March 6th 1954
Ruskin Bond, Esq.,
124 Haverstock Hill
London N.W.I

My dear Ruskin,
I have read The Room (and it must be The Room—it is the inevitable title for it), and I like it. I gave it to someone else to read yesterday, and they brought it back to me saying 'I think it's a lovely story'. Andre hasn't read it yet, however, so you will just have to make do with this much at present.

I am not without criticism, however, and two I can give you straight away. 1. The end is a bit too fairy-tale. The coincidence of your meeting with Kamini by the river strains the credulity at a point when it is absolutely vital that it should not be strained. I thought that this could be avoided fairly easily by making something like this happen. Perhaps a neighbour to the house where she had been with her mother in Hardwar could chip in and say that she had an idea where the girl might be found—she had felt sorry for her, and had tried to help her, but Kamini had not accepted it (excepting, perhaps, for once or twice taking food from her) and had slipped off into the town: but she had seen her about occasionally, and thought that she often hung about the steps to the river ... You could still be pretty hopeless about finding her, and so have the hopeless feeling of page 121, but when you did find her it would not make the reader feel 'how very convenient!' in that disturbing way.

The other thing is that you have been too ruthless in your pruning away of inessentials. What you have done, in fact, is write as though your medium was the short story, not the novel. You don't give time enough time to pass in! (I'm not sure that that isn't a meaningless remark!) What I mean is, that some incidents and people could be, perhaps, a little enlarged, so that the reader had time to settle down in them. Particularly, this applies where you first go to live with Somi. This is a crux point, new life, and you dismiss that week in a page or two. I think you could enlarge here quite a lot, with benefit. Somehow the feeling of strangeness and excitement at the small things being different, the eating and the sleeping and the washing... You are taking your reader from one world (superficially speaking) into another, as well as yourself, and you must allow them more time to get the feel of it.

I wonder what you will feel about that. Does it make sense to you?

I shall try very hard to get you the final decision as soon as possible, and no doubt we'll be talking more about the book soon. Meanwhile, I do think you have done wonders.

Yours,
Diana

P.S. I'll tell you one thing that I missed—the original Kapoor family. You'll begin to wonder why I don't sit down and write the book myself, soon; but couldn't Somi's family have such neighbours, who could come into that chapter? Kishen could still be their spoilt son. Your pupils rather materialize out of thin air, as it stands, and they would be more explained if you had two families backing you as a teacher, and telling people about you. And that old drunk father was a good solid character—an excellent filler in of atmosphere and background.

I must say I worked harder on that book than on anything else I have written; and there was a time when I thought it had all gone to waste. Because Deutsch just could not make up his mind about it. His readers (Walter Allen, the famous critic, and Laurie Lee, the writer) said it was full of promise but that it would be premature to publish a work that was, in many ways, still immature. They were probably right; but I think that 'immaturity' was one of the appealing things about the book, for it was, after all, a story of adolescence written by an adolescent.

Anyway, it led to several meetings with Diana Athill, and our enduring friendship. She was sixteen years older than me, and I wasn't really her type, and I was past the stage of puppy love, so there was no question of a romantic or physical relationship. I looked upon her as a literary person, even as a mentor, which she was, and then as a smart and sensitive friend whose company I enjoyed. She was fond of me, and she could see I was neglecting myself, so she would invite me to her flat sometimes and share her meals with me—wholesome English food she cooked herself. When it grew very cold, she gave me an overcoat.

Many years later, Athill took to writing herself, and published a series of remarkable memoirs (the last of these at ninety-eight). In some of these she describes her life with several lovers, and writes about being 'the other woman' very often and finally going off sex at age seventy-five. But at the time I knew her, I did not see evidence of this. She was sharing her York Terrace flat with her cousin Barbara, who was working for *The Economist*, and it was Barbara who was having an affair with a writer called Anthony Smith—who was having an affair with a hot-air balloon. He took off in his balloon and landed somewhere in Iran or Afghanistan. However, he came back to write a book about it, and to marry Barbara.

On a couple of occasions, I took Diana to an Indian restaurant—there were only about half-a-dozen to choose from in the London of the 1950s—and sometimes we went to the cinema together. We usually went to see French films, which had English subtitles.

After I took her to see a particularly silly film called *Aan*—the first Indian feature film to be shown in London—she became a bit wary of my choice of films, but got her revenge by taking me to see Eisenstein's *Battleship Potemkin* and the unfinished *Que Viva Mexico*. The latter had been edited by Marie Seton, whom I was to meet in Delhi and Darjeeling several years later, when she was working on her biography of Satyajit Ray.

A film buff from my time in Delhi with my father, I explored the suburbs of London, visiting cinemas which were showing offbeat films that might not have benefited from a West End release. And when I had some money to spare, I went to the theatre. I saw a great production of *Porgy and Bess*, brought to perfection by the two great Black singers Leontyne Price (singing 'Summertime') and William Warfield ('Bess, You Is My Woman Now'), and by an old film favourite, Cab Callaway, with his rendering of 'Ain't Necessarily So'.

The old Scala theatre was close to the Photax office on Charlotte Street, and around Christmas time I dropped in to see the annual production of *Peter Pan*, Barrie being one of the playwrights whose plays I had lapped up when I was at school. Playing Peter was Margaret Lockwood, one of the most popular British film stars of the 1940s; not so young any more, but still beautiful and very accomplished. I was the envy of my office colleagues. Most of them lived in the suburbs and went straight home after work. Also, they saved their money, whereas I spent mine.

The movies and musicals provided some relief from the otherwise monotonous routine of near-endless hours in the office, followed by hurried sandwich or beans-on-toast dinners and a lot of typing and revising of my manuscript. After a year of drudgery, juggling with figures (no calculators and no decimal system as yet), I stepped out of that office looking for a different sort of life. And in due course I found it.

DOWN TO KEW WITH VU AND GOODBYE TO ENGLAND

TODAY, AS I LOOK OUT OF MY WINDOW AT THE MOUNTAIN MIST curling up from the valley, I am reminded of a different mist—not so much the London fog of 1953, as the mist that was gradually obscuring the vision in my right eye.

It began with black spots that kept dancing in front of my eye, like Fred Astaire in top hat and tails. Well, we all see spots from time to time. But these were there in all my waking hours—in the office, on the streets, in cinemas, restaurants, and in my little room. They were very irritating.

'It's probably due to malnutrition,' I told myself, and began dosing with vitamins.

But gradually the spots grew bigger until they coalesced into a shifting cloud, and there wasn't much else that I could see with my right eye.

Fortunately, the left eye was unaffected, and I used it to guide me to the consulting room of an eye specialist. After various tests and examinations, which involved several visits, he declared that I was suffering from 'Eale's Disease', a rare condition of the retina, and had me admitted to the Hampstead General Hospital for further observation and treatment.

I spent a month in the general ward, a guest of Her Majesty's Government and the National Health Insurance, which meant I did not have to pay a penny for my stay and treatment. The latter consisted of cortisone injections to the eye, and a diet designed to build up my resistance to infection—for I was right in thinking that malnutrition was at the root of my problem. For almost a year I had been living on Mars Bars, beans on toast, cheese sandwiches, and the occasional 'meat and two veg' dinner. I had never been so skinny in all my life. And now, to the envy of the other patients in the ward, I was provided with a bottle of Guinness (light ale) with my substantial lunch. This was designed to buck me up—and it did! 'God bless Her Majesty', I toasted the Queen as I gulped my Guinness, although I should really have been blessing the Labour Government, which had just been voted out of power.

While recuperating in the Hampstead General, I wrote a story and read several books, brought to me on a trolley every morning. I discovered the detective novels of Josephine Tey, and a book on the Buddha (by Robert Payne) which helped me to take a philosophical view of my situation. I received visits—Diana Athill (with flowers), my new landlady (with a cake), and my office manager (with my salary packet). As I had no expense at all that month, I had saved twenty pounds of my salary.

My vision did improve slightly. The cloud dispersed. But it never went away completely, and even today I do not see much with my right eye. Well, as long as my left eye and my writing hand continue to serve me well, I consider myself lucky, or rather, blessed by a benign providence.

And in London there were soon to be other distractions.

One of the patients in my ward in the Hampstead General hospital was George, a man of about thirty who had come to England from Trinidad and worked as a ticket-collector at one of the underground stations. He had been suffering from fever and a stiff neck and the doctors suspected meningitis. He was a large, stout man with a gentle, kindly expression on his mobile face, and he was always smiling—except when he had to be given a rather painful lumbar puncture. He would set up quite a commotion then, and I would go over and sit on his bed and try to calm him down. When I left the hospital, I gave George my home address, although I didn't expect to see him again.

A few months later, I found him on my doorstep, fully recovered and smiling. We repaired to a nearby pub and drank rum. He invited me to a party in Camden Town, and when I arrived, I found I was the only 'white' in a gathering of handsome Black men and women determined to have a good time. We drank and danced into the early hours of the morning, when I fell asleep on a sofa, and someone fell asleep on top of me.

I went to two or three more of these calypso parties—I didn't really have the stamina to become a regular—and George and his friends poured sunshine into my rather dreary life.

And then, along came Vu.

Or rather, her cousin Thanh, who introduced me to her.

Thanh was a Vietnamese youth of my age, but younger-and better-looking, delicate and androgynous. His family was well-to-do, and lived in France (Vietnam had been a French colony and many Vietnamese had settled in France). He was in London because he wanted to be a pianist and he wanted to speak English fluently. Both his piano-playing and his English were rudimentary. He had met Praveen somewhere, and when Praveen told him that I was a writer of sorts, he turned to me for help with his English.

Thanh was a complicated person, but I didn't see this at first. I was attracted by his exotic looks and a sort of sophisticated aloofness he cultivated. He didn't like Asians very much, though he was one himself, and when I told him I was Indian—very much an Asian—he looked disappointed but seemed to get over it. He said he liked me, and despite myself I was flattered. We grew close; I stayed with him in his rooms and enjoyed his cooking—he was a better cook than a pianist—and conversed with him in English.

Sometimes he would complain that I wasn't a good friend, that I did not respect him, and thought too much of myself though I knew so little and spoke English like a Welshman, not a proper Englishman. But he would turn affectionate soon after and cook me delicious pork and fried rice.

Sometimes he would be gloomy and tell me he didn't have long to live.

'There is something in my chest. It is always ticking,' he would say and bare his bony, pale chest for me. I would put my ear to it and hear nothing. I would ask him to go to a hospital and get an X-ray done, but he would turn away in irritation.

Our association ended abruptly one day when he realized my accent wasn't even Welsh—as, I later gathered, Praveen had told him—but Indian. He felt that I had betrayed him in some way. Indians, he said, were not to be trusted.

'Find someone who can speak real English,' he demanded. 'Otherwise you are not my friend.'

So I introduced him to a boy who spoke 'real English'—a Cockney youth who worked for the British Railways. They hit it off splendidly, and months later dear Thanh was speaking pure Cockney. I suppose I'd had my revenge.

Before he terminated our friendship, Thanh had introduced me to Vu Phuong—a pretty, petite, sweet, intelligent nineteen- or twenty-year-old, who was on her own in London, studying something or the other—it was a mystery to me what some of these young people were studying, they seemed to have an endless amount of time on their hands. But at least Vu did not ask me to teach her English. She knew enough to be able to charm anyone who met her. And I found myself at ease in her company. This was unusual, because I was usually shy and self-conscious with girls of my own age.

Vu liked visiting parks and public gardens, and I was quite happy to accompany her on these little expeditions—strolling through Regent's Park; feeding the ducks at the pond on Hampstead Heath; lying on the grass on Primrose Hill; exploring the hothouses at Kew.

The botanical gardens at Kew always attracted me, because there I could return to the tropics simply by entering one of those steamy hothouses where tropical plants grew in profusion. It was the Amazon basin rather than the Ganges plain that was re-created here, but that was good enough for me; anything to get away from the London drizzle and the fogs that came in from the Atlantic.

'We'll go down to Kew in lilac time,' were the words of an old song, but I was glad to go down to Kew at any time.

On Primrose Hill, Vu took my hand and held it seemingly for ever, and naturally I fell in love with her. It was the first time a girl had shown me undisguised affection and a desire to be with me. I did not take her back to my rather gloomy room (my landlady had forbidden visitors), but she took me to hers (no sign of a fearsome landlady) and we spent hours together, drinking tea and playing simple card games. I must have been madly in love with her in order to play cards; I hated card games—my time with Miss Kellner being the only exception. But during those idyllic few weeks I was ready to do anything to please Vu.

We drank innumerable cups of chrysanthemum tea, and told each other's fortunes from the tea-leaves. You need proper tea leaves for this, not tea-bags. When the leaves settle at the bottom of the cup, they take on unusual shapes and patterns, and those who can interpret these patterns predict the future from them. Vu was an expert at doing this, and predicted all sorts of interesting things for me—that I'd be a successful writer some day (but not in the near future), that I'd travel to distant lands (maybe India, maybe Africa), and that I'd have many love affairs.

'Never mind the love affairs,' I said. 'What about us—will you marry me?'

She studied the tea-leaves in her cup for some time and said, 'It's not in the tea-leaves. So sorry.'

'Try again. Read my tea-leaves this time.'

So she studied the pretty chrysanthemum leaves at the bottom of my empty cup, and made the same pronouncement: 'So sorry, Ruskin. It's not in the tea-leaves.'

After that I refused to look at the tea-leaves.

She really was a lovely person, and I was deeply in love with her. But it often happens that I overdo things, get carried away by my infatuation or passion and make a mess of everything. I finally taught myself to take things somewhat lightly, not to scare people away with the intensity of my feelings, and even to have no expectations from others, but it took me many, many years.

When Vu told me that she was going into the country for a couple of weeks to pick strawberries with a group of students, I should have left it at that. Strawberry-picking was an annual ritual with foreign students who made a little pocket money working on farms in the English countryside. But a week without Vu was too long for me. I knew where they'd gone—a village called Kintbury in Berkshire, only an hour or two from London—and on a desolate weekend I bought a rail ticket and travelled up to Kintbury.

It was a pretty little place, Kintbury, a real old-fashioned English village, with a homely pub decorated with prints of hunting-scenes. I had a light lunch, and set off for the farm where I was told the girls were staying.

I found them all right, all gathering strawberries—pink-cheeked English girls, tall willowy Scandinavian girls, handsome smiling African girls—and Vu in the middle of them, having the time of her life.

I don't think she was pleased to see me—she'd have to explain my sudden arrival to all her companions—but she was never unkind, and she greeted me with her usual sweetness and asked me why I was there.

'Just wanted to see you,' I said.

'Well now we have seen each other. I have to be with the girls. You go back to London and I will see you next week.'

I went back, feeling rather foolish. I called at her lodgings the following week but was told by her landlady that she had not returned. Three days later, when I telephoned, I was told that she had moved elsewhere. The landlady wasn't sure where. Somewhere in South London—Tooting or Clapham—she was very vague about it. I had changed my own lodgings several times, but I had always lived mostly in north London. Except for Kew Gardens, south London was unfamiliar territory to me.

Disheartened and downcast, but still hopeful, anxious to clear up any misunderstanding and reinstate myself in Vu's affections, I made a serious attempt to locate her. A sympathetic Thai student gave me an address, and off I went to track it down. I had a fortnight's leave that year, and I spent most of it in a frustrating endeavour to find Vu Phuong, to whom I had surrendered my heart.

It was clear that she no longer wanted my heart, if she ever had at all, but I persisted. Was I becoming a stalker? The thought did not occur to me then, but looking back, I feel I came near to being one.

At the new address I was told that Vu and her student friends had gone to Paris. Apparently her sister ran a restaurant there. I walked across the street and spent some time walking up and down the pavement. I had a feeling that Vu was in the house. And when I crossed the road and looked up at the building, I saw her face at one of the windows, looking down at me. She withdrew as soon as I raised my hand to wave to her.

I walked away, and took the train back to London. Walking back to my empty room from the Swiss Cottage station, I stopped at a pub and had a few brandies, but of course that didn't help.

Some days later, I received a postcard from Vu, telling me that she was with her sister in Paris, and they might go back to Vietnam. Obviously I did not fit into her scheme of things. There would have been no future for me in her country, and I suppose she saw no future with me. I tried to forget her. But it wasn't easy.

She held my hand on Primrose Hill,
I loved her then and love her still.
Although she had sworn we never would part
She went away with the shreds of my heart.
But I loved her then and love her still,
And I see her still climbing up Primrose Hill.

~

It was a year of disappointments, and Andre Deutsch did not make things any better by refusing to make up his mind about *The Room on the Roof*. He'd given me twenty-five pounds as an option on the book, and I was supposed to receive another fifty pounds as an advance against royalties. But he hesitated to commit himself to publication—he thought he would lose money on the book (after all, it was a first novel by a complete unknown), and he felt, too, that I should wait a year or two before making authorship my profession.

I wasn't the only writer with whom Andre had trouble making

up his mind. None other than Orson Welles, the great director who had transformed cinema with *Citizen Kane*, had come up with a novel called *Mr Arkadin*, and it appeared that nobody at Deutsch wanted it! Orson Welles may have been a great filmmaker (though not always), but as a writer he was something of a flop. But you couldn't tell him so. He was a big man with a bad temper. And like most actors, he was extremely vain. A polite letter of rejection was mailed to him. His response was to come storming into Andre's Thayer Street office, denouncing two-bit publishers and their lackeys in no uncertain terms. Chairs were overturned, manuscripts flew out of windows, and poor little Andre Deutsch (who was only five-and-a-half feet or thereabouts) dived for cover. (I received a blow-by-blow account from Diana a few days later.) In the end Andre agreed to publish the wretched book.

I suppose that's one way to get your masterpiece accepted—terrorize the unfortunate publisher.

Andre and Diana were right in thinking that *Mr Arkadin* had little merit as a novel. The book never really took off, and when Welles obstinately transferred it to the screen (in the process wasting the talents of some good actors, including Michael Redgrave), it did no better; the master had clearly lost his touch.

As a publisher, Deutsch was going from strength to strength, roping in such writers as Jack Kerouac, Wolf Mankowitz, Mordecai Richler, and, a little later, V. S. Naipaul and his talented but short-lived brother Shiva. But of my little book there was no sign—though I did finally receive the fifty-pound advance—and I began to see the future as year after year of totting up sales figures for Photax Ltd., good people though they were. Surely I could do as much, if not more, back in India, where I would at least have friends to cycle around with, and the freedom that comes from being a nobody in the great grey multitude that makes up the country.

For some time I had almost resigned myself to a lifetime of clerical servitude—it would have been bearable had there been someone, a Vu Phuong, to take my hand occasionally—but now, once more, I began to think seriously of returning to India; although, when I mentioned this to anyone—Indian students, my mother, or friends back in India, they expressed alarm at the thought and did their best to dissuade me. What was the point in coming all the way to England if I was going to return home because I felt lonely and because I thought I was a failure?

'Home'—that was the magnet. Not the 'home' of my mother and stepfather, but the larger home that was India, where I could even feel free to be a failure. The Land of Regrets, someone had called India; but for me it was a land of acceptances. For hadn't I, a mixed-up colonial castaway, an accident of history, found acceptance on the streets and in the tea-shops and the wayside haunts of Dehra? I wasn't looking for a palace or a hilltop retreat. All I really wanted was my little room back again.

~

I left London without any planning; I made up my mind on the spur of the moment. I gave my office a week's notice, and they had a little party for me, gave me a travel bag, and the head of the office said if I changed my mind and returned to London, I could have my job back.

Diana Athill didn't know I was leaving. She found out only when I wrote to her from Dehradun to tell her, 'So I'm back in India. Are you going to publish my book?' I suppose I should have behaved better after all the kindness she had shown me, and gone and met her before I left London for good. But I did hear back from her some months later, when she sent me copies of *The Room on the Roof*. We still write to each other every eight or ten years (Diana will be a hundred this winter; 2017).

From Vu I heard nothing more. Her life, it seemed, was to go in another direction—to war-torn Vietnam, where her parents were still living in Hanoi, the Communist stronghold. Or she stayed on in Paris; perhaps she came back to London. I never found out.

Thanh died shortly after I returned to India. A common friend wrote to tell me it was something to do with his heart. A stopwatch had been ticking away in his chest after all. He had died in Paris, looked after by his sister.

The voyage back from England was on a cheaper liner than the one that brought me to the country. It was a Polish ship, the *Batory*, which had been in the headlines just some weeks earlier because most of the crew had taken political asylum in England.

My cabinmate was an Indian student, Raghuvir Narain, who was coming back home for a break. We discovered a cheap but rather nice Polish vodka in the bar, and would pool our money to buy a couple of drinks every other evening. When we stopped in Gibraltar, we went ashore together and spent some time walking around. There were a lot of shops and almost all were Indian-owned—even at that time, 1956. At Port Said, we went ashore again, and were cheated—it served us right—by a couple of Egyptian men who promised to take us to a place where a woman and two donkeys did intimate things to one another. We returned to the ship considerably poorer, having bought the men many rounds of drinks before realizing we'd been had.

The *Batory* was a jinxed ship. As we were passing the Suez Canal, a crew member jumped overboard and was never seen again—it was a Communist ship and the man was probably desperate to get away. Some days later, when we were in the Arabian Sea, the ship's alarm bells began to ring in the middle of the night and there was much panic; no one knew what was happening; and hardly anyone knew how a life jacket should be worn, as there'd been no lifeboat drill. There were shouts of 'Abandon ship!' and then 'Man overboard!' and some children had begun to wail. Someone said the ship's engine had gone silent, and it did appear that we were drifting in the immensity of darkness and sea. Finally, we were told it was a false alarm and we could go back to our cabins. We later heard that a passenger had fallen overboard. Who it was, or how he or she had ended up in the sea, we never found out.

Our last stop before Bombay was Karachi, where again I

went ashore, already feeling I was home. I bought some Karachi newspapers to see if there were any I could send my stories to for publication, but the few that I picked up didn't seem to have any space for stories or essays. I never did manage to get published in any papers in Pakistan,

Then we were in Bombay's Ballard Pier. And as we were getting off, a fire broke out on the *Batory*. People rushed out while the Bombay fire brigade trucks drove into the docks with their bells ringing. I was glad to be off that ship!

This time I didn't stay in Bombay. I went straight to the Bombay Central Station and took the slow train to Delhi.

Mr H met me in Delhi at the station, which was very good of him. Time had indeed made us all better people—him more responsible than before, although I was being more reckless than I had ever been. Did my mother have something to do with him being there? She hadn't followed the rules, after all, and maybe she understood me better at that time than others would have. Of course, it may just have been that Mr H happened to be in Delhi for some other work. Even so, he needn't have come to receive me. So there he was, and we travelled together by train from Delhi to Dehradun.

As we approached Dehradun, the train entered a forest of familiar green. Every click of the rails brought me closer to all that I had missed and was now coming back to reclaim as my own. I belonged to the hot sunshine and muddy canals, the banyan trees and the mango groves, the smell of wet earth after summer rain, the relief of a monsoon thunderstorm, the laughing brown faces. And the *intimacy* of human contact—that was what I had missed the most in England. The orderly life, the good sense and civility were all admirable, but they did nothing for the soul. I missed the freedom to touch someone without being misunderstood; the freedom to hold someone's hand as a mark of affection rather than desire, but also to show desire without reserve and find fulfilment. I missed being among strangers without feeling like an outsider; I missed everything that made it all right to be sentimental and emotional.

In Dehra, Somi's cousin Dipi was at the station with his bicycle. I put my suitcase and travel bag in my stepfather's second-hand car, pulled myself onto the crossbar of Dipi's bicycle, and we rode through the streets of the town that had shaped my life, and brought me home.

BEGINNING AGAIN

I HAD LEFT LONDON FEELING A LITTLE DEPRESSED, BUT AS WE entered the Red Sea my spirits had soared with the temperature. At the end of the voyage, stepping off the gangway in Bombay, I was a happy young man, and happier all the way to Delhi and onwards to Dehra. The passage home had cost me about forty pounds, and I had a similar amount in cash with me. That would see me through the coming month, perhaps two, and that was as far as I dared to think.

Sometimes I feel my life has been a saga of new beginnings. Setbacks, failures, and then small successes to spur me on to other failures. In the beginning, I had to come to terms with the loss of my father, then create an identity for myself in my stepfather's home. Off to Jersey to make a beginning of sorts in an atmosphere that was completely alien to me. Another beginning in London; small achievements amounting to nothing. And now back to India, and starting all over again.

And what was I, anyway? English, like my father? Or Anglo-Indian, like my mother? Or Punjabi Indian, like my stepfather and half-brothers? Or a London Indian, like so many of my friends who had settled there, in body and in spirit?

Well, I was back in India, and I had no intention of going elsewhere, and as the land was full of all kinds of people of diverse origins, I decided I'd just be myself, all-Indian, even if it meant being a minority of one.

And ever the optimist, I was convinced that I could make a living from my writing, even though I could not see anyone else doing so.

I had my small typewriter, the one Mr Bromley had helped me purchase in Jersey, and I was soon putting it to good use. Although book publishers were in short supply, I was able to make a fairly impressive list of English-language magazines and newspapers to whom I could sell my wares, and it went something like this:

The Illustrated Weekly of India (first choice)
The Sunday Statesman (second choice)
Sport and Pastime
Sainik Samachar (armed forces weekly)
The Deccan Herald
The Tribune (Ambala)
Shankar's Weekly
My Magazine of India (if it still exists)

Most of these publications included fiction in their supplements and magazines, so there was a ready market for my short stories. *The Illustrated Weekly*, I had found out, still paid Rs 50 for a story or article; *Sainik Samachar*, Rs 30; the others, Rs 25.

Before leaving London I had sold a story to the *Young Elizabethan*, a British literary magazine for older children, and I planned to send them more. And of course to the BBC, which paid fifteen guineas—fifteen pounds and fifteen shillings—for a fifteen-minute story. Back then, the rupee was stronger and the 180 or 190 rupees per story would keep me in some security, if not comfort, for a month.

Encouragement came from C.R. Mandy, the genial Irish editor of *The Illustrated Weekly*. He had published some of my early work, and now he accepted the first two stories I sent him. I would soon be bombarding him with almost everything I wrote.

But where was I to live?

Though my mother and stepfather had welcomed me back, they were already packing to leave for Delhi. Mr H's business dealings had gone awry yet again. He was now bankrupt; his workshop had closed down, he owed money to various people, and there were heavy demands from the income tax department. An old friend who ran a car business in New Delhi had offered him a job as a workshop manager, and he was glad (and wise) to accept it. As he and my mother were in financial difficulties, I could not expect much help from them; nor was I in a position to do much for them. They suggested that I accompany them to Delhi, but I hadn't come back to live in Delhi. I wanted to stay on in Dehra, at least for the time-being. I wanted to be near old friends; I wanted new friends. I wanted the proximity of the hills and rivers. And above all, I wanted the freedom of being my very own person.

This was when Bibiji came into the picture.

~

Bibiji had a name of course, but everyone called her Bibiji. She was my stepfather's first wife, the woman he had abandoned for my mother, and she became a guardian angel of sorts during those two and a half years in Dehra when I struggled to make a living as a freelance writer. If this sounds complicated, I suppose it was. It is the kind of thing that can only happen in India, or at least it was when I was twenty-one.

I got on rather well with this hardy, industrious lady, and sympathized with her predicament. In order to sustain herself and two small children after Mr H deserted her, she had started a kirana shop, a small provision store, in a corner of the Astley Hall shopping arcade, thus becoming Dehra's first lady shopkeeper. She was a sturdy woman of balloon-like proportions, very strong in the arms, who could fling sacks of flour around as though they were shuttlecocks. On one occasion, early into Mr H's affair with my mother, she had gone looking for them armed with an axe. I could see that she had probably been a little overwhelming for my diminutive stepfather.

Bibiji had rented a couple of rooms above the kirana shop and, as she lived alone, she offered to sublet one of these rooms to me for a nominal sum. I took it without hesitation, for it would have been impossible to find anything else in the centre of town that didn't cost at least twice as much. Bibiji's profits from the store were meagre, and she should really have been charging me more, but I think having me stay on her premises in Dehra, and not with my mother or stepfather in Delhi, gave her a victory of sorts.

My room was bright and airy, with a balcony in front and a small veranda at the back. A neem tree grew in front of the building, and during the rains, when the neem-pods fell and were crushed underfoot, they gave off a rich, pungent odour which I can never forget. There were flats on either side of my room, served by a common stairway, which was blocked, at night, by a sleeping cow, over whom one had to climb, for it would move for no one. In the evenings I lit a kerosene lamp if I wanted to read or write, as there was no electricity—the bills having gone unpaid for several years. The amount due was now astronomical, and no one could afford to clear the arrears, so I had to manage without lights or a fan or a radio. Most of my writing was done in the mornings at my desk, especially during the hot summer months when I would fall asleep at mid-day.

My 'desk' was a large dining table on which I spread out my notebooks, papers and typewriter. A couple of smooth rounded stones from the Rispana riverbed acted as paperweights. There was a framed photograph of my father and one of Vu Phuong. Daddy's photograph is still on my desk. Vu's moved from its frame into my album some months later, and there it has remained as a distant memory.

All my memories I examined, rearranged, edited, or sometimes just reproduced, for my stories. I was diligent about this, but I certainly did not burn the midnight oil in my striving to make a living as a writer. If I could manage one thousand words a day, I was satisfied. And this could be accomplished in a couple of hours. Afterwards, I would drop in at a café for a cup of coffee, and in the evenings I would walk to the bazaar for tikkis or kababs, and to look at strangers with whom I would imagine conducting intensely physical, clandestine affairs. Then I would return to light my kerosene lamp for an hour at night and jot down stray thoughts and ideas, or write a letter, before getting into bed alone.

I used to breakfast with Bibiji downstairs, behind the shop, where she had a small alcove to herself. Breakfast would consist of aaloo or mooli parathas (as many as I could consume) with a sabzi and pickles—all manner of pickles. I soon became a pickle aficionado, my favourites being shalgam (turnip), a very Punjabi pickle; or stuffed red chillies; or jackfruit pickle. It was very substantial fare and I usually didn't need another meal till the evening, when I went down the road and took my dinner in a small restaurant or a dhaba. I was never any good as a cook, and these eating places were quite cheap—for five rupees I could have a decent non-vegetarian meal, and if I stuck to the basics—daal, rice and a vegetable—I could eat in three rupees.

During the day, Bibiji had no time to cook, as she had to run the shop, and that too without any help. I would come by and help her with bills and invoices and haphazard accounting. She was barely literate, but an astute shopkeeper; she knew instinctively who was good for credit and who was strictly nakad (cash), and she measured out quantities of rice, potatoes and lentils with the professionalism of any bazaar shopkeeper. I soon learnt the names of all the different, colourful daals that she displayed—moong, arhar, masoor, malka, etc (but alas, I can no longer tell one from the other). Her rajma (red beans) was in great demand, and people from Delhi would buy quantities of it. Dehra was also famous for its basmati rice, which was grown all over the Doon. Today, there are very few rice fields, the builders having taken over most of the countryside.

Once or twice a week, at the crack of dawn, Bibiji would set off for the wholesale market to procure her supplies. Normally, this was a bit too early for me to be up and about, but on a couple of occasions I made a special effort, got up and dressed and accompanied her to the wholesale market, in the depths of the Paltan Bazaar. This entailed a forty-minute march along deserted roads, then an hour of negotiating with vendors from the rural surroundings offering green peas or cabbage or cauliflowers, or mounds of rice, flour and daals, or onions and potatoes, all at fluctuating rates. Bibiji was of course good at bargaining, and hiring a push-cart, would soon have it loaded up with her purchases. Her favourite coolie, Mumtaz, would then trundle the cart back to Astley Hall and the provision store.

Who was Astley, and why was this shopping centre so named? Foreign road and place names have, over the years, come and gone, but Astley Hall is still (as I write) Astley Hall, just as Connaught Place in New Delhi remains Connaught Place. No one knows who Astley was; I don't, either. Those who might have known are long ago gone. I can only speculate that Astley was a favourite son of one of the owners of the property on which this commercial centre came up, back in the early 1900s.

'Astley', of course, is often mispronounced, and Bibiji always called it 'Asli' Hall—'asli' meaning the 'real thing'. Which was how she described my father, whom she had met just once, she said, when he had come to the old photo studio before Mr H sold it.

'Your father was an asli Angrez (an Englishman),' she would say, implying, I think, that he was a man of honour and good conduct. She didn't have a good word for my mother, but that was understandable. When she referred to my father as a 'Juntalman', it was meant to be a judgement delivered about my mother and her—Bibiji's—ex-husband.

Bibiji's pronunciation was distinctly Punjabi. To her I was always 'Rucksun', not Ruskin.

'Rucksun,' she would say, 'one day you must write my life story.'

And I would promise to do so.

~

Of the book that I *had* written, there was no news, and I had, in fact, forgotten all about it, being far too busy trying to sell my stories to magazines and make a living. I had made it my duty to study every English language publication that found its way to Dehra (most of them did), to see which of them published short fiction. A surprisingly large number of them did; the trouble was, the rates of payment were not very high, the average being about twenty-five rupees a story. Ten stories a month would therefore fetch me two hundred and fifty rupees—just enough for me to get by.

Only *The Illustrated Weekly*, as I have said, paid Rs 50 per story, and fortunately quite a few of my stories appeared in the paper. One day, a letter from C.R. Mandy informed me that he was going to serialize *The Room on the Roof*—and that was how I knew it had been published. Even Diana Athill had neglected to inform me. Copies of the book finally turned up, but I first saw it when serialization began in the *Weekly*, with lively illustrations by Mario Miranda, the *Weekly*'s well-known cartoonist and illustrator. That was in 1956, and I recall the morning well, because I wrote about it soon afterwards. I was twenty-two then and I am eighty-two now; a lot has happened since then, and if I sat down to make a list of all my mornings, I would probably remember more eventful ones. But as it was my first book, I suppose it deserves commemoration, so here's the piece I wrote:

> *I was up a little earlier than usual, well before sunrise, well before my buxom landlady, Bibiji, called up to me to come down for my tea and parathas. It was going to be a special day and I wanted to tell the world about it. But when you're twenty-one, the world isn't really listening to you.*
>
> *I bathed at the tap, put on a clean (but unpressed) shirt, trousers that needed cleaning, shoes that needed polishing. I never cared much about appearances. But I did have a nice leather belt with studs! I tightened it to the last notch. I was a slim boy, just a little undernourished.*
>
> *On the streets, the milkmen on their bicycles were making their rounds, reminding me of William Saroyan, who sold newspapers as a boy, and recounted his experiences in* The

Bicycle Rider in Beverley Hills. *Stray dogs and cows were nosing at dustbins. A truck loaded with bananas was slowly making its way towards the mandi. In the distance there was the whistle of an approaching train.*

One or two small tea shops had just opened, and I stopped at one of them for a cup of tea. As it was a special day, I decided to treat myself to an omelette. The shopkeeper placed a record on his new electric record player, and the strains of a popular film tune served to wake up all the neighbours—a song about a girl's red dupatta being blown away by a gust of wind and then retrieved by a handsome but unemployed youth. I finished my omelette and set off down the road to the bazaar.

It was a little too early for most of the shops to be open, but the news agency would be the first and that was where I was heading.

And there it was: the National News Agency, with piles of fresh newspapers piled up at the entrance. The Leader *of* Allahabad, *the* Pioneer *of* Lucknow, *the* Tribune *of* Ambala, *and the bigger national dailies. But where was the latest* Illustrated Weekly of India? *Was it late this week? I did not always get up at six in the morning to pick up the* Weekly, *but this week's issue was a special one. It was my issue, my special bow to the readers of India and the whole wide beautiful wonderful world. My novel was to be published in England, but first it would be serialized in India!*

Mr Gupta popped his head out of the half-open shop door and smiled at me.

'What brings you here so early this morning?'

'Has the Weekly *arrived?'*

'Come in. It's here. I can't leave it on the pavement'.

I produced a rupee. 'Give me two copies.'

'Something special in it? Did you win first prize in the crossword competition?'

My hands were not exactly trembling as I opened the magazine, but my heart was in my mouth as I flipped through the pages of that revered journal—the one and only family magazine of the 1950s, the gateway to literary success—edited by a quirky Irishman, Shaun Mandy.

And there it was: the first instalment of The Room on the Roof, that naïve, youthful novel on which I had toiled for a couple of years. It had lively, evocative illustrations by Mario, who wasn't much older than me. And a picture of the young author, looking gauche and gaunt and far from intellectual.

I waved the magazine in front of Mr Gupta. 'My novel!' I told him. 'In this and the next five issues!'

He wasn't too impressed. 'Well, I hope circulation won't drop,' he laughed. 'And you should have sent them a better photograph.'

Expansively, I bought a third copy.

'Circulation is going up!' said Mr Gupta.

The bazaar was slowly coming to life. Spring was in the air, and there was a spring in my step as I sauntered down the road. I wanted to tell the world about my triumph, but was the world interested? I had no mentors in our sleepy little town. There was no one to whom I could go and confide: 'Look what I've done. And it was all due to your encouragement, thanks!' Because there hadn't been anyone to encourage or help, not then nor in the receding past. The members of the local cricket team, among whom I had friends, would certainly be interested, and one or two would exclaim: 'Shabash! Now you can get us some new pads!' And there were other friends who would demand a party at the chaat shop, which was fine, but would any of them read my book?

But perhaps one or two would read it, out of loyalty.

A cow stood in the middle of the road, blocking my way.

'See here, friend cow,' I said, displaying the magazine to the ruminating animal. 'Here's the first instalment of my novel. What do you think of it?'

The cow looked at the magazine with definite interest. Those crisp new pages looked good to eat. She craned forward as if to accept my offer of breakfast, but I snatched the magazine away.

'I'll lend it to you another day,' I said, and moved on.

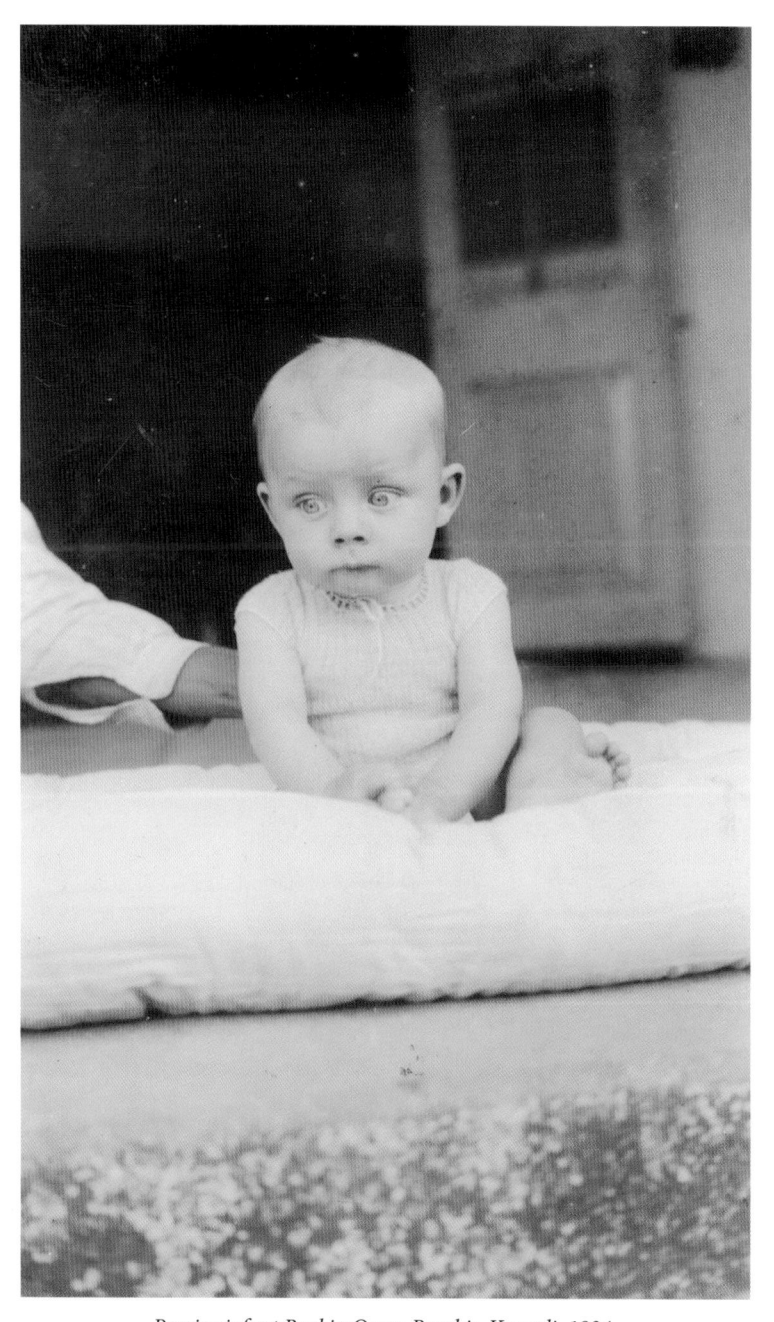

Pensive infant Ruskin Owen Bond in Kasauli, 1934.

Top left: With my mother in Kasauli. Top right: Daddy.

On the beach in Jamnagar.

Left: The little devil in Jamnagar.

Top: With my sister Ellen; taking a break from pushing her tricycle around the garden.

Top: The Jamnagar Palace. The old palace, on the right, was where my father ran his school for the children of the royal family.

Left: The Jamnagar princesses: Manha, Jhanak, Ratna and Hathi; my father's pupils.

Top: My mother at the Jamnagar aerodrome, before she went for a spin in a Tiger Moth plane with a prince from one of the neighbouring states.

Right: Dehra Granny with my mother (who would have been in school when this picture was taken).

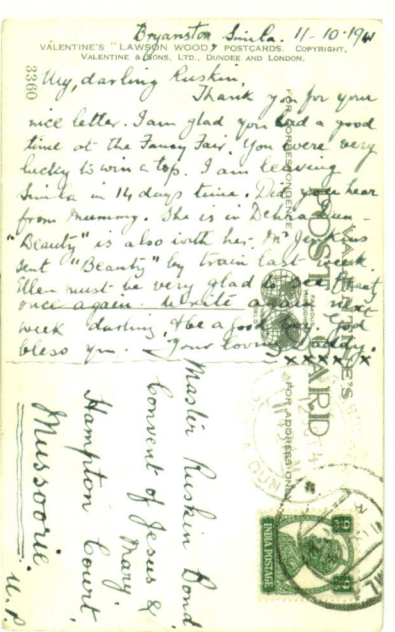

A postcard from my father, sent in 1941, when I was at school in Mussoorie.

Left: In Daddy's RAF cap, outside the Humayun Road hutment in Delhi.

Top: In my room on Atul Grove Road, with the gramophone (the black box standing on the left), bagatelle and dart board.

Top: A rare picture of my friends at Bishop Cotton's, taken with a 'Baby Brownie' camera, which was popular in the 1940s and '50s. Sitting in front of the Sikh boy standing on the bench is Azhar.

Right: Receiving a trophy on sports day in senior school.

The last picture of my father, taken when he was posted in Karachi.

Top: My mother and Aunt Enid on a picnic in Dehra in the mid 1940s.
Above: Ellen and I with some young friends near the Jamuna river just outside Dehra.

My house in school, Ibbetson. This photograph was taken just before Partition. Several of the boys here would soon leave for the newly created state of Pakistan.

The Bishop Cotton's football team of 1950. I'm in the centre, with my good friend Kasper, a German, standing behind me. The others are Boga, an Irani boy; Lama, from Nepal; Plunkett, an Anglo-Indian boy; a Sikh boy, Jogi, and his brother Nepinder; Shakalpa, a Tibetan boy; Hemender, one of the sons of the late Maharaja of Patiala; an Austrian boy, Kruschandel; and Hilton, an English boy.

Top: Haripal, reading a National Geographic *issue, outside my room on the roof in Dehra, 1951.*

Left: Somi.

With Somi, Dipi and Daljit on one of our excursions from Rajpur to Mussoorie.

Top left: With Aunt Emily and her son in Jersey.

Top right: Possibly the only photograph of me in London.

Left: Diana Athill, my first editor.

Left: With my Sikh friends in Dehra after my return from England in 1955.

Bottom: And as a Sikh myself.

My stepfather with Ellen, William, and my half-brothers Harold and Hansel.

Bibiji and I in the Ganga—I ventured a little further into the water than she did!

In the fields near Rajouri Garden in Delhi, with Kamal (in the centre) and one of his brothers. This was back in the late 1950s; there are now shopping malls and flyovers where this picture was taken.

The poet of Delhi, in Patel Nagar. (Ghalib would have approved!)

Top: On a picnic in Tughlakabad, Delhi.

Left: At the end of a trek to the Pindari Glacier in 1960.

Top: With a friend outside the CARE office in the old Theatre Communications Building in Delhi's Connaught Place area.

Left: The 'blue-eyed' buffalo I bought for young farmers in Ropar as part of my duties with CARE.

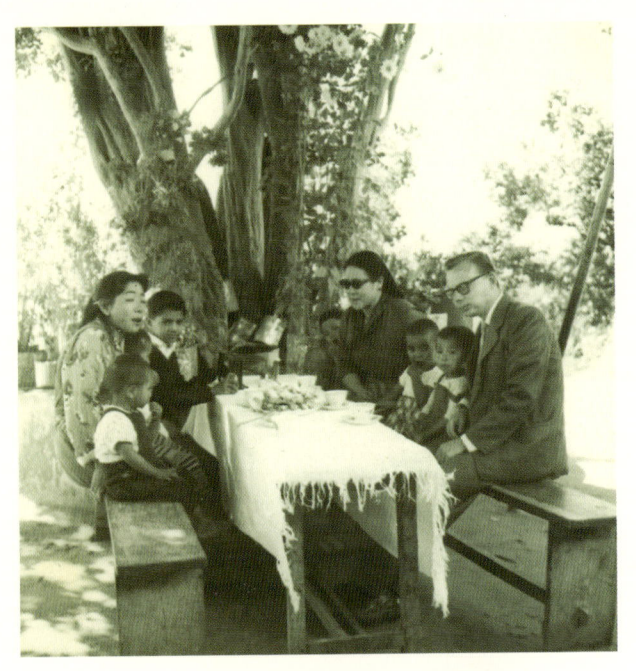

Top: With the Dalai Lama's sister, whom I met as a representative of CARE in Dharamshala in 1960 or '61.

Left: Father and son— Tibetan refugees in Darjeeling.

Top: *Writing in Mussoorie.*

Left: *Reading in Mussoorie.*

Suzie the cat listening to the radio.

Top: On the telephone in Maplewood in the 1970s—probably speaking to R.V. Pandit, proprietor of Imprint *magazine, who was responsible for my joining the tiny club of Mussoorie residents with a phone connection.*

Above: Preparing for a picnic below Maplewood Lodge with Hetty Pimm, Surekha Sikri and other friends.

Right: Surekha and her younger sister Phoolmani

Top: Prem and Chandra; the beginning of my family.

Left: Prem with his children—Rakesh, Mukesh and Dolly.

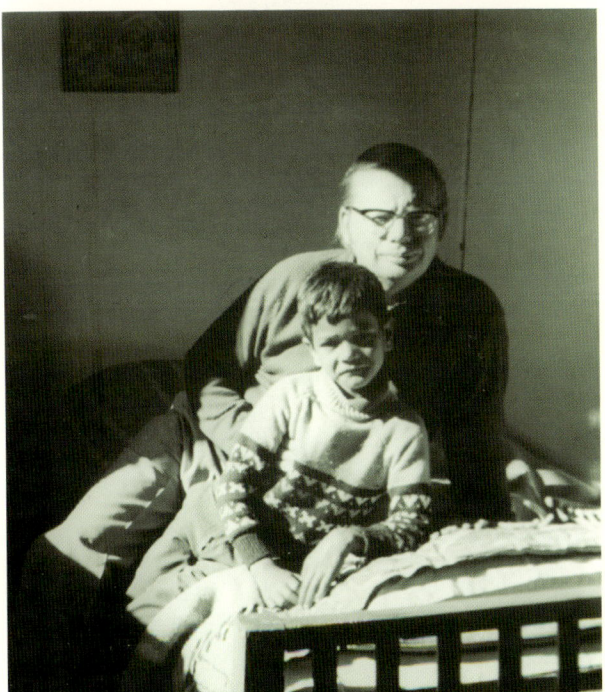

Top: Out on a walk
with Rakesh and
his brother Suresh,
whom we lost when
he was barely two.

Left: With Rakesh,
shortly after
we moved to
Ivy Cottage.'

My mother in her final years—with Ellen (above) and just before her operation.

With my family—Rakesh and Beena, and their children, Siddharth, Shrishti and Gautam.

The view from my window

The following year, Mandy serialized the sequel, *Vagrants in the Valley*, another of my productions from Bibiji's flat. *The Room* had been written out of my homesickness and longing for India. *Vagrants* was written in Dehra, after my return, and lacked some of the youthful optimism of my first book; but it had more of my sensuality, for Dehra was a sensual sort of place, the summers steamy and subtropical. Andre Deutsch wasn't enthusiastic about this second novel, and it was never published outside India.

Another story that Deutsch turned down (and lost the manuscript), because it was too short to make a book, was a little novella called *Leopard in the Lounge*. Fortunately, I had made a carbon copy of the typescript (no photocopiers in those days), and as it was too long for a Sunday magazine, I sent it to P. Lal, who ran a small literary publishing house in Calcutta called Writers Workshop. He sat on it for twenty years. Like 'The Green City', I presumed that it had been lost forever, and I was quite philosophical about the loss of manuscripts in publishers' offices. Then one day in the early 1970s, I received a packet from P. Lal enclosing the story, with a rejection slip attached! I put it aside for another ten years. Then in the late 1980s, when Penguin India was publishing collections of my short stories, I revised and edited the story a little and changed the title to 'Time Stops at Shamli'. It became the title story of a new collection, and till today it remains a favourite with many of my readers.

Chance gives, and takes away, and gives again!

To return to Bibiji.

She had acquired a certain amount of independence with her little provision store, and she certainly did not miss her husband. She was in her mid or late forties now; her daughter was married to someone in Amritsar, and her son was in a boarding school. Her closest friend was Mrs Singh, who lived in the adjoining flat and was ten or twelve years younger. Bibiji and Mrs Singh got on beautifully. You could say they were made for each other. Mrs Singh was married to a police inspector, who came home occasionally from wherever he was posted, and she had a son, Ajay, a boy of twelve who was addicted to lollipops and thoroughly spoilt.

During the day Mrs Singh sat in the shop, smoking a hookah, a custom apparently quite common amongst the villagers of her district, and observing the customers. And afterwards she would entertain us with clever imitations of the more odd or eccentric among them. In the evening she would help Bibiji prepare dinner, and sometimes I would join them after my dhaba dinner for a story or gossip session. The two friends would make themselves comfortable on the same divan, wrap themselves in a razai or blanket and invite me to sit on a charpai next to them and listen to their yarns or tell them a few of my own.

I would climb up to my room, but they would continue talking late into the night, and afterwards there would be a good deal of activity in that divan bed. Mrs Singh would double up with Bibiji even when her police inspector husband was home on leave. He did not appear to find anything unusual in his wife's intimate relationship with Bibiji. His mind was obviously on other things, or he was a good man who understood a thing or two about love.

Mrs Singh was an attractive woman, and a rather good storyteller who entertained me with stories, mostly of the supernatural kind, about life in her village near Agra. At twilight, sitting on her charpai and puffing at the hookah, she would launch into accounts of the various types of ghosts that one might encounter: prets (mischievous ghosts), churels (the ghosts of immoral women, who had their feet facing backwards), various other spirits and goblins, and people who were reincarnated as buffaloes or snakes or sarus cranes. She once told me of the night she had seen the ghost of her husband's first wife. The ghost had lifted Ajay, then a few months old, out of his cradle, rocked him in her arms for a little while, and announced that she was glad the child was a boy and a sweet one, too—a sentiment not shared by those who knew the brat.

Mrs Singh gave me some of my early 'ghost' stories—'The

Haunted Bicycle' (those buffalo children), 'Have You Ever Been In Love With a Ghost?' (sadly, I've lost this one), 'A Face in the Dark' (that faceless school boy), 'The Bent-Double Beggar', and others. I don't think she had been to school, and she spoke in her own quaint village dialect, but I had no difficulty in following her; her gestures and facial expressions always helped the stories along.

She always referred to me as 'the road inspector' because of my habit of walking all over the town—through the bazaars, to the railway station, into the tea gardens…In quest of what, she would ask. What could I tell her? That I went looking for stories, adventure, romance? But these things usually came to me when I wasn't looking for them. I gave her the only reason I could think of: I was just a champion walker! Mrs Singh did not approve, and together with Bibiji, she would make plans to get me married. When I protested, saying I was only twenty-three, they said I was old enough. Bibiji had an eye on an Anglo-Indian schoolteacher who sometimes came to the shop, but Mrs Singh turned her down, saying she was too thin and would have trouble bearing children. Instead, she suggested the daughter of the local padre, a glamourous-looking, dusky beauty, but Bibiji vetoed the proposal, saying the young lady used too much make-up. Both finally agreed that I should marry a plain-looking girl who could cook, use a sewing machine, and speak a little English.

They did not know it, but I was enamoured of Kamla, a girl from the hills, who lived with her parents in quarters behind our rooms. Whenever I passed her on the landing, we exchanged pleasantries and friendly banter; it was as though we had known each other for a long time. But she was already betrothed, to a much older man, a widower, who owned some land outside the town. Kamla's family was poor, and it was to be a marriage of convenience. There was nothing much I could do about it—landless, and without prospects—but after the marriage had taken place and she had left for her new home, I befriended her younger brother and through him sent her my good wishes from time to time. She is just a distant memory now, but a bright one, like a forget-me-not blooming on a bare rock.

Mrs Singh left Dehra some years later. Bibiji continued to run her shop for several years, and it was only failing health that forced her to close it. She sold the business and went to live with her daughter, who was by then in New Delhi. There she lived on into her eighties, despite very high blood pressure and diabetes.

~

Most of my old Dehra friends had finished their schooling and joined colleges in other parts of the country. Except Krishan, and he too would soon be leaving.

But there were others to take their place—teenagers struggling to do their matric or intermediate, or young men in college, aspiring for their arts or science degrees. College was a bit of a dead end. But those who had their schooling in Dehra and then moved on usually did well for themselves.

Like the Dilaram Bazaar boys, Gurbachan, Narinder and Sahib. Gurbachan was an average student, but after doing his intermediate he went to stay with an uncle in Hong Kong. Ten years later, he was a superintendent in the income tax department. Narinder was always having to take tuitions to scrape through his exams. But he spoke English quite well, and he had a flair for business. Today, he owns the largest wholesale wine business in the UK (and as he doesn't drink himself, it's profit all the way). Sahib went off to England, and for some years worked as a clerk in an office and wasn't doing very well. Then he started making samosas and supplying them to various cafes and restaurants, and soon became the samosa king of London.

These boys, and others like them, came from middle-class families. It was impossible, then, to foresee what life held in store for them. And it wasn't always happy endings. Sudheer, a charming young scamp, went on to become the assistant manager of a tea estate in Jalpaiguri, and was bludgeoned to death by the tea garden labourers.

My own future was a little easier to predict. In a sense, I had already arrived. At twenty-two I was a published author and had written many stories for newspapers and magazines, although not many people had heard of me. Of course, I wasn't making much money then, and probably never would, but it was the general consensus among my friends that I was an impractical sort of fellow and I would be wise to stick to the only thing that I could do fairly well, which was putting pen to paper.

At the time, I was the only one earning any money, and I would pay for the chaat and tikkis we consumed near the clock tower. Sahib and I had tikki-eating contests, which I usually won, and regretted the feat immediately after, when it was time to pay the bill. But it was good to have fun, and soon I would be walking up to Mussoorie with my friends for some more loafing about and eating snacks. We would walk up quite regularly from Rajpur to Mussoorie on the old bridle path. By this footpath it was just seven miles to Mussoorie. In two and a half hours we would be in the Mall, where we would loiter, have a cheap lunch of puri-chhole at the Sindhi Sweet Shop, and then go back in the evening to Rajpur and catch a bus into Dehradun.

There were a couple of other interesting friends I acquired during this time—older, with respectable-sounding jobs and expensive habits, but often broke and in need of money, which they seldom returned.

There wasn't much work for anyone in Dehra. Only lawyers seemed to thrive there in those days, possibly because they also doubled up as property dealers. My neighbour, an income-tax lawyer, spent more time wheeling and dealing over property sales or disputes than he did in the income-tax offices which were next door. Although he had an office right next to my room, he was usually to be found in the bar of the Royal Café, downing countless whisky-and-sodas with his clients or cronies. This was just routine drinking. If he collected a large fee, he would go on a real binge and we wouldn't see him for days.

He employed a Nepali messenger boy, Sitaram, who had nothing to do except sit on a chair on our shared balcony—in the shade if it was summer, in the sun if it was winter, and just inside the door in the monsoon. Sometimes I shared my boiled eggs with him (I was good at boiling eggs) and we became friends, and he ended up doing more work for me than he did for his employer.

The lawyer's name was Suresh Mathur, and he was a fan of P.G. Wodehouse's humorous novels. When talking to me he would address me as 'dear old chap' or use expressions such as 'Good egg!' or 'Tally-ho!' He must have been an Englishman in a former existence. He was the Bertie Wooster type, but unfortunately he did not have a Jeeves to keep him out of trouble. Staggering into his office after a morning's hangover, he would sometimes be wearing the wrong socks—a purple sock on one foot and a yellow sock on the other. With that combination, Wooster would never have got past Jeeves.

Suresh liked wearing a tie, but it was usually the same tie—a ragged affair which looked as though it had also served as a collar for a dog. It had been given to him by a lady-love many years ago, and Suresh liked to wear it for sentimental reasons, even though the lady had married someone else.

'What ho! What!' Suresh would greet me in true Wooster fashion, proof, if it were needed, that the last Englishmen were to be found in India. He would arrive in his office at noon, drop all his mail, unopened, into a waste paper basket, and invite me to join him for a drink at the Royal Café. After a couple of large gin-and-tonics he would expound on the English poets of the 1890s (he had studied them at college), the state of the universe, and his favourite topic, the 'fourth dimension'. Till today I have no idea what he meant by the fourth dimension, but he would hold forth on the subject for an hour or two, finally ending by staring gloomily into his empty glass where, presumably, the fourth dimension revealed itself to him.

But Suresh was a survivor. He owned an old house in Rajpur which he had inherited from his father. A year or two after I'd left Dehra I heard he'd sold the property for a good sum to a prosperous widow, a former princess, who lived nearby. Not long after, he married the widow, his senior by some years, and got the property back (for nothing). When I met him in the Royal Café a couple of years later, I told him he'd made a smart move, a remark which seemed to offend him: he assured me that he was genuinely in love with the princess. And he paid for the drinks—a rare event—and told me that the house was up for sale again! Apparently, they were thinking of moving to Delhi. Good old Suresh. I don't think he ever did a stroke of work in his life.

If a lawyer could be hard up, what chance had a journalist? William Matheson, in his mid-thirties, had everything going for him when he came out to India as an assistant to Von Hesseltein, a correspondent for some of the German papers. Von Hesseltein passed on some of his assignments to William, and for a time all went well. William lived with Von Hesseltein and his family, and was also friendly with Suresh, often paying for the drinks at the Royal Café. Then William committed the folly of sleeping with the boss's wife. He justified this indiscretion by telling us that Von Hesseltein was sleeping with a strapping young man in his twenties whose father owned a dairy near the bazaar. William obviously felt that the wife was getting a raw deal, and if his boss preferred the roller to the brush, the arrangement would make everyone happy. But Von Hesseltein was not the understanding sort. He threw William out of the house and stopped giving him work.

William hired an old typewriter and set himself up as a correspondent in his own right, living and working from a room in the Doon Guest House. He bombarded the Swiss and German papers with his articles, but there were very few takers. No one then was really interested in India's five-year plans, or the Bhakra-Nangal Dam. William wanted to write a book about his experiences in the French Foreign Legion, which he was convinced would be both a critical and a commercial success, but the book never got written. After two or three drinks at the Royal Café he would regale us with tales of his exploits in the Legion, before and after the siege of Dien-Bien-Phu in Vietnam. Some of his stories had a ring of truth, others (particularly his sexual exploits) were obviously tall tales; nevertheless, I was happy to pay for the beer in order to hear him spin them out.

Another reason why I didn't mind paying for William's drinks was his rather good literary judgement. In Dehra in the mid '50s there were few, if any, literary influences and certainly no literary atmosphere. William would dissect and tear my stories to bits, and this had a salutary effect on my over-writing. His praise was so sparing, that when he did say something was good, I knew it was good.

William shifted to Meerut a little later. He married and moved in with an Anglo-Indian girl from a fairly affluent family who had fallen for him. I was living in Delhi then, and he would invite me to his 'marital home' whenever I had a free weekend, Meerut being just two hours by bus from Delhi.

William lived with his wife and father-in-law in the Meerut cantonment, in a large bungalow with stables at the back. The father-in-law, Captain Sualez, retired from the army, was a legendary racehorse owner and trainer—in those days, the Meerut racecourse was even more popular than the Delhi racecourse, because it was patronized by the army. The captain was an eccentric old man who moved about town in a pony trap, and preferred horses to people. Except his daughter, a lovely dusky girl of whom he was very fond. He had married an Indian lady who worked as an ayah, but she was long dead and he had raised his daughter on his own. He resented William and put up with him only out of love for her.

None of this affected my stay there; the captain seemed happy to have me, if it meant I would keep William out of the house!

When Captain Sualez died, the daughter inherited his considerable money and properties and lucky William took her with him to scenic Switzerland, where they lived happily ever after.

Some people got by on their charm and their wits.

Not having much of either, I had to bang away at my typewriter and turn out four or five stories or articles every month—in order to pay my rent; keep myself in clothes; buy the odd book and see the odd film (sometimes a late-night film with Sitaram); make the occasional small loan to Bibiji and treat myself to the occasional beer or ham sandwich; have something for postage on my manuscripts to the BBC or the *Weekly* or anyone who would publish them; and get myself a pair of spectacles, for my eyesight was getting weaker by the day.

'Sir, do you see those pretty girls walking down the road?' Sitaram would ask me from his chair on the balcony. I could barely make out that they were girls, let alone pretty ones, and so I went to the local optician and started wearing glasses. The girls immediately came into focus, and of course they were all pretty.

In spite of turning out stories and articles for magazines and newspapers on a regular basis, it was becoming increasingly difficult to earn enough to cover my modest expenses. *The Room* had brought in very little in the way of royalties, although a generous advance for a German translation (*Die Strassezum Bazar*), and fifty pounds that came with the John Llewellyn Rhys Prize the novel had won, had made things easier for a few months. But Rs 50 from the *Weekly* was about the best I could get in India for a short story. I did receive Rs 750 for the serialization of *The Room*, and roughly the same amount for its sequel, *Vagrants in the Valley*, but I ran through that money fairly quickly.

My mother kept urging me to come to Delhi where, it seemed, jobs were to be had for anyone who could speak and write English. Today, hundreds of thousands of boys and girls come out of English-medium schools, but in 1959 there were barely half-a-dozen of these schools in Delhi; if you came from an affluent family you were sent to a school in the hills (such as my old school), or to Doon School in Dehra or Mayo College in Ajmer.

In Dehra, I supplemented my income by giving a couple of tuitions to children at Cambrian Hall, a new school being run by the Mainwarings, the Anglo-Indian couple who had advised me to do the sensible thing and go back home the time I had quarrelled with my mother and left home. I received Rs 50 per month for giving the children an hour every morning. They learnt absolutely nothing from me but I persisted with them for three or four months, before Mrs Mainwaring took pity on me and ended my services.

Then there was Mr Dutta, who brought out a small weekly newspaper called *The Frontier Mail* (originally published from Quetta, I think), and once a week I would drop in at his press, in a gully off Paltan Bazaar, and help him with his editing and proof-reading. He did not provide anything new; just a rehash of stuff taken from the national newspapers. For my help, Mr Dutta gave me Rs 100 per month.

I wasn't earning much, but I was certainly getting experience!

Mr Dutta had a fifteen-year-old son—frequently thrashed by his father but well-spoilt by his mother. Sudhir had wicked ways and an odd sense of fun. He had kept a young monkey and trained it to—putting it delicately—pleasure itself in public. Sudhir would ride around town on his bicycle, the monkey in a shopping basket strapped to the handlebar, and would stop outside shops or at street-corners, where the monkey would soon draw a small crowd, grinning mischievously while it proceeded to give a demonstration of what the Bible called 'wasting'.

One day the boy was chased down the street by some angry shopkeeper. He parked his bicycle outside Bibiji's shop, ran upstairs, and hid the monkey in my bathroom; then he took off from the back stairs. I was out at the time, but Bibiji had spotted Sudhir's coming and going, and she came upstairs to see if all was well. Meanwhile the monkey had escaped from the bathroom and entered Suresh Mathur's office, where it was greeted by a somewhat inebriated Wooster with a 'What ho! How are you, old boy?' Sitaram tried to drive the monkey away, but it simply made an amorous grab at him. Then Bibiji marched in with a jhaaroo, her small hand-broom, and gave it a wallop on the backside. The monkey leapt over the balcony, landed on the roof of a taxi that was probably heading for Mussoorie, and was never seen again in Dehra.

Sudhir's exploits were many, and he was expelled from at least two schools, but this is my story, not his, and I shall keep him for another time.

And returning to my story—it was time to move again, for my earnings were becoming more uncertain by the week. I wasn't unhappy about the prospect of moving to Delhi, but I wasn't entirely happy, either. Would my freelancing days be over? What would Delhi make of me, and what would I make of Delhi, a city I hadn't seen for fifteen years, and never as an adult…

But before I left there was an amusing 'literary' encounter. Dehra had a visitor, and a rather well-known one—G.V. Desani, who had written a wildly eccentric novel, *All About H. Hatterr*, in the late 1940s, which had got him a lot of attention. There was a Hindi writer, Bramh Dev, who ran a photo studio next to Bibiji's shop, and it was at Bramh Dev's that I met Desani. He was going around with a petition nominating himself for the Nobel Prize for Literature. He had already got Bramh Dev's signature, and Nergis Dalal's (Nergis, who lived in Rajpur, had published some stories by then, and would soon publish a novel). Then he must have been told about another writer in the area, so he got Bramh Dev to send for me. I don't think Desani knew anything about Bramh Dev or me, but he was looking for any and all writers to sign his petition. Everyone was so flabbergasted, no one refused!

A very odd man was Desani. He'd had a coffin made for himself and would sleep in it, dressed in his best clothes. I never saw this, of course. I never saw him after that day, in fact. He went away to teach in a university in America and spent time in some Buddhist monasteries. He wrote another book, a collection of short stories, when he was eighty or eighty-five, and that was all.

Well, I had neither the qualifications nor the desire to teach at fancy universities. I didn't have the luxury of writing a book and a half and basking in the glory for ninety years.

'Delhi is yet far,' said a famous saint; but that was four hundred years ago. Now Delhi was just six-and-a-half hours from Dehradun, and to Delhi I went.

A RELUCTANT DELHI-WALLAH

But in Delhi, during those early months, I was miserable. The words were not coming. I couldn't write a thing. I was troubled by a recurring stomach ache. And the promised job had faded away, and so had my savings; not that I had anything to save, but there had at least been the occasional cheques and even those had dried up. Moreover, we were living (my mother and stepfather, brothers and sister) in the furthest outpost of what was then New Delhi, in a refugee colony on the Najafgarh Road called Rajouri Garden.

This was 1959 and Rajouri Garden was just a scattering of small houses put up by Hindu and Sikh refugees from those parts of the Punjab that were now in Pakistan. Needless to say, there were no gardens. The treeless colony was buffeted by hot, dusty winds from Haryana and Rajasthan. The residents were having a hard time readjusting to life in India, getting work or setting up small businesses, and they had little time for flowers, even less for outsiders. But some of them let out portions of their houses, and as the rents were comparatively low, my stepfather rented a three-room set which included a small courtyard and a hand-pump.

That hand-pump made all the difference, because water was always a problem in Delhi (and continues to be to this day). The water from the hand-pump was clean, and could be used for cooking, washing clothes, bathing, even drinking if boiled. It wasn't the water or the food that gave me stomach trouble (no one else was having a problem), it was just plain discontent and frustration.

To visit a bookshop or a cinema I had to travel to Connaught Place, and the journey by bus took about an hour. But buses were few and infrequent; one would have to stand on the roadside for a long time, waiting with a small crowd of commuters, and then struggle to get on to the bus which was usually full. You had to be a straphanger for most of the journey.

A couple of years previously the motor scooter had been invented, and this had resulted in the auto-rickshaw which could accommodate a couple of passengers. I would use auto-rickshaws whenever I could get one, but they were seldom to be found in Rajouri Garden. On several occasions, after seeing a film at one of the Connaught Place cinemas, I walked all the way back to Rajouri, a distance of five or six dusty miles, for the last bus would have returned to its depot.

This was not the Delhi of my childhood—that charmed circle of Atul Grove, Humayun's Tomb and Connaught Place, where all good things were within easy reach. Everything was too much work now! And where were all the trees? How I longed for those idle hours at Dehra's little Royal Café. How I missed my bicycle-riding friends from the Dilaram Bazaar. And Dehra's little bookshops, and the litchi trees, and my lamp-lit room above Bibiji's love den and kirana store.

I longed to return, but I felt I had to stick it out for a couple of years, find a job that would pay me a decent salary, and save a little money before making another bid for freedom, the sort of freedom that only successful freelancing could bring me.

I finally made my peace with Delhi—even with the harsh summer, when muggy nights would end in the briefest of dawns and then the sun would come shouting over the rooftops. Gradually, I grew to like the smells of summer: The delicate odour that arose when water was sprinkled on the hot terrace floor in the evening, before it was time to lie on a charpai under the open sky. The smell of a freshly cut cucumber and of khus- and rose-sherbet syrup. The sweet, fleeting scent of raat ki rani, the night-blooming jasmine, on the evening breeze, along with the stronger scents of mango blossom and cowdung smoke—for this was long before LPG cylinders, and kerosene stoves were infrequently used. Chulhas, clay ovens fed with wood and dried cowdung cakes, were popular and economical.

But it was my old trick—walking—that I finally used to ferret out Delhi's elusive charms. Summer and winter, I scorned the dust and the traffic, and walked all over Delhi—from Rajouri Garden to Connaught Place, of course, but also from Daryaganj to Chandni Chowk, and from Ajmeri Gate to India Gate—investigating historic streets and buildings, or simply sitting on the grass near the India Gate canal and eating purple, tangy jamuns with a little salt.

In Kashmere Gate, there was a quiet restaurant near the Ritz cinema hall—already decrepit—which I began to frequent. After a film show or a good meal of kababs and tandoori rotis, I would walk on to Maiden's Hotel, once the most popular hotel in Delhi. It had come up during the Delhi Durbar, I think, and it was named not after a pretty milkmaid, but after its owner and founder, John Maiden. Its architecture was most impressive, and I would visit it from time to time to gaze upon its façade—but I did not step in, for fear of losing a lot of money.

About that time the Maiden's was being used as a set for a British film about World War II called the *The Wind Cannot Read*, which starred Dirk Bogarde and the beautiful Yoko Tani. Most of the hotel had been converted into a wartime hospital for the purposes of the story. There was also a scene at the Red Fort, which I witnessed. It depicted the Diwan-i-Khas, a pavilion where the Emperor Shah Jahan would spend a couple of hours every evening before retiring for the night. The words of the poet Amir Khusro, which I had seen inscribed in Urdu above the arches of the pavilion as a child with my father, were still there (as they are today): 'If there be a paradise on earth, it is here, it is here, it is here.'

The view across the winding Jamuna must have been a splendid one six hundred years ago; but by the late 1950s the Jamuna was already a polluted river, and the colonies across it, such as Shahdara, were drab and depressing.

Far better views, I discovered, were to be had closer to Rajouri Garden. The houses were built on one side of the Najafgarh Road. On the other side, as yet uncolonized, were extensive fields of wheat and other crops that stretched away to the west and the north. I would walk across the main road and into the fields, finding old wells, irrigation channels and the occasional scarecrow, and sighting birds and small creatures that no longer dwelt in the city.

Some way down the Najafgarh Road was a large village pond and beside it a magnificent banyan tree—the kind you wouldn't find in any city today, for healthy banyans need so much space in which to spread their limbs and live comfortably. That was the biggest banyan I had ever seen, and I got to know it quite well. It had about a hundred pillars supporting the boughs, and above them there was a great leafy crown, an enormous, generous canopy. It has been said that whole armies could shelter in the shade of an old banyan, and probably at one time they did. I saw another sort of army: mynahs, sparrows, rosy pastors, crested bulbuls without crests, brown-headed and coppersmith barbets, jungle babblers and many other birds crowding the tree in order to feast noisily on big, scarlet figs. Squirrels darted up and down the great bark of the tree, stopping now and then to sniff the air. Flashy parakeets wheeled in and shot out, screeching just because they wanted to screech.

Even further down was a large jheel. One could rest in the shade of a babul or keekar tree and watch kingfishers skim over the water, making just a slight splash as they dived and came up with small glistening fish. I would spot one of these beautiful birds perched on an overhanging bush or rock, and wait patiently to see it plunge like an arrow into the water and return to its perch to devour the catch. It came over the water in a flash of gleaming blue, shrilling its loud 'tit-tit-tit'.

Late one morning, in the midst of a sea of wheat I found a camel going round and round a well, pulling up buckets of water. At my approach the pigeons flew out of the well, and a flock of parrots set up a racket in a nearby banyan tree, this one a little smaller, but no less hospitable to birds and squirrels. A village boy was sleeping in the shade of the tree, his striped pyjamas rolled up to his thighs. A flute lay beside him. Here, suddenly, I had come upon a corner of India that hadn't changed in hundreds of years. It would change before long, but at that moment it was a picture caught in time: the old well, the camel, the pigeons, the parrots, the banyan tree, the boy and the flute. And I wrote a little story around it, called 'The Flute Player'.

The boy, when he woke up, was friendly enough, and introduced me to his camel. The camel acknowledged my presence by continuing to look bored and supercilious and to traverse slowly around the well. The parrots returned to the tree to gossip, the pigeons to the dark recesses of the well to meditate. The boy even played his flute for me. I noticed that he had two thumbs; one large and one small. He seemed quite proud of them. Two thumbs are supposed to be lucky.

'Don't you go to school?' I asked

He gestured towards his village, a speck in the distance. 'When the school is ready I will go to it.' And meanwhile he could look after the camel and sleep beneath the banyan tree.

'Stay lucky,' I said. And I saw him from time to time.

~

The transistor radio was another nice distraction in those years. It was a relatively new innovation, and a real craze. Just as today every youngster carries a mobile phone, in the late 1950s and early '60s, everyone had his or her portable transistor radio. Whether you were in a bus or an office or a roadside café, you were forced to listen to the latest cricket commentary, even though Indian victories were infrequent, to say the least.

The stars and heroes of the era were Vinoo Mankad, a great all-rounder; Vijay Manjrekar and Chandu Borde, both stylish batsmen; Vijay Merchant, a fine opener; Polly Umrigar, a big hitter once he got going; and Subash Gupte, a wily spinner. Our fast bowlers were mere trundlers. When the powerful West Indies team came to Delhi, and was leading the series 3-0, I had just arrived in the city, and I joined the hordes at the Feroze Shah Kotla grounds to watch the final Test. The seats were all sold out, but I managed to climb the walls of the Kotla, where I joined a rowdy crowd of young men armed with oranges—just in case India lost, which seemed likely. From this vantage point (unpaid for) you could see only one end of the pitch, the bowler but not the batsman, or vice-versa at the end of an over; but this was good enough to keep you in the picture as far as the progress of the match was concerned. I had the satisfaction of seeing Chandu Borde score a century (or was it 98?) and J.K. Holt of the Windies do likewise, but my hero, Vinoo Mankad, was out for a duck. (During my sojourn in England I had kept up with his century at Lord's). Anyway, India managed to draw this final Test match, and the crowd left the grounds in good humour. The oranges were consumed, or kept for the following week's football tournament.

I did not see much football, but I did see some high-quality hockey matches at a little stadium just off Connaught Circus, behind the Madras Hotel. Here, young Ashok Kumar, playing for Indian Airlines, would display some of the wizardry of his father, the legendary Dhyan Chand.

Always eager to escape from Rajouri Garden, my life would revolve around Connaught Place—its cinemas, bookshops, cafés. Here I met my old friend Krishan again ('Kishen' of *The Room on the Roof*, if you haven't yet guessed). Once a duckling with modest looks, he had grown into something of a swan; a very presentable and good-looking young man of nineteen. He had been an engineering student in Calcutta and was now planning to go to England for 'further studies'. He was good company and we spent several evenings together, seeing films and frequenting the United Coffee House. Then he went away. He was always coming into my life at crucial junctures, and then disappearing again.

A new friend I made at this time was Kamal, a young man of about eighteen, and we were to be travelling companions for some years. His family lived in a flat down the road from us in Rajouri Garden—Bhabiji's house, which became a second home for me in Delhi, but I'll come to that shortly.

After six months or so in Rajouri Garden, we moved to Patel Nagar, which brought my stepfather a little closer to his place of work. He was working as a sales manager for Sikand & Co., on Janpath, and later with another firm that dealt in cars, Pearey Lal & Sons, as a works manager.

And, finally, I found employment too.

I was offered a job with CARE (Cooperative for American Relief Everywhere), which had only been active in India for a couple of years, and had a small office and staff of about a dozen people in the old wartime Theatre Communications Building in the Connaught Place area. The chief of CARE was a man called Oden Meeker who had set up offices in Hong Kong, Laos and other Southeast Asian countries, and had written a book called *The Little World of Laos*. His secretary, Hermie Michael, an Anglo-Indian lady, had given him a copy of *The Room On the Roof*. He had liked it and asked to see me. So I dropped in at the CARE office, had a chat with Oden Meeker, and was taken on as an administrative assistant, or field officer, on a monthly salary of Rs 500. Two months later I was given charge of CARE's Tibetan relief programme, and my salary was upped to Rs 800, which was a princely sum in those days.

It was 1959, and the Dalai Lama and his followers had sought asylum in India after China annexed Tibet. Several thousand men, women and children had fled Tibet and trekked great distances to reach India, and they were given sanctuary in various hill-stations—Mussoorie, Shimla, Dalhousie, Darjeeling—as well as in the steamy jungles of Bylakuppe near Mysore, down south. CARE was among various foreign agencies providing food aid or equipment for these settlements, and my job was to visit these centres, assess their needs, make reports, even at times make deliveries.

There was a fair amount of travelling to be done; the job certainly kept me on my toes, for Oden Meeker was a man of impulse, and sometimes he would send me haring off to the hills in the middle of winter because there were children who needed bathtubs, or carpet-makers who needed handlooms, or old folk who needed beds and blankets and woodcutters who needed axes.

CARE was to keep me busy for four years, and it wasn't easy to find the time to write. I tried to put down at least a few hundred words a day, but few of them rang true.

The Dalai Lama himself was in Mussoorie's Happy Valley at first. But it was too public. The government didn't want him too much in the way, and there were also concerns about security, so he was shifted to Dharamshala, a charming little cantonment town in the Kangra Valley, barely on the map those days, which became the headquarters of the Tibetan government in exile. I visited Dharamshala just once, and it wasn't my first tour for CARE, either. It was to Bylakuppe, in Karnataka, that I went first, and then to Dalhousie and Shimla in Himachal Pradesh.

The Indian government had settled a large number of Tibetan refugees in Bylakuppe. It had been just jungle till then, and the refugees had to clear it themselves and build their hutments—right inside the Coorg forest—and start agriculture. Sturdy Tibetans of the warrior Khampa tribe were mainly responsible for the clearing, and they went about their job cheerfully and efficiently. The refugees were having a tough time adjusting to the heat and many were falling ill. The government and relief agencies like CARE were doing what they could to help, and although my own role was very limited, it gave me a sense of satisfaction to be part of these efforts. Some of the frustration of being unable to write went away as I got more involved in CARE work. And the Tibetans were handsome people, smiling easily despite the hardship, welcoming me wherever I went.

An Indian organization that was also helping the refugees was The Council for Tibetan Relief, run by Sucheta Kripalani, wife of the prominent freedom fighter Acharya Kripalani, who had been president of the Indian National Congress at the time of Independence, but had resigned from the party soon after. That year, returning from Bylakeppe, I found Acharya Kripalani in the same compartment on the train from Bangalore to Delhi. Also with us was a young American man working for some other relief agency. The American got into an argument with Acharya

Kripalani—a Gandhian Socialist who believed in swadeshi and the village economy and cottage industries. The American disagreed with him, saying India was going backwards, not forward, and spirituality and socialism were not going to bring any development. He was very passionate about India, and angry with a lot of people and a lot of things. But Acharya Kripalani was a very calm and reasonable man. He never got excited, and listened with interest to the young man, replying patiently and at great length, explaining why he thought the Western model of development—which Nehru was adopting—was not good for India. The argument went on late into the night, and never any good at arguments and confrontations, I remained just a listener. Kripalani finally persuaded the young American—or just let him tire himself out! In any case, the American finally went to sleep, and I turned to look at the dark night outside the window, where India, vast and timeless, slumbered.

Unlike Bylakeppe, Dalhousie was cooler, and easier for the Tibetan refugees to adjust to. There were about 2,500 of them in this beautiful but deserted hill-station. Before Partition, it had received most of its visitors from Lahore; now the hotels lay empty, even in summer. The Tibetans brought some colour and new life to the place. By mid-winter they were busy on their handlooms, weaving carpets and rugs.

I made three official visits to Dalhousie, and on one of these, I was branded a spy. You took a bus or taxi from Pathankot to Dalhousie, and I'd been told to meet the PWD people in Pathankot, also for some CARE work, before I carried on to Dalhousie. The PWD offices were by a canal that ran along the border with Pakistan. I did not know that it was a sensitive area, and decided to take a stroll along the pretty canal, taking pictures with my camera (I had developed a serious interest in photography around this time). This caused a bit of a stir, and I was sent for and the PWD engineer got very angry. I didn't understand what the fuss was about, there was nothing secret there or anything of importance. I told the engineer this and went on my way. But I was reported to the local Intelligence department, on suspicion that I was an American spy, and when I reached Dalhousie, I noticed a couple of men lurking around in the hotel where I was staying. I wouldn't have guessed they were intelligence men if they hadn't done such a bad job of concealing themselves as they followed me everywhere I went for two or three days. Or maybe that was the idea—to let me know that I was being watched.

Finally, one evening, I asked the men to join me for a drink in the hotel bar. We finished a bottle of Rosa rum, and I was able to convince them that I was an Indian working for a foreign relief agency. It's wonderful what a bottle of rum can achieve!

In Shimla, to my surprise, I found the Tibetan children living and learning in the premises of the old BCS prep school. The buildings had been deserted during the disturbances of 1947, when it was thought the prep school children would be safer in the main school, some distance away. Now, standing on the high ground above the playing field, memories came flooding back to me. This was where I had stood with my father in the summer of '43, watching a medley of small boys shouting and running about on the dusty flat. Scores of small Tibetan children were doing the same thing now. Here, fifteen years earlier, I had fought or wrestled with other boys, or played hop-scotch, or sat in a quiet corner and read a book or a comic...

And the names, which I thought I'd forgotten, came back to me like a roll-call: Abbot, Blake, Bland, Chauhal, Kellnar, Mirchandani. And dear Azhar. I turned away with a dull ache in the heart.

But I was comforted by the sight of the new children in the old field. It is good that life carries on. Those who had replaced us, from toddlers to teenagers, had come trudging through the snows and high mountain passes, accompanied by parents who had followed their revered Lama into a land which had its own myriad problems but which nevertheless gave them food and shelter and sanctuary. I sanctioned whatever they had requested from CARE—writing materials, and more tubs and beds—and returned to my hotel without visiting my old school, the senior school, probably because I was reluctant to stir up more memories of lost faces and times long gone.

On a similar expedition to Darjeeling, I was taking an evening stroll along the Mall when I heard a familiar voice call out: 'Do you have my Henry Green?'

Henry Green was a novelist, now forgotten, popular with highbrows around that time. And the person who had accosted me was none other than Marie Seton, a person closely connected to films and film people. When I was in London I had been to see her edited version of Eisenstein's uncompleted film, *Que Viva Mexico*, a semi-documentary work by the great Russian director who had made the silent classic *Battleship Potemkin*. Now Marie Seton was in India, writing a book on the films of Satyajit Ray, who had achieved international recognition with his Apu trilogy.

I had met her in Delhi—a woman full of enthusiasms (and criticisms), a little past middle-age, who loved talking. Someone, possibly Oden Meeker, had given her a copy of *The Room*; she had been enchanted by it (or so she said) and insisted on meeting me. We met several times, usually in the evenings at Hotel India in Connaught Place—which later became Nirula's—only a short distance from the CARE office. She could talk for hours, so you had to sit right opposite her for comfort. On the first occasion, I had sat beside her, and after half-an-hour had developed a severe crick in the neck. She talked about everything under the sun—films, film people, the British royal family and their little foibles, the intrigues that revolved around the Academy awards, British actors who were alcoholics, American actors who were gay, Italian directors who were sex maniacs—and I listened fascinated, because she was never dull. She seemed to know everyone who was anyone, from the Pope to Pandit Nehru, and knew a good deal that others did not know. Sometimes she would give me such details of what went on in the casting rooms of Hollywood and the bedrooms of the English royalty, that I blushed—and I don't blush easily.

So what was she doing in the Darjeeling Mall, demanding the return of a book which I had never borrowed?

It turned out that she was watching Satyajit Ray at work—'studying his methods', as Watson would have said. Ray was making a film called *Kanchenjunga*, named after the majestic peak that was visible from parts of Darjeeling, and he and his crew were filming on the Mall, just around the corner from where I was talking to Marie Seton. In a break between takes she took me over and introduced me to the great man. Of course he'd never heard of me—I was little more than a failed author at the time—but he was very courteous, friendly, and invited me to watch the proceedings. I did for some time, but as I had to visit the Tibetan Centre, I left Mr Ray to the mercy of Marie Seton—she finally did write a book about him—and went about my business.

The funny thing was that we were all staying at the same hotel, a rambling old place called the Everest—not just Ray and his crew, but also a film crew from Bombay consisting of Shammi Kapoor and an actress called Kalpana, making a pot-boiler called *Professor*. While Ray was filming a realistic scene on the Mall, Shammi & Co were engaged in a sunny song-and-dance number on the railway tracks that served Darjeeling's little toy train. The contrast in methods could not have been sharper.

I did not meet Mr Kapoor. But I did talk to his charming wife, Geeta Bali. She was not in the film, having given up acting due to poor health, but I remembered having seen her in a couple of films in 1949-50, before I left for England, and she was a good actress, very lively and spontaneous. She sat in the sun on the hotel lawns, looking rather lovely (the others were away, filming), and she smiled and took my compliments very graciously. A few months later she had passed away.

~

My tours were not limited to Tibetan relief centres. CARE's donors, back in the USA, were keen on supporting educational, health and self-help programmes in India. I was given additional responsibility of the self-help programme, where my job was to visit village communities, doing things as varied as buying buffaloes for young farmers in Ropar, expounding on the merits of a steel plough as opposed to wooden ploughs (CARE was giving away steel ploughs), or providing sewing machines to groups of young women intent on subsidizing the family income. I had to pretend to be knowledgeable on many unfamiliar things. When, at the Ropar cattle fair, an elderly famer told me that buffaloes with blue eyes gave more and better milk than buffaloes with grey eyes, I believed him. I bought the blue-eyed buffalo and presented it to the young farmers—a group of village boys who had formed their own cooperative. They told me I had been fooled, but nice boys that they were, they also added that it was nice to have a pair of blue eyes to gaze into!

The self-help programme took me to many places in Punjab and Uttar Pradesh, and I would often take detours to places of historical interest. I went to Lucknow a few times by road, and stopped at Shahjahanpur. It had been my father's birthplace, and it was also the scene of a well-documented massacre in the cantonment church during the 1857 rebellion. A girl of mixed race had survived the killings and had left some account of her escape and the refuge given to her by local people, both Hindu and Muslim, and I had been toying with the idea of writing a novel inspired by her story. So I took the opportunity to visit the area where these dramatic events had taken place—the church, the parade ground, the neighbouring mango-tope or 'bagh'. Very little had changed in this sleepy old town. A monument to the fallen (since removed, I'm told) stood near the church. And there was still a bridge of boats across the little river Khanaut. The visit helped me to flesh out the story, and it was published as a short novel, *A Flight of Pigeons*, some years later.

I was going through my 'historical' period, as far as my writing was concerned. Free on most weekends, I would make short visits to places within a day's bus-ride of Delhi: Agra, where I found the grave of John Mildenhall, the first Englishman to spend some time in that city, during Akbar's reign; Sardhana, where the remarkable Begum Samru, a former nautch girl, had ruled with her mercenary army in the eighteenth century and amassed great wealth; Hansi, where Irish adventurer George Thomas had once held sway. And, of course, sacred Mathura and Brindaban, so closely associated with the youth of Lord Krishna. The fields and lakes around Mathura still teemed with bird life—acrobatic blue jays, large parties of screeching parrots, peacocks flaunting their beautiful tail-feathers, herons perched on the backs of buffaloes. Sarus cranes—usually in pairs—waded in shallow water-bodies, and golden orioles and scarlet minivets sat in the ancient trees, like jewels set in a green canopy. A feast for bird-watchers, but my time was always limited, and I could only dwell briefly on these avian delights. One day, I would tell myself, perhaps I would live closer to Nature's beauty.

Meanwhile, some of my historical essays went into *The Illustrated Weekly*. That august periodical never received much respite from my attentions, at least not until the 1970s, by which time good Mr Mandy had retired and gone to live alone in a tiny uninhabited island he had bought in the Indian Ocean. It could only be accessed by boat when the tide was high. He fled some years later, having had quite enough of his own company.

And I was always running away from Delhi—unable to cope with the chaotic city and my chaotic family for very long. On weekends, I went to nearby small towns, and on longer holidays, to places further away—once as far as the Pindari glacier in Kumaon. I trekked up with some college students I barely knew. It was a four-day adventure which culminated in our sunbathing in the nude on the glacier, and on my way back I had to pay for that pleasure by selling my wristwatch for the bus fare. This picturesque trek was to give me the background for my first children's book, *The Hidden Pool*.

Naturally, with all this travelling, very little writing got done—even most of those historical pieces were not written or published till a couple of years later. The little that I did manage to place in magazines got me some appreciation, which kept my spirits up. Dr Karan Singh, a scholar and son of the former Maharaja of Jammu and Kashmir, wrote me a nice letter after reading one of my essays. And Khushwant Singh, who published me in *Yojana*, the magazine he was editing at the time, invited me home.

Khushwant Singh's home in Sujan Singh Park—an upmarket colony built by his contractor father in the 1940s—hadn't yet become quite as famous as it soon would, when Khushwant's friends and admirers and visiting writers and artists from Pakistan and other countries would drop in every evening for some Scotch whisky and lively conversation. I only met him during the day. I remember one small lunch party. There was no Scotch but beer. Khushwant had a very large Alsatian, much loved, who sat next to his chair and Khushwant poured half a bottle of beer into his bowl, which the Alsatian lapped up and then dozed off.

Khushwant Singh's wife was a striking lady with a sharp mind and strong opinions. One day she said to me, 'A writer should not write to make money from his writing. He should do it simply because he loves writing.' I didn't argue the point. They owned a lot of nice property, and I was sitting in one of these, being fed a nice lunch, and they had always been very nice to me. I would go back and write a little story and send it to *Yojana*, and gratefully accept the small fee I would be paid for it.

~

I was keen to rent a place of my own in Delhi, but in those days it was extremely difficult for a bachelor to find accommodation. Inevitably the landlord had daughters, and if a young male tenant was not to be trusted on the premises it also implied that the daughters were not to be trusted.

So I continued staying with my mother and stepfather, first in Rajouri Garden, then in South and West Patel Nagar. I had a room to myself, and contributed to the rent and household expenses, but even so, we were rather cramped. In addition to us human inhabitants—seven in all—there were by now several noisy dogs, as my mother was breeding (and occasionally selling) Pomeranians, a neurotic breed, popular in Delhi at the time. No wonder I was glad to be 'on tour' from time to time.

When not on tour, I would spend many hours with my friend Kamal's family in Rajouri Garden, occasionally spending the night there. It was a large middle-class Punjabi family—a 'joint family', few of which now remain. With twelve residents, the house was far more cramped than my family home, but I didn't feel frustrated or trapped—I was always a visitor; there by choice. It was a miracle that everyone managed to fit into that small flat, especially at night—there would be charpais everywhere, with some of the children sleeping on mattresses laid out on the floor. You had to step gingerly, weaving your way through sleeping forms, if your bladder had not been disciplined to shut itself down till it was morning—when all but one bed would be carried outside and stored in a small shed in the garden.

The undisputed head of Kamal's family was his mother, Bhabhiji—all her children and daughters-in-law called her that. Recently widowed, she was in her late fifties and ran the house like a benevolent (and sometimes slightly malevolent) autocrat. She would be the first to wake up, even before the community of sparrows burst into noisy conversation in the guava tree in the little courtyard-cum-garden. She did this mainly to show up her two daughters-in-law. No matter how hard they tried to be up first and get to the kitchen, Bhabhiji would forestall them. It gave her the satisfaction of saying, 'What use are daughters-in-law if I have to wake up before the birds to cook for their husbands!' The daughters-in-law were now resigned to the morning ritual, and actually quite happy to be spared the breakfast duty—Bhabhiji would make sure they had not a moment of rest once their husbands had left for the day.

I became a confidant of all of them—Bhabhiji complaining about the daughters-in-law, they complaining about her. The younger daughter-in-law would also complain about her husband because he never stood up to his mother in her defence. 'I don't think he loves me,' she would sniffle, and I would assure her he did. I was pampered by all three women—there would be aaloo parathas and omelette and pickle for breakfast when I stayed over, and tea in a brass tumbler before that, because Kamal had told them, 'My friend is an Angrez. He likes bed tea.'

Kamal had recently joined an art college, which no one in his family had quite understood. I think we became friends because no one else in the neighbourhood understood this, either. My support mattered to him; and I had good company in him, especially on my travels to the small towns outside Delhi, where I would look for material for my stories and essays. You could say we were two artists giving each other some moral support.

Kamal was painting regularly, but sometimes he wondered if he had made the right choice. He was impatient and unsure of himself—when would he start making money? Would he ever really achieve anything? I organized two exhibitions for him, at the AIFACS Gallery on Rafi Marg, close to the Parliament building, and in a little gallery in Shankar Market. When we travelled, I would encourage him to sketch the people and places we saw. But it was a losing battle, because he was always torn between his family's wishes and his own.

Kamal and I saw a lot of each other over the next few years, and he would come over to stay with me in Mussoorie after I went to live there, still painting half-heartedly. And then we drifted apart.

It happened because I fell in love. The girl was a cousin of Kamal's—let us call her Sushila—who used to visit his home in Rajouri Garden when I was living there. It wasn't love at first sight, for she was very young then, still in school. She was just another child to me, twelve or thirteen years my junior. But in just two years, everything had changed, and I was caught in a storm of emotion.

That dance of passion—mercifully brief—was yet in the future. And that future, as it turned out, was not too distant.

After serving in India for three years, Oden Meeker left for

CARE Hong Kong, or CARE Manila, I'm not sure which, and his place was taken by a Dr Kline, a totally different sort of person, more career diplomat than dispenser of aid. He shifted the office from Connaught Place to his own house in Friends Colony, where he threw parties for Delhi's social and political elite. He was a fiend for publicity, and when he discovered that I was a writer, he took me off all self-help and donor programmes and had me write and send out innumerable press releases describing the good work being done under his aegis. This was self-defeating because they were obviously propaganda and were published by no one apart from *The American Reporter*, a publication of the United States Information Service (USIS).

If I was going to write reams of self-congratulatory hand-outs I might as well be doing my own writing, even if it meant a drop in my income. I began thinking of leaving CARE. Of course, my mother and everyone else was against it. Giving up a good job with a foreign relief agency, and for no reason other than that I was bored with the work they were now giving me, didn't make much sense to anyone. I allowed myself to be persuaded, and remained with CARE for almost another year, until a visit to Mussoorie decided it for me.

For yet another publicity brief, I was asked to visit the hill resort and write about CARE's Tibetan relief programme there, especially for the refugee children, and I was only too happy to go. The education of many of the children was being sponsored at the Wynberg Allen School, where I was to meet the principal, an Australian gentleman called Mr Kidd, and he asked me to lunch. He had also invited an old lady, Miss Bean, whom he introduced me to. She lived in a cottage below the school, and the teachers at the school were kind to her because she had very little money. The principal had told me, before she arrived, that she had lost all her property and had no relatives.

Something about Miss Bean reminded me of Miss Kellner, my friend of long ago—she wasn't physically handicapped in any way, but like Miss Kellner, she was slightly built and looked fragile, yet sprightly. She told me she had lived in Mussoorie all her adult life, and though she'd had to sell her house, she was lucky that friends who owned a couple of homes in Mussoorie had asked her to stay rent-free in one of these cottages and look after it. When I mentioned that I was thinking of giving up the CARE job and moving to Dehradun or anywhere nearby, she said the cottage was vacant, except for the little corner where she lived, and would I like to see it. I said I would, and after lunch we walked down to her abode.

The cottage was in an isolated spot, sheltered by oak and maple trees, just off the old bridle path that I used to take from Dehra, trudging up to Mussoorie with Somi, Krishan and Sahib. It was late spring, and the oaks and maples were in new leaf—the oak leaves a pale green, the maple leaves red and gold and bronze, turning to green as they matured. A woodpecker was tapping away at the bark of a maple, trying to prise out an insect.

The vacant rooms were on the first floor. I helped the old lady up the steps and she opened the door for me. It led into an L-shaped room. There were two large windows, and when I pushed the first of these open, the forest seemed to rush upon me. The maples, oaks, rhododendrons, and an old walnut, moved closer, out of curiosity perhaps. A branch tapped against the windowpanes, while from below, from the depths of the ravine, like a sweet secret, rose the indescribably beautiful song of a whistling thrush.

'I'll take it, Miss Bean.'

I had no doubts, but even if I had, the delighted look I saw in her eyes would have wiped them all away.

I gave Miss Bean a year's rent to pass on to her friends—Rs 400, which was modest even for those days—and returned to Delhi to give CARE a month's notice and to inform my mother. She wouldn't approve, but she also knew that once my mind was made up about something, it was very hard to make me change it—and in her case, pretty much impossible.

I had no illusions about what lay ahead. But my lifelong feeling of insecurity had come up against a dream I had—an old dream of living only by my writing; a dream of freedom. Lack of money had made it difficult for me to realize it. But then, I knew that if I was going to wait for money to come, I might have to wait until I was old and grey and full of sleep. I was almost thirty—still young enough to take a few risks. If the dream was to become reality, this was the time to do something about it.

PART IV

LONE FOX DANCING

MAPLEWOOD LODGE, MUSSOORIE.
The summer of 1963.
The forest is still, silent; until the cicadas start tuning up for their performance. On cue, like a conductor, a barbet perched high in the branches of a spruce tree begins its chant: '*Unneeow—unneeow-unneeow!*'

Now the forest begins to pulse with the hypnotic buzzing of the cicadas.

Big white ox-eye daisies grow on the hillside. The sorrel—'Almora grass'—has turned red. I sit in my garden, contemplating my old Olympia typewriter. Still writing stories, still trying to sell them.

As a boy, loneliness. As a man, solitude.

The loneliness was not of my seeking. The solitude I sought. And found.

I am to spend many summers, monsoons, winters in this cottage. Mornings in the sun. Evenings in the shadows.

Some mornings I carry my small table, chair and typewriter out on to a knoll below one of the oaks, and take a little help from the babblers and bulbuls that flit in and out of the canopies of leaves. White-hooded babblers; yellow-bottomed bulbuls. Never still for a moment, they help me with my punctuation.

For dialogue I depend more on the crickets, cicadas and grasshoppers who keep up a regular exchange, debating the issues of the day. But for reflective and descriptive writing I look into the distance, at the purple hills merging with an azure sky; or I examine a falling leaf as it spirals down from the tree and settles on the typewriter keys.

The sun bathes everything with clear, warm light. Somewhere high up on the hill, cows are grazing. I don't see them, but I hear the bells tied around their necks.

I write in leisure; there is no hurry.

I write *Panther's Moon* and *Angry River*. I meet a lovely, smiling girl on the hillside, twirling a blue umbrella, and she becomes Binya of *The Blue Umbrella*.

A crow visits me from time to time, and tells me his story. I call it 'A Crow for all Seasons'.

I discover a small stream at the bottom of the hill. An abundance of ferns—dark green and pale—flourish in the shady places along its banks, where the grass is moist and speckled with tiny white flowers.

A spotted forktail hops from boulder to boulder, uttering its low pleasant call, talking to itself.

A pair of pine martens are drinking at the stream. They see me and go bounding across the ravine and into the trees.

I walk downstream, and one day I discover a little waterfall. The sun strikes it from behind an overhanging rock and creates a tiny rainbow. I bathe beneath the rainbow. I lie on the grass, while a pair of dragonflies hover above me, making love. I could go looking for love. But you don't find love by searching for it.

Across the stream is a grassy knoll where a single pine tree grows—a stranger among oaks, spruce, and maple. Pine trees straddle the top of the opposite hill, but this one has escaped from the community and asserted its independence, rather as I have done; so I've adopted it, and I come here often, to sit beneath its blue-green branches, compose a poem or simply contemplate my navel. I call it my Place of Power. I'm reading Gurdjieff.

I spend a night on the pine-knoll, stretched out beneath a cherry tree. I'm awake for hours, listening to the chatter of the stream and the occasional tonk-tonk of a nightjar, and watching, though the branches overhead, the stars turning in the sky.

The window at which I work faces the slope of the hillside, Bala Hissar, where an Afghan king lived in exile. There's a wind humming in the pines and deodars. A small, plump squirrel climbs on the window sill, a little out of breath with the effort.

He's been coming every day, and has learned to eat from my hand. I feed him groundnuts, bread crumbs and peas.

I have no groundnuts today. He sniffs and probes my palm and wrist, then reconciles himself to nibbling at the peas. He's an uncomplaining sort of fellow.

A spectacular electric storm last evening. The clouds grew very dark, then sent bolts of lightning sizzling across the sky, lighting up the entire range of mountains. When the storm was directly overhead, there was hardly a pause in the frequency of the lightning; it was like a bright light being switched on and off with barely a second's interruption. There was thunder and rain all night.

But the morning is gloriously fresh and spirited. A strong breeze is driving the clouds away, and the sun keeps breaking through. The mynahs are very busy, very noisy, looking for a nesting site in the roof. The babblers are raking over fallen leaves, snapping up absent-minded grasshoppers.

A whistling thrush is drying himself on the broken garden fence. He's a deep, glistening purple, his shoulders flecked with white. He sits silently for a while, then flies up to the roof, from where he treats me to an enchanting musical performance. He starts with a hesitant whistle, as though trying out the tune; then, confident of the melody, he bursts into full song, a crescendo of sweet, haunting notes and variations ringing clearly across the hillside.

There's a flurry of alarm calls in the forest. A young kakar deer strays into the garden, fleeing something. It runs around in confusion for some time till it finally finds its way into the jungle again.

Towards sunset, I watch the owlets emerge from their holes in the trees. They put out their little round heads, with large staring eyes, before shuffling out. After they have emerged they sit very quietly for a time, as though only half-awake. Then, all of a sudden, they begin to chuckle, finally breaking out in a torrent of chattering, before spreading their short, rounded wings and sailing off for the night's hunting.

Silence descends. Only the shuffling of porcupines, and the soft flip-flop of moths beating against the window panes.

The power goes off. A yellow moon blooms above the hill.

~

When I moved in, Maplewood Lodge had been nestling there among the old trees for over seventy years. It had become a part of the forest. Birds nestled in the eaves; beetles burrowed in the woodwork; a jungle cat lived in the attic. Some of these denizens remained even during my residence.

I'd first seen the cottage, as I've written, in spring, when the surrounding forest was at its best—the oaks and maples in their fresh green raiment; flashy blue magpies playing follow-the-leader among them. There was one very tall, very old maple above the cottage, and this was probably the tree that gave the house its name. A portion of it was blackened where it had been struck by lightning, but the rest of it lived on, a favourite of woodpeckers— the ancient peeling bark harboured hundreds, perhaps thousands, of tiny insects. It was the Himalayan maple, of course, which is quite different from the North American maple; only the winged seed-pods are similar, twisting and turning in the breeze as they fall to the ground, for which reason the Garhwalis call it the Butterfly Tree.

A steep, narrow path ran down to the cottage from the main path that went past the Wynberg Allen School. During heavy rain, it would become a watercourse and the earth would be washed away, leaving it very stony and uneven. Actually, the path ran straight across a landing and up to the front door of the first floor, where I had my rooms. It was the ground floor that was tucked away in the shadow of the Bala Hissar hill; it was reached by small a flight of steps going down, which also took the rush of water when the path was in flood. Miss Bean, who was in her mid-eighties, lived in two small rooms on the ground floor.

Maplewood was the first place I saw, and I did not bother to see any others. The location wasn't really ideal. The cottage faced east, and as it was built in the shadow of the hill, while it received the early morning sun, it went without the evening sun. By three in the afternoon, the shadow of the hill crept over the cottage. This wasn't a bad thing in summer (even though Mussoorie summers were never hot), but in winter it meant a cold, dark house. There was no view of the snows from inside the house, and no view of the plains. But the forest below the cottage seemed full of possibilities, and the windows opening on to it probably decided the issue. And the whistling thrush, which had sent its song up the ravine to enchant me at exactly the right moment that afternoon.

I made a window seat and through the changing seasons, I wrote more—and I think better—than at any other time of my writing life. Most of my stories were written in Maplewood—the stories that went into *Our Trees Still Grow in Dehra*, *The Night Train to Deoli* and *Time Stops at Shamli*. The journals from that time provided material for the non-fiction books that followed the novellas and story collections. That old cottage was kind to a struggling young writer.

There were very few distractions. Not only was I mostly on my own for the first couple of years—except in summer, when some visitors came up—Mussoorie itself was a very quiet place, especially in the rains and in winter. Like all hill stations set up by the British, Mussoorie was in decline in the 1950s and '60s; the Mall was not half as busy at it is today, and in winter all the hotels and most of the shops would shut down. Only a couple of restaurants would stay open for the local residents. It wasn't tourism that sustained Mussoorie in those days; the boarding schools were the main economy, and when these, too, closed for the winter holidays, the little town would be deserted.

On the outskirts of the town there were a number of abandoned houses. Most of Mussoorie's older cottages had been built by British residents, and all but a few of them had left in a hurry after 1947, giving their houses away or making distress sales.

Property prices went down sharply, so that the houses were of little value, and as there were few takers as tenants either, many of the vacant houses were sold by the new owners to the kabaris. And the kabaris didn't want them as residences; they proceeded to dismantle the houses, taking out the doors and windows, all the metal, the wooden flooring, the tin from the roofs, the bathroom fittings, and anything else that could be recycled or sold as scrap. Empty shells—just stone walls and bits of roof—dotted the outskirts of Mussoorie, inhabited by wild cats, bandicoots, owls, goats and the occasional coal-burner or mule driver, or the rare vagrant.

Among these ruins, some of the older British and Anglo-Indian residents like Miss Bean lived out their final years.

'I'm the last Bean in India,' she would say. 'And I'll be gone too, before long.'

She was eighty-six, but looking at her you wouldn't have guessed—she was spry and took some care to look good. Not once in the five years that we spent together did I find her looking slovenly. The old-fashioned dresses she wore were clean and well-ironed, and sometimes she added a hat. Her memory was excellent, and she knew a great deal about the flowers, trees, birds and other wildlife of the area—she hadn't made a serious study of these things, but having lived here for so long, she had developed an intimacy with everything that grew and flourished around her. A trust somewhere in England sent her a pension of forty or fifty rupees, and this was all the money she had, having used up the paltry sum she'd received from the sale of her property.

She'd had a large house, she told me, which she had inherited from her parents when they died, and she'd had an ailing sister whom she had nursed for many years before she too passed away. As she had no income, she kept boarders in the house, but she had no business sense and was losing money maintaining it. In the end, she sold the house for a song to one of the local traders and moved into two small rooms on the ground floor of Maplewood Lodge, a kindness for which she remained grateful to her friends, the Gordon sisters.

It must have been lonely for Miss Bean, living there in the shadow of the hill, which was why she had been excited when I moved into the floor above her. With age catching up, she couldn't leave her rooms and her little garden as often as she would have liked to, and there were few visitors—sometimes a teacher from the Wynberg Allen School, the padre from the church in town, the milkman twice a week and, once a month, the postman. She had an old bearer, who had been with her for many years. I don't think she could afford him any longer, but she managed to pay him a little somehow, and he continued out of loyalty, but also because he was old himself; there wouldn't have been too many other employment opportunities for him. He came late in the morning and left before dark. Then she would be alone, without even the company of a pet. There'd been a small dog long ago, but she'd lost it to a leopard.

It had happened late one afternoon. She was in a rickshaw on Camel's Back Road, going to a tea party at a friend's house, the dog sitting in her lap. And suddenly, from the hillside above her, a leopard sprang onto the rickshaw, snatched the dog out of her hands, and leapt down to the other side and into the forest. She was left sitting there, empty-handed, in great shock, but she hadn't suffered even a scratch. The two rickshaw pullers said they'd only felt a heavy thump behind them, and by the time they turned to look, the leopard was gone.

All of this I gathered over the many evenings that I spent chatting with Miss Bean in her corner of the cottage. I didn't have anyone to cook for me in the first few years at Maplewood. Most evenings I would have tinned food, and occasionally I would go down to share my sardine tins or sausages with Miss Bean. She ate frugally—maybe she'd always had a small appetite, or it was something her body had adjusted to after years of small meals—so I wasn't really depriving myself of much. And she returned the favour with excellent tea and coffee.

We would have long chats, Miss Bean telling me stories about Mussoorie, where she had lived since she was a teenager, and stories about herself (a lot of which went into some of my own stories). She remembered the time when electricity came to Mussoorie—in 1912, long before it reached most other parts of India. And she had memories of the first train coming into Dehra, and the first motor road coming up to Mussoorie. Before the motor road was built, everyone would walk up the old bridle path from Rajpur, or come on horseback, or in a dandy held aloft by four sweating coolies.

Miss Bean missed the old days, when there was a lot of activity in the hill resort—picnics and tea parties and delicious scandals. It was a place of mischief and passion, and she enjoyed both. As a girl, she'd had many suitors, and if she did not marry, it was more from procrastination than from being passed over. While on all sides elopements and broken marriages were making life exciting, she managed to remain single, even when she taught elocution at one of the schools that flourished in Mussoorie, and which were rife with secret affairs.

'Do you wish you had, though,' I asked her one March evening, sitting by the window, in the only chair she had in her bedroom.

'Do I wish I had what?' she said from her bed, where she was tucked up with three hot-water bottles.

'Married. Or fallen in love.'

She chuckled.

'I did fall in love, you know. But my dear father was a very good shot with pistol and rifle, so I had to be careful for the sake of the young gentlemen. As for marriage, I might have regretted it even had it happened.'

A fierce wind had built up and it was battering at the doors and windows, determined to get in. It slipped down the chimney, but was stuck there, choking and gurgling in frustration.

'There's a ghost in your chimney and he can't get out,' I said.

'Then let him stay there,' said Miss Bean.

Above us rose an uninhabited mountain called Pari Tibba, Fairy Hill. The villagers said only aerial spirits dwelt there. Miss Bean called it Burnt Hill or Witch's Hill. Burnt Hill, because it was frequently struck by lightning; Witch's Hill because it was supposedly haunted.

'You know about Pari Tibba, don't you?' she asked.

I said I didn't, so she told me.

In the early days, when Mussoorie was being settled, a few houses had come up on Pari Tibba but they were frequently hit by lightning and burnt down, so people stopped living on it. Then there was a young couple who fell in love and wanted to marry, but they were of different faiths and their families opposed their union; so they ran away together, and took shelter at night in one of the ruined houses on Pari Tibba, where no one would stop them from consummating their love.

'Then a storm came up—as it often does here—the building was struck again by lightning, and the lovers perished in each other's arms. A shepherd found their charred bodies many days later.'

'A romantic tale,' I said.

'But a true one,' she averred.

It was said the star-crossed lovers haunted the hill. Miss Bean herself did not believe in ghosts, but she had seen a few. Her family was haunted by a malignant phantom head that always appeared before the death of one of her relatives. She said her brother saw this apparition the night before their mother died, and both she and her sister saw it before the death of their father. The sisters slept in the same room, and they were both awakened one night by a curious noise in the cupboard facing their beds. One of them began getting out of bed to see if their cat was in the room, when the cupboard door suddenly opened and a luminous head appeared. It was covered with matted hair and appeared to be in an advanced stage of decomposition. And as they crossed themselves, it vanished.

The next day they learned that their father, who was in Lucknow, had died suddenly, at about the time that they had seen the head.

~

Mussoorie only had about three cars that year, all owned by doctors, and there may have been a taxi or two. There were rickshaws, but hand-drawn, and sometimes, on steep ascents, you needed three people to pull one. The rickshaw pullers were poor men from the villages of Tehri Garhwal, who continued to make a precarious living in this way till hand-drawn rickshaws were abolished in the 1970s and the men were given cycle rickshaws.

But you used rickshaws only if you were in a hurry or had a medical emergency, or if the distance to cover was considerable, or if you had a load too heavy to carry. Mostly you walked.

Two or three times a week I would walk into town, to visit the Allahabad Bank, the post office, and the bookshop, occasionally stopping at Kwality's for a coffee or a snack. By mid-November the main town would be deserted. If it snowed, youngsters trudged up from Rajpur to revel in snow-fights on the Mall, but no one stayed overnight. The few people who had nowhere to go would ask me why I wasn't going anywhere for the winter. Even Miss Bean went away for a month, to the YWCA in Dehradun.

Winter or summer or rain, I was happy to write or laze in my rooms, or to step out and take a path, any path, and follow it till it led to a forest glade or stream or hilltop. I liked walking at night. There would be no one else about at that hour, except the odd drunk who usually needed guidance, and as I always had time on my hands, I would help him find his way home. But for that, my walks were solitary, quite peaceful and pleasant. No one ever bothered me, neither man nor beast.

I was conscious all the time of the silent life in the surrounding trees and bushes, and on the road. I smelt a leopard on a couple of occasions, but did not see it. I felt the warmth of a body very close behind me, but when I turned there was no one.

Sometimes the silence was broken: jackals barked and howled in the distance; a nightjar announced itself with a loud grating sound, like a whiplash cutting the air. A little scops owl, which spoke only in monosyllables, said 'Wow', softly but with great deliberation. He would then continue to say 'Wow' every other minute for several hours throughout the night.

Or there would be a rustling overhead and I would look up to see a flying squirrel glide from the top of one deodar tree to another. (On a moonlit night, it was a beautiful scene.)

And sometimes I stood and stared. Because far above the trees, streams of stars were overlapping in the sky. If I was lucky, I also caught the wash and glow of the Milky Way.

A solitary man, I met solitary people. Fleeting encounters.

One evening I wandered much further down the Tehri road than I had intended to, and by the time I returned, it was very late. Some lights still twinkled on the hills, but shopfronts in the old Landour Bazaar were shuttered and silent. The people living on either side of the narrow street could hear my footsteps, perhaps, or they might have been asleep, for it was a cold night; doors and windows were shut. A three-quarter moon was up, and the tin roofs of the bazaar, drenched with dew, glistened in the moonlight. Although the street was unlit, I needed no torch.

The rickshaw stand was deserted. A jackal slunk across the road like a thief or an adulterer. A field rat wriggled through a hole in a rotting plank, on its nightly foray among sacks of grain and pulses.

As I passed along the deserted street, under the shadow of the clock tower, I saw a boy huddled in a recess, a thin shawl wrapped around his shoulders. He was awake and shivering. He was aware of my presence, but he did not look up at me; he continued to shiver, and I passed by, my thoughts already on the warmth of the little cottage. Until something stopped me—it wasn't anything I had seen in his face, there wasn't light enough for that. I think it was the fact that he hadn't looked up—he was resigned to his abandonment; he expected nothing at all from the world.

I walked back to the shadows where the boy was crouched. He didn't say anything when I sat down next to him, but this time he did look up, puzzled and a little apprehensive, ready to shrink away or even to beg forgiveness for a crime he hadn't committed. I could tell from his features that he had come from the hills beyond Tehri. He had come here looking for work and he was yet to find any.

'Have you somewhere to stay?' I asked. He shook his head; but something about my tone of voice gave him confidence, because now there was a glimmer of hope, a friendly appeal in his eyes.

'If you can walk some way,' I offered, 'I can give you a bed and blanket.'

He got up immediately—a thin boy, wearing only a shirt and a pyjama. He wrapped his thin shawl around himself and followed me without any hesitation.

He had trusted me. I couldn't now fail to trust him.

So now there were two in the sleeping moonlit bazaar. I glanced up at the tall, packed, haphazard houses. They seemed to lean towards each other for warmth and companionship.

The boy walked silently beside me. He was a quiet one. Soon we were out of the bazaar and on the footpath. The mountains loomed over us. And although no creature of the forest had ever harmed me, I was glad to have a companion walking next to me.

In the morning, I gave him hot water for a bath. He made us tea, I brought out some old buns, and we made a breakfast of these. Then he went away. It was only later that it occurred to me I could have offered to take him on as a cook or bearer. I didn't have the income to pay him a respectable salary, but he wouldn't have starved, and he would have had a place to stay, while he looked for something more suitable.

But something about him, and the circumstances of our meeting, prevented me from doing that. It seemed to me that an act of charity, or anything transactional, would have ruined whatever it was that had brought us briefly together. Perhaps he had felt the same, because I never saw him again.

~

Without a cook, unwilling to learn to cook myself, and tired of tinned sardines and sausages, I would walk into town in the evening, to the Kwality restaurant, give myself a drink, have dinner and walk back home at about ten. I never carried a torch; it was a good road up to the Wynberg Allen School, where there was a lone street lamp at the gate—which worked sometimes and sometimes not, and lit a tiny bit of the path going down to the cottage, but then it was quite dark as the path went through a bit of jungle, and up to the landing—you walked by memory and habit.

One night, the lamp at the school gate was working, and a little distance from it, three or four red foxes were prancing and dancing around in a small clearing. I walked quietly down the path, not wanting to disturb them. I had walked a fair distance, and when I was halfway down, I looked back from the dark, and there was a single fox, still dancing in the diffused light. He gave me a little poem:

As I walked home last night
I saw a lone fox dancing
In the bright moonlight.
I stood and watched,
Then took the low road, knowing
The night was his by right.
Sometimes, when words ring true,
I'm like a lone fox dancing
In the morning dew.

Winter was a good time for writing poetry.

The knoll beneath the pine tree was too windy; the garden was too cold; the sun did not reach the stream for long. It was better to sit by a charcoal brazier with a pen and notebook—just as I am doing today, fifty years later, only now it's a large stove burning firewood, and I have my adopted children plying me with cocoa or my favourite onion soup. It's mid-January, and we expect snow; but a good snowfall has been elusive during the last two years.

I remember the first time it snowed in Maplewood. From the windows I could see, up at the top of the hill, the deodars clothed in a mantle of white. It was a fairyland: everything still and silent. The only movement was the circling of an eagle over the trees.

But it was very cold and I stayed in bed most of the time. A boy from a nearby bakery would come down occasionally, bringing bread or buns or biscuits. Sometimes his sister came instead. She was a lively, precocious girl, always ready to sit and talk and even flirt a little. I called her Miss Bun.

One morning, I opened the door and there was several inches of snow on the ground; fresh snow, and a leopard's pug marks along the pathway and up to the front door. Up at the school, closed for the winter, the chowkidar's mastiff had disappeared. I had no dog for the leopard, but I decided to stay indoors after dark for some days. Do leopards hunt foxes? Probably not. But they might hunt a writer if there's nobody else available.

FRIENDS AND LOVERS IN MAPLEWOOD

I WOULD BE GIVING THE READER A WRONG IMPRESSION IF I TRIED to present myself as another Thoreau, living alone beside Walden Pond with only birds and beasts for company. I was on my own quite often, particularly in the early days at Maplewood, but there were human companions too.

Maplewood Lodge was in a slightly isolated spot, but it was a sociable little corner. Along the stretch from the clock tower down to the Wynberg Allen School, all the houses were occupied, many of them by school teachers, and a few by Anglo-Indians or long-time British residents, many of them quite old and living alone. They were a friendly lot, and they would come to see me at Maplewood, or invite me over for small get-togethers. A little further away lived some ex-royals, usually a migratory species, and I got to know at least one of them quite well.

I had many friends among the local families, too, and people from the nearby villages who came selling milk, or students who came to the government school nearby. And there were outstation boys studying in Mussoorie's private schools who dropped in from time to time, to show me their essays or raid my larder when they felt hungry. Spending time with them—and, later, with the young ones in my adopted family—I began writing stories for children. And became a child myself!

But it was old people I befriended first. There was Miss Bean; and then, along came Sir Edmund Gibson, an eighty-six-year-old bachelor, whom I'd met a couple of times in my Dehradun days. He'd been the British Resident in the Kathiawar states during the Raj, where he'd known my parents, though I have no memory of him from that time. After Independence, he had retired in Dehradun, where he was running a large farm, but at a loss—he was doing it more as a hobby. He didn't want to go back to England, and divided his time between the Dehradun farm and a sprawling bungalow close to Maplewood Lodge, maintaining a large retinue of servants and their dependants like an eighteenth-century nawab.

'I'm at the mercy of my servants,' he would complain, but he had placed himself at their mercy long ago. One or two of them, like his Gurkha manservant, Trilok, were genuinely fond of him; the others hoped to get bits of his farm and would have preferred that he made an early exit.

But like his old Hillman car, which he kept in Dehradun because it couldn't get up the hill, Sir Edmund had a rugged constitution; despite his many illnesses, it looked as though he would outlive his hardy servants. He had come to India in 1910, and survived cholera, typhoid, dysentery and malaria. Now, despite congested lungs, a bad heart, gout, weak eyes, bad teeth, recalcitrant bowels, he was still deriving some pleasure from living. Many mornings I would find him sitting under an oak tree—probably as old as him—and looking timeless. One day he said to me, 'I don't mind being dead, Ruskin, but I shall miss being alive.' Which was a good summing up of his attitude to life.

I think the secret of his longevity was that he refused to go to bed when he was unwell. Nothing would prevent him from getting up, dressing up, writing letters, or getting on with a Wodehouse or the latest *Blackwood's* Magazine, to which he had been subscribing for fifty years (he was pleased to find that some of my own essays were appearing in *Blackwood's*).

And nothing would keep him from his afternoon tea, or his evening whisky and soda, which he sometimes shared with me.

When he was Resident in Kathiawar, he was once shot at from close range. The man took four shots and missed every time. He must have been a terrible shot, or perhaps the pistol was faulty, because Sir Edmund was a big man and should have made a large target. Sir Edmund loved to recount this to everyone he met. That an attempt was made to assassinate him was proof that he was a mighty man; that he had survived the attempt made him mightier still.

He also treasured two letters from Mahatma Gandhi—which were written from prison—although he had himself arrested Gandhi in Rajkot on one occasion.

'I liked Gandhi,' he said. 'He had a sense of humour. No politician today has any humour. They all take themselves far too seriously. When I went to see Gandhi in prison, I asked him if he was comfortable, and he smiled and said, "Even if I was, I wouldn't admit it!"'

Sir Edmund wasn't without humour himself. When someone asked him for permission to shoot a bird on his land in Ramgarh, he refused.

'I need it for a biology class. It's in the interests of science and humanity,' protested the man. 'Do you think a bird is better than a human being?'

'*Infinitely*,' said Sir Edmund. 'Infinitely better.'

When he was bored, he went down to his farm in Dehra and to his beloved Hillman, but he would be back sooner than he'd have said he would. And I was always happy to have him back, for his wit and the whisky he generously shared with me, even though it was a strange local brew that could give you a nasty hangover.

Sir Edmund finally died of a stroke, and according to his wishes, he was cremated on his Dehra farm.

A couple of years later, Miss Bean passed away in her sleep, and I never found old friends like them again.

~

Sometime in 1964, an interesting family from Almora moved into the neighbourhood—Zohra Verma and her four children. Zohra's husband had died and left her a cottage just above Maplewood Lodge, which she hoped to sell. It took her over a year to find a suitable buyer, during which time her children stayed with her, two of them attending school in Mussoorie.

Zohra had been an English teacher at Aligarh University, and was very opinionated about books and writing—in fact, about everything under the sun—but she was good company despite this. The child of a Hindu-Muslim marriage, she herself had been married twice—first to a Muslim, from whom she'd had a daughter, and then to a Hindu, who was in the air force, and from whom she had two daughters and a son. All four children were quite bright and talented—even a little eccentric, as bright people often are—and for this, I'm certain, they had their mother to thank; the fathers would have been no match for her. She was a tough, spirited little woman—a tiny bundle of energy, and rather overwhelming. You could see she must have been a very passionate person too, when she was younger.

All the daughters took after Zohra, but it was the second daughter, Surekha, who seemed to have inherited her passionate nature more than the others. Surekha was a bit of a free spirit, of a sensual and artistic nature, whom sleepy Mussoorie would have found difficult to contain, and it was a good thing that she soon went to Delhi and joined the National School of Drama. I lost touch with her after her marriage, but I would keep hearing about her work. She acted in a film during the Emergency, but it was never released because it was a satire on Indira Gandhi and it got into trouble with Indira's hot-headed younger son, Sanjay

Gandhi. The film was called *Kissa Kursi Ka* and Surekha had played Mrs Gandhi. She didn't get many film roles after that, but she was very active in the theatre in Delhi. Later, she had some good character roles in films, which brought her recognition and awards, and now I see her on television, playing the strong older woman in a couple of those interminable soap operas that would be difficult to watch if it were not for some fine actors like her.

Surekha's younger sister, Phoolmani, was very charming, still in school at the time. But it was the eldest sister with whom I was more friendly. We called her Punni. She was about my age and had recently returned from London, where she had studied to become a doctor. She was something of a tomboy, almost always dressed in trousers and shirts, and smoked very heavily. She was also rather strong-willed, not really interested in running a home or settling down with anyone, so I was surprised when I heard some years later that she had married someone several years her junior, a man I had met when he would visit Zohra's family in Mussoorie. His name was Naseeruddin Shah and I think he was still in college when I first saw him. The marriage didn't last very long, and Punni went away to Iran. Naseer went on to make quite a name for himself in Hindi cinema and theatre.

Naseer had a Mussoorie connection too—his father owned a house here. He was a nice old gentleman whom I had met just once, when I was looking for a place to rent. The house was sold when he died and I didn't see Naseer for many years after that.

But I've almost forgotten about Zohra's youngest, her son. And that isn't surprising because he was a quiet boy, and with the three dominating sisters and a dominating mother, almost invisible! Fortunately for him, there was no lasting damage—he went into the army and ended up as a general.

Strong, dominating women seemed to find me all the time. One day I received an invitation to a party from Robin Jind, one of the sons of the erstwhile Maharaja of Jind, and a well-known announcer on Doordarshan in the 1960s. A very good-looking man, he was also a talented painter who'd had a few exhibitions in Delhi, and it was at one of these that I'd met him.

On one of his visits to Mussoorie, Robin ran into me on the Mall and said, 'Come over in the evening, my mother is giving a party.' That was the first time I went over to the Maharani of Jind's place—Her Highness Prithvi Bir Kaur; HH to her friends. She was Robin's stepmother, the Maharaja's second wife (the first having died in mysterious circumstances).

It was quite a wild party. There were all sorts of strange people, and an hour into the merriment, HH was walking around balancing a bottle of expensive whisky on her head. We met regularly after that. She was a very social person; she liked company and would come down to see me in Maplewood, but more often I would drop in—or rather she would order me to come. We would drink together, though I could never keep up with her—she was a daytime drinker, like her husband, who had died from too much alcohol; sometimes she would start after breakfast, have a late lunch, at around four, and start drinking again in the evening. But it didn't seem to affect her in any way.

HH was great fun over a few drinks, especially when she got going on all the disasters that had overtaken her friends and acquaintances: someone had been knocked down by a truck; someone else had been sucked into the fuselage of an aeroplane; and a dear old friend, a retired mountaineer, who was suffering from Alzheimer's, poor man, had died searching for the Annapurna base camp on the Delhi Ridge. She recounted all these tragedies with great sympathy and great relish.

She hadn't yet found Bill Aitken, the writer who would also become a good friend of mine. He was still living the ascetic's life in an ashram up in the mountains above Almora, and she was having an affair with the Peruvian chargé d'affaires, a typical Spanish type, with the money to go with his charm. He used to supply all the imported booze for her wild parties. He had rented a cottage for his wife and children who went to school in Mussoorie, but he hardly ever visited them. He would come to see HH, however, and they would go off on trips together. That stopped after he went back to Peru and she began to visit the ashram in Almora, where she met Bill, and they became partners for life.

Bill was a calming influence on HH, and I think after a long time she found genuine companionship in him. I don't suppose it was always easy for him, but Bill had been wandering too long himself, and once he had made the commitment, he stuck to her.

HH had two sons who gave her a lot of trouble. This was partly her fault—she had indulged them to begin with, and then suddenly cut them off. But you couldn't tell her that. She was, after all, a maharani. I tried not to contradict her, and for that reason she remained fond of me till the end.

Bill continues to live in their home in Mussoorie, though we rarely see each other, age having caught up with both of us.

~

When summer came around and tourists flocked to the hill station, there were friends and their families from Rajouri Garden and Patel Nagar who would turn up, often unannounced, to prevent me from being too much of a recluse.

Kamal would come up on and off, sometimes staying for several weeks at a stretch, so that he wasn't so much a visitor as a roommate. I got used to having him in the house and soon we were spending a lot of time together; he would paint, while I wrote, and then we would take a break and go for long walks, or on treks into the neighbouring hills and mountains.

It was a busy little household, for apart from the two of us, there were two black Pomeranians my mother had given me on one of my visits to Delhi, and a Siamese cat, and all of us got along quite well. The Poms—Toffee and Pickle; brother and sister—insisted on being taken along when we went out walking; the cat, being a cat, preferred some independence and would stay back, wanting to do her own thing.

She was a pretty cat, and deserves a proper introduction; and you must indulge me as I turn to my old Maplewood journal for a small tribute to the only pet who became intimate enough with me to share my bed.

Suzie came into my life when she was just three weeks old. I'd been in Maplewood for a few months and it was beginning to get a little lonely, so I told a friend that I needed a pet. I had expected to receive a dog; but when the kitten arrived, its small questing head with the chocolate-tipped ears thrust out of the friend's coat pocket, I fell in love at first sight. And, taking its sex for granted, I named the kitten Suzie.

Suzie spent her first night curled up in a tea cosy. She showed her good breeding right from the start by selecting a commodious pot of geraniums for her morning ablutions, and then I loved her even more, because I had no idea how to train a cat.

But, like most Siamese cats, she showed a dislike for milk; and I was faced with the problem of obtaining a regular supply of meat. As I lived two miles from the nearest butcher, I took meat only once or twice a week; but Suzie disdained a vegetarian diet. I solved the problem by purchasing a month's supply of tinned sardines and feeding her exclusively on fish. She liked butter too, and used it to polish her coat. All this proved expensive, but I was hoping that as she grew older her natural instincts would result in her bringing in her own supplies.

I was not disappointed. She was barely a month old when she snapped up a large moth that flew in through the open windows on a balmy September night. A few days later I found, on the kitchen floor, the head and tail of a mouse. The bright innocence of Suzie's sky blue eyes told me where the rest of the mouse was now lodged.

Cats rarely answer to their names; but Suzie often did. Moreover, I had tied a little bell to her neck, and this generally told me where she was. Her favourite haunt was a cherry tree. When a pair of thrushes were building a nest, she learnt to climb this tree beautifully—and the birds went elsewhere.

If a cat and a dog are properly introduced to each other, they make the best of friends. It did not take Suzie long to develop a playful, nose-tapping relationship with a neighbour's dog, a Peke. Another dog, a rather doleful, good-natured Cocker Spaniel, permitted Suzie to sleep beneath her on cold days. Such was Suzie's charm that she was soon being fed by my neighbours, and this generosity solved my food problems. People took pity on us. Bachelors and kittens are suitable objects for compassion.

Suzie must have been about five months old when I discovered, to my dismay and embarrassment, that she was really a male. But I scorned all suggestions for a change of name: he had been Suzie from his infancy, and he would keep his girl's name. And if this confused the world, it was the world that needed to sort itself out; I was all right with this ambiguous state of affairs. (When Kamal came to stay, he suggested we change Suzie's name to Souza. But I had a friend called D'Souza who was built like a wrestler, and it would have been odd to have D'Souza jump into my lap or nuzzle my chest.)

I had been warned that as soon as Suzie was eight months old he would start staying out late at nights, or even remaining away for several days in his search for a suitable mate. But Suzie was not like other males. He stayed at home, and the queens came to him. There was a beautiful black creature with yellow eyes, straight out of Edgar Allan Poe, and a handsome wild cat from the forest, who came to the front door on alternate nights (never together). Suzie would go out and meet his admirers, and frolic with them in the long, dew-drenched monsoon grass, before returning indoors to sleep deeply and sweetly at the foot of my bed.

Suzie liked people. I think he found them comfortable. If there were guests, he would always choose the one with the broadest, most accommodating lap. At night, he usually slept on my tummy (he liked its rise and fall, as I breathed) and if it got cold, he curled up in the hollow behind my knees. One morning, when there was a small blizzard blowing outside, I woke up to find he had somehow crawled under my shirt and woollen vest and was splayed out on my chest, his head tucked under my chin.

In the house, during the day, he was unobtrusive. Outside, he had his own pursuits and pleasures, whether it be stalking garden lizards or too familiar mynahs and crows. Sometimes I found him curled up on my typewriter, reminding me that I had not been working regularly of late. He liked music, and a favourite spot of his, ever since childhood, had been beside the radio. That's where I found him one morning, and he stayed there while I brought out my camera and took a picture. It will always be my favourite picture of Suzie.

So we lived happily, Suzie, Pickle, Toffee and I, and Kamal, whenever he same to spend time with us. But good things, like bad things, must come to an end, and one by one, over the next couple of years, we all went our separate ways

Pickle was the first to go. It was a November evening, a little after sunset. The kitchen door opened out to the forest, and the young cook we had recently employed had left it open. Suddenly, Pickle charged out barking, and the bark became a yelp—and we ran out, Kamal and I, to see what had happened. There was no sign of Pickle. The cook came running after us and said, '*Baghera le gaya!*'—A leopard's taken him! We took our torches and all three of us went looking, all the way down to the edge of the ravine, but there was no sign of Pickle. The next morning, when we went to search again, we found his paws in the gully.

Some months later, Suzie disappeared. It couldn't have been a leopard, because leopards, as far as I know, don't eat cats. I never found out what happened. I consoled myself with the thought that someone had seen him on the road, fallen in love with him, like I had, and taken him home, to look after him better than I had done.

Kamal brought home four rabbits—thinking this would cheer us up. We let them roam around in the garden for much of the day and brought them in for the night, but they made a mess inside. One day we bought a wire cage and put them inside and left them in the garden. By morning they were gone. A leopard—or jackals, perhaps—had dug under the wiring. Two of the rabbits had been carried away, and two had died of fright.

Only Toffee lived to a healthy old age, and when she died, we buried her in the garden.

~

Late in the summer in 1964, Sushila came up to Maplewood. I had last seen her, after a gap of over two years, on a recent visit to Delhi, and perhaps because I was thirty—a dangerous age for dreamers, when youth is beginning to say goodbye—and because I had lived a hermit's existence for months, I lost my heart to her. She was sixteen; dark and slender, with large expressive eyes; and I became aware of her in a way I hadn't been when I used to spend time with Kamal's family. Perhaps subconsciously I had always been aware of her, but in a somewhat paternal way, because she was often in her school uniform then. She still had three years of school left, but only because she'd been failing her exams.

She lived with her parents and brothers in a dusty, flyblown locality somewhere on the fringes of Delhi, where many of the poorer refugees had settled after Partition. I had always been drawn to people from backgrounds very different from my own, and who seemed to be a little out of step with the world, as I was; and Sushila, in her hand-me-down clothes, dreaming of one day travelling the world and happy to spend time with the boys and get up to mischief, began to occupy my thoughts that fortnight in Delhi.

I was living with Kamal's family (I was on reasonable terms with my own family, but this was only possible from a distance), and Sushila was staying there too—she was on a long visit with her mother, who frequently came to Rajouri Garden to recover from the toil and drudgery of her marital home. I looked for ways to be close to Sushila and talk to her alone, but this was impossible in a house overflowing with busy women, noisy children and men who sat around doing very little. So I would take her, with Kamal and her ten-year-old brother Sunder, to Connaught Place for coffee and snacks. Once, I took them to see a movie, where I had thought I would hold her hand, but Sunder sat between us.

He had grown very fond of me, as small boys will of anyone who buys them sweets and takes them to the pictures.

When I left Delhi for the hills that time, Sushila cried. At first, I thought it was because I was going away. Then I realized it was because she couldn't go anywhere herself. I think she both envied and resented me that freedom. But she gave me a garland of marigold flowers as a parting gift, which I wore, feeling like a groom, though nothing had been said.

So I was happy when she turned up at Maplewood sometime later with Kamal and her little brother. Sunder insisted on sleeping with me, and he wouldn't let his sister leave his side at night, so the three of us slept in my bed, and Kamal shifted to the second room, which he had converted into his studio. I was tense with longing through the first night, like some wound-up machine. I stayed awake, looking at her dark, long-fingered hand on Sunder's chest, till sleep finally came to me in the early hours.

The next day we went to the stream for our first picnic, where again we were surrounded by people—Kamal, Sunder, and a couple of our Maplewood neighbours. But that night, I put my hand on Sunder sleeping between us, and my fingers brushed hers, and she took my hand and held it against her soft warm cheek. I reached across and kissed her eyes and her neck. Sunder woke up and I pulled back. He put his arm and a leg around me and after a while Sushila turned her back to us and was soon fast asleep.

We began to take long walks after that, at all times of the day, when I would tell them love stories disguised as fairy tales—which confused Sunder and amused his sister. And they bored Kamal, because he began to absent himself from these walks, saying he wanted to focus on his painting. (Stories, in any case, didn't interest him; in all the time I knew him, he never read any of mine, or indeed anyone else's.)

He wasn't with us on our next picnic at the stream, and there were no neighbours. Sunder and I bathed in the cool, refreshing water while Sushila sat on a rock, with her feet in the water. I splashed water on her and she threw a small stone at me. I begged forgiveness and she asked me to kiss her feet, which I did and we all laughed and went back to the cottage, where Kamal scolded me for neglecting my writing. I was hardly ever in the house, he said, something had happened to me. I laughed it off, saying I was entitled to a holiday, but some stories were brewing. I didn't like lying to him, and to cover my guilt I asked if he had made any progress at all on the painting he'd been struggling with for days. He looked angry, but decided to let it be.

I couldn't write; it was true that something had happened to me. I wanted to be with Sushila all the time; I imagined her standing naked in the stream, or lying naked in our bed, or walking naked in the garden with flowers in her hair. When she showed me a boy's photograph and told me he was in love with her and wrote her letters, I was jealous. I tried not to show it, but became gloomier every minute, till she sensed my dismay and tried to make amends. She assured me the correspondence was one-sided and she was no longer interested in the boy. I was elated again. Euphoric one minute and in deep despair the next—I had never known such upheaval.

One morning, Kamal took Sunder to the skating rink on the Mall. It was a warm day.

'Let's go to the stream,' Sushila said, snatching the book I was reading out of my hands. 'I'll bathe you.'

We went down the steep path, and I took her to the waterfall, and showed her the small cave behind it. We lay down on the damp rock and I kissed her. I kissed her eyes, lips and her long, slim neck, till her shy responsiveness turned to passion and she clung to me, and suddenly I became afraid of myself and broke free of her embrace. I told her it wasn't safe outside.

That night, in whispers, I told her I had never loved anyone in my life as much as I loved her. I wanted to spend my life with her, and I would take care of her. I must have sounded like Majnu or Romeo, and I wanted to say much more, but there are no words bigger than these in love, and I think I was truly in love. No woman had responded to me as tenderly as she had.

'Do you love me?' I asked her, and there was silence. I asked again, telling her I wanted to marry her and I would wait for her all my life if I had to, and then I convinced myself that she had nodded yes and I hadn't seen it in the dark.

We were lying on the bed one afternoon, Sushila's head on my arm, and Sunder sleeping beside us, when Kamal walked in unexpectedly. We were too startled to react. He didn't say anything, merely passed through the room to his studio. Sushila pulled away and looked afraid. 'He knows,' she said. I said he would understand; I would tell him I wanted to marry her and meant to talk to her mother.

I asked Kamal out for a walk, and when we were some distance from the house, we had a row. He said I had deceived and used him. He also accused me of seducing an innocent girl.

'She's hardly a child,' I said in my defence. 'And I'm not exactly old. I'm thirty.'

'She's still almost half your age,' he said. 'Does she love you?'

'I think so.'

'You think so? You are a fool. Look at her, look at yourself. This is India.'

'I want to marry her,' I said to stop him. 'Will you help me?'

I didn't know what I was doing; I hadn't thought it through, but if it was marriage that would keep Sushila with me, I would marry her.

Kamal took her and Sunder back to Delhi two days later. And I was left with the brooding mountains and a house that seemed emptier than before. I kept finding things that she'd left behind—strands of hair on the pillow, a broken bangle, a little box of kajal. At night I drank brandy and wrote listlessly, while the rats scurried about on the rafters.

In the monsoon there was a constant drizzle and drumming on the corrugated tin roof. The mist rose at intervals through the day, thin vapour one minute and dense cloud the next. It covered the trees and made the forest ethereal, but I couldn't respond to the beauty.

Then a letter came from Kamal, saying that he wanted to move out and live on his own. He couldn't afford the rent and wanted me to share a flat with him in Delhi for a year. During that time he would help me to convince Sushila's family and arrange the marriage. I packed a few things and took the bus to Delhi.

We found a flat, but I could hardly meet Sushila there. In fact, through the weeks I was in Delhi, I saw her just once, in Kamal's family home, which was full of people for some celebration. We did not speak, but I spoke to one of her uncles. He seemed happy on his sister's behalf. The girl had to be married soon, he said, and it might as well be me; I was almost a part of their extended family already. It would happen; I should be patient.

I had little reason to stay in Delhi after that. I could only wait now, and I would rather wait in my quiet corner in the hills. Kamal didn't seem to enjoy being with me, either. He used to joke that it was unnatural for me not to have a girl in my life; now that I had found one, I had obviously done it all wrong. But neither of us wanted to be the first to express our unhappiness. It was the landlord who put us out of our misery. He asked us to vacate the place—Kamal's nephews and cousins, who would stay with us all day and sometimes at night, made too much noise, he said, and used up all the water.

I returned to Mussoorie with half an assurance from Sushila's uncle. But I didn't hear from anyone for months after that. When I couldn't wait any longer, I took the bus to Delhi again, and when I reached Kamal's family home, I wasn't welcome anymore. One of his brothers met me outside the door and told me I should go back to Mussoorie and stay away for some time. There had been a mistake; Sushila was engaged to be married.

She was married off some months later, to a man with better prospects, and from their community. She's still married and lives somewhere in the great sprawl of North India (for which reason I have had to disguise her identity). Whether she wears bangles anymore, or strings marigolds into garlands, I do not know. She's probably a grandmother now. It's the grandchildren who keep us going!

Kamal didn't continue his painting and went into more commercial work, something to do with textiles and garment design, after he too married. We rarely met after that year, but I would hear of him from time to time because one of his nephews, Anil, lived with me for a couple of years to complete his education. Anil's family had come on hard times after his father abandoned them, and the boy was pulled out of the private school he was attending in Delhi. I got him admitted to Wynberg Allen, where he did well and later he joined a medical college in Dehradun. He became a doctor and settled in America some years later.

~

One way to get over a failed love affair is to get married. Another is to trek into beautiful, deserted places.

In the months after I returned from Delhi, turned away by Sushila's relatives, I began frequenting uninhabited spots high up on the hills of Mussoorie. There was a hill called Cloud's End. From its naked, windswept crest, one had a view of the plains on one side, and of the snow peaks on the other. Wild sorrel grew among the rocks, and there were many flowers—clover, wild begonia, dandelion—sprinkling the hillside.

On the spur of the hill stood the ruins of an old brewery. Some enterprising Englishman had spent a lifetime here making beer for his thirsty compatriots down in the plains. Now, moss and ferns grew from the walls. In a hollow beneath a flight of worn steps, a wildcat had made its home. It was a beautiful grey creature, black-striped, with pale green eyes. Sometimes it watched me from the steps or the wall, but it never came near.

No one lived on the hill, except occasionally a coal burner in a temporary grass-thatched hut. But villagers used the path, grazing their sheep and cattle on the grassy slopes. It was mostly young boys and girls who brought their families' cattle and sheep there. I found a boy who played a flute. Its rough, sweet notes travelled clearly across the mountain air. I saw him often, and he would greet me with a nod of his head, without taking the flute away from his lips.

And there was a girl who was nearly always cutting grass for fodder. She wore heavy anklets on her feet, and she did not speak much either, but she had a wide grin on her face whenever she met me on the path. She was always singing to herself, or to the sheep, or to the grass, showing me how much I still needed to learn about contentment. What's all the running around for, she seemed to say. Sit down, stop chasing, and the words will come, and maybe love, too.

There was a boy who carried milk into town, who would often fall into step with me. He had never been away from the hills. He had never been on a train. He asked why my hair wasn't black, and seemed to understand easily when I told him why—there was no surprise or wonder (a lesson for those who think cosmopolitanism is acquired in big cities and universities). He told me about his village; how they made rotis from maize, how fish were to be caught in the mountain streams, and how bears came to steal maize from their fields and pumpkins from the roof of their house.

On Pari Tibba, I walked among the abandoned buildings, many struck by lightning. I saw no ghosts or witches, but one day I saw a bear. I was sitting in an oak tree, just to see if I was still as agile as I used to be as a boy, when I heard a whining grumble, and a small bear ambled into the clearing beneath the tree. He was little more than a cub, not threatening in the least, and I sat very still, waiting to see what he would do.

The young bear put his nose to the ground and sniffed his way along, until he came to an anthill. And here he began huffing and puffing, blowing rapidly in and out of his nostrils, and the dust from the anthill flew in all directions. But the anthill was a ruin, too, deserted by the ants long ago! And so, grumbling and whining, the bear made his way up a nearby plum tree and soon he was perched high in the branches. He had only just made himself comfortable, when he noticed me in the neighbouring tree.

The bear at once scrambled several feet higher up his tree and lay flat on a branch. It wasn't a very big branch, so there was a lot of bear showing on either side. He tucked his head behind another branch, and as he couldn't see me, he seemed to be satisfied that he was hidden. But like all young ones, he was full of curiosity. So, slowly, inch by inch, his black snout appeared over the edge of the branch, and as soon as he saw me, he drew his head back and hid his face.

He did this several times. I waited until he wasn't looking, then moved slowly some way down my tree. When the bear looked over again, and saw that I was missing, he slowly stretched across to another branch and helped himself to a plum, and whined in pleasure. At that, I couldn't help bursting into laughter, and the startled bear tumbled out of the plum tree, landed with a thump on a pile of dried leaves on the ground, and fled from the clearing, grunting and squealing. He looked determined to complain to his mother, so I quickly clambered down the oak tree and hurried downhill (someone had told me bears find it difficult to run downhill).

I was whistling and smiling when I reached my study, and I sat down and wrote a story about bears. The next day, I wrote a second story, and began an essay. Words came easily, and I was singing Nelson Eddy and Eartha Kitt songs and making myself mugs of tea and coffee.

How to mend a broken heart and get past the dreaded writer's block? Find a young bear in a plum tree.

AN END AND A BEGINNING

BY MY MID-THIRTIES, I WAS LOSING MY OLD RESTLESSNESS, and writing regularly, although there was little money. English-language publishers in India were only interested in textbooks, and newspapers and magazines didn't pay very much. In order to survive, I had to produce as many stories, essays and middles as possible, so I kept banging away at my sturdy old typewriter.

It might have been a little easier if I'd shifted to Delhi or Bombay or Calcutta. But now the mountains were in my blood. The changing seasons of Mussoorie determined the rhythm of my life and writing. Even in the bitter winter months, I looked out for the white-capped redstart that would perch on the bare branches of the pear tree in the garden and whistle cheerfully at me, giving me the opening lines of a poem. And I looked out for the milkman who came on his old bicycle, his milk-cans crowned with snow, to sell me water adulterated with cow's milk and teach me Garhwali love songs.

I only left the hills to make the occasional trip to Delhi to see my family—mainly my mother, and Ellen. William had left for England around the time that I came to live in Mussoorie, and from England he had emigrated to Canada.

~

In the summer of 1969, I received a letter from my mother. She had been diagnosed with breast cancer. She was fifty-four, and I had never seen her in bed with an illness, and when I went to see her, she dismissed the diagnosis as a nuisance rather than a worry. She looked a little older than her years, but her liveliness was undiminished.

At home, Mr H was trying to take charge of the situation. He didn't expect much support from me, for which I couldn't really blame him. My half-brothers, like my mother, were in denial; and William couldn't afford a trip to India. The only reliable support Mr H had was from Premila, my step-sister—Bibiji's daughter—who was living with him and my mother after an unsuccessful marriage. She had found a job with the YWCA in Delhi and was becoming a sort of anchor for the family.

I returned to Maplewood to lock up the place and come back to Delhi in time for my mother's operation. The doctors had said her left breast would have to be removed if she was to have any chance of survival.

Before leaving Mussoorie, I gathered some old photographs I had kept from the days when Daddy, my mother and I were still together. Perhaps she'd like to have them—it was my small gesture of reconciliation. There was also a faded negative, yellow and spotted with age. It was a picture of my maternal grandparents which my mother had given me long ago but I hadn't bothered to get a print made. I did now, and when I got the photograph and saw Granny's face for the first time in twenty-two years, I was immediately struck by my resemblance to her. I had become a little like her, without realizing it—I led a Spartan life, I lived tidily, and I had grown to like gardens. But I hadn't realized the physical resemblance was so close—the fair hair, the heavy build, the wide forehead. She looked more like me than my mother.

In the photograph, she was seated on her favourite chair, at the top of the veranda steps, and Grandfather was standing behind her in the shadows thrown by a large mango tree which was not in the picture. He was a slim, trim man, with a drooping moustache that was fashionable in the 1920s. By all accounts he had a mischievous sense of humour, although he looked unwell in the picture. He appeared to have been quite swarthy. No wonder he had been so successful in dressing up 'native' style and passing himself off as a street-vendor. My mother had told me stories of his escapades. In his own way, he had been a little wild, his character in strong contrast to my grandmother's forbidding personality and Victorian sense of propriety. So it was him you took after, I said to my mother in my head, and I put the picture and the negative in my suitcase with the others.

I got off the bus in Delhi and went straight to the Lady Hardinge Hospital, where my mother had been admitted the previous day. It was early August and the sweat oozed through my shirt as I sat in the back of a stuffy little taxi taking me through the busy roads leading to Central Delhi.

I found my mother in a small ward, a cool, dark room with a ceiling fan whirring overhead. A nurse was writing something on a chart tied to the side of the bed, and I stood behind her. When she left, my mother saw me, standing there with my small suitcase.

She gave me a wan smile and beckoned me to come nearer. Her cheeks were slightly flushed, possibly due to fever; otherwise she looked her normal self. I found it hard to believe that the operation she would have the following day would only give her, at the most, another year's lease on life.

I sat at the foot of her bed. 'How do you feel?' I asked.

'All right. They say they'll operate in the morning. They've stopped my smoking.'

'Maybe they'll let you have your rum,' I said.

'No. Not until a few days after the operation.'

She sat up and put the pillow behind her to support her back. I produced her parents' photograph and handed it to her.

'The negative was lying with me all these years. I had it printed recently. I thought you'd like to have it.'

'I can't see without my glasses,' she said.

The glasses were lying on the locker near her bed. I handed them to her. She put them on and studied the photograph, and laughed. 'Look at him!'

'You resemble your father,' I said. 'And funnily enough I look like Granny.'

'Your grandmother was always very fond of you.'

'It was hard to tell. She wasn't a soft woman.'

'It was her money that got you to Jersey. The only person who ever left you anything. I'm afraid I've nothing to leave you, either.' She sounded almost apologetic, which didn't suit her.

'You know very well I've never cared about money. Daddy taught me to write. That was inheritance enough.'

'And what did I teach you?'

'I'm not sure…Perhaps you taught me how to enjoy myself now and then!'

She looked pleased at this. 'Yes, I've enjoyed myself between troubles. But your father didn't know how to enjoy himself. That's why we quarrelled so much.'

'He was much older than you. You were different people.'

'You've always blamed me for leaving him, haven't you?'

'I was very small at that time. You left us suddenly. He was sick and he had to look after me. Naturally I blamed you.'

'He wouldn't let me see you. He kept you away from me, did you know that?'

'Because you were going to marry someone else—'

I broke off; we had been over this before. I wasn't there as my father's advocate, and the time for recrimination had passed.

It began to rain outside, and the scent of wet earth came through the open doors, overpowering the odour of medicines and disinfectants. The nurse, a pleasant Malayali woman, came in to inform me that the doctor would soon be on his rounds. I could come again in the evening, or early morning before the operation.

'Come in the evening,' my mother said. 'The others will be here then.'

'I haven't come to see the others.'

'Won't you be staying with them?'

'I don't know. I might.'

'As you like.'

I got up to leave.

'Ruskin,' she said, as I picked up my suitcase. 'Will you look after Ellen?'

'You shouldn't worry about that. I will. You need to think about getting better.'

I promised to see her in the morning, and then I was on the road again, standing on the pavement, on the fringe of a chaotic rush of traffic, with a vague fear—apprehension, more than fear—that I may not see my mother again.

To everyone's relief, the operation was successful, and when she was discharged, I went back to Maplewood. But the cancer returned within a few months. The round of tests began again, and one evening someone from the family phoned a neighbour with a message for me, saying I should come to Delhi. When I phoned back, my half-brother Harold took the call.

'You'd better come, Ruskin,' he said. 'She won't last long.'

She was back in hospital the night I reached the Patel Nagar flat. Harold was with her. Sometime after we'd finished dinner, he called to say that she had died.

We cremated her at Nigambodh Ghat the following morning, and immersed her ashes in the Jamuna.

For better or worse, we are all shaped by our parents. My mother's sensuality, I think, was stronger than her intelligence; in me, sensuality and intelligence have always been at war with each other. And I probably also inherited her unconventional attitude to life, her stubborn insistence on doing things that respectable people did not approve of—traits that she probably got from her father, a convivial character, who mingled with all and shocked not a few. She must have been quite a handful for my poor father, bookish and intellectual, who probably wanted her to be a 'lady'. But this was something that went against her nature.

I like to believe I had mended my relationship with my mother before she died. It wasn't about forgiveness, there was nothing to forgive. If I did not, as a child, receive the same love from her as I did from my father, it was not entirely her fault. As she had married again and was engaged in bringing up my stepbrothers, a clash of interests was only to be expected. A note of resentment creeps in here. I did resent my stepfather, stepbrothers and the whole unwanted step-scene that I had to live with after my father's death. It had also affected my relationship with William, whom I identified with a family that I couldn't relate to. Perhaps that was my failing—after all, if I was living in a kind of no-man's-land, so was he. (William has never returned to India, and we've exchanged a handful of letters in fifty years.)

I had a better connection with Ellen, and now that our mother was no more, I felt responsible for her. I asked Mr H if I should take Ellen with me, but he said he would keep her. The RAF allowance was for her lifetime, and that would allow him to keep an ayah to look after her. He kept his word, and after he died, Premila took over the responsibility of looking after Ellen, and she did it far better than I could have done. Ellen lived to the age of seventy-eight, spending her last years in Ludhiana, where Premila had shifted after her retirement.

My mother had been worried about Ellen when she realized she was dying; it must have been a lifelong worry. But at least she was spared the heartache of burying her sons. Both Harold and Hansel died tragically young some years after her.

It was late Christmas Eve in 1975, when Harold set out from Dehra in his father's car, to try and get to Delhi in time for a party at the Anglo-Indian club. Although he was a good driver, having taken part in car rallies and other tests of speed and endurance, he had become a heavy drinker and he was in no condition to undertake a long and arduous drive late at night. He was alone, and he was killed instantly, or so we were told. Apparently, his car had been caught and crushed between two trucks, which had speedily disappeared into the night.

Harold had been a bit of a tearaway. He was attractive to women, but they had a hard time looking after him. And he wrecked their lives in addition to his own. There were lessons about life and highways that he never learnt.

But perhaps there aren't any lessons to learn. A few months after Harold, my second half-brother Hansel, who had emigrated to Australia, was killed in a motorcycle accident. He was the careful one, who seldom took risks. He was sober, but someone else on the road was not.

~

After my mother died, even the tenuous connection I had with the world beyond Mussoorie was gone.

And then, with the coming of Prem, life changed again, and for the first time in my life I became a family man.

Prem was seventeen or eighteen when I first saw him. I was still in Maplewood, and had finally acquired a cook and helper who would often take off for days without warning, but he wasn't a bad cook and he was an honest man, which was reason enough to put up with him. So when I found this boy—tall, dark, with good teeth and brown, deep-set eyes, dressed smartly in white drill—on the landing outside the kitchen door, looking for a job, I had to refuse.

'I already have someone working for me,' I said.

'Yes, sir. He is my uncle.'

In the hills, back then, everyone was a brother or uncle.

'You want me to dismiss your uncle?' I asked.

'No, sir. But he says you can find a job for me.'

'I'll try. I'll make enquiries and let you know. Have you just come from your village?'

'Yes. Yesterday I walked ten miles to Pauri. There I got a bus.'

'Sit down. Your uncle will make some tea.'

He sat down on the steps, removed his white keds and wriggled his toes. I liked his ease of manner and his easier confidence.

'I need to know something about you, If I'm going to recommend you to people,' I said. 'Do you smoke?'

'No, sir.'

'It is true,' said his uncle, who had joined us on the steps. 'He does not smoke. All my nephews smoke, but this one is a little peculiar, he does not smoke—neither beedi nor hookah.'

'Do you drink?'

'It makes me vomit.'

'Do you take bhang?'

'No, sir.'

'You have no vices. It's unnatural.'

'He is unnatural, sahib,' said his uncle.

'Does he chase girls?'

'They chase him, sahib. So he left the village and came looking for a job.'

The boy grinned, then looked away, began rubbing his feet.

'Your name is?'

'Prem Singh.'

'All right, Prem, I will try to do something for you,'

I did not see him for a couple of weeks. I forgot about finding him a job. But when I met him again, on the road to the bazaar, he told me that he had got a temporary job in the Survey, looking after the surveyor's tents.

'Next week we will be going to Rajasthan,' he said.

'It will be very hot. Have you been in the desert before?'

'No sir.'

'It is not like the hills. And it is far from home.'

'I know. But I have to collect some money in order to get married.'

In his region, there was a bride price, usually of two thousand rupees.

'Do you have to get married so soon?'

'I have only one brother and he's still very young. My mother needs a daughter-in-law to help her in the fields and with the cows.'

I had travelled up to the villages of Garhwal beyond and above Mussoorie, and seen how little the villagers had to live by—the mountains were immense and beautiful, but, as a villager had said to me, 'You can't eat mountains.' No family had more than a few terraced fields, and these were narrow and stony, usually perched on a hill or mountainside, above a stream or river. The villagers grew rice, barley, maize and potatoes—just enough to live on. Even if they produced sufficient quantities for sale, the absence of roads made it difficult to get the produce to the market towns. There was no money to be earned in the villages, and money was needed for clothes, soap, medicines, and recovering the family jewellery from the money-lenders. So the young men left to find work in the plains. The lucky ones got into the army. Others entered domestic service or took jobs in garages, restaurants and hotels, dhabas and wayside teashops. Some of this has changed, but not very much.

In Mussoorie the main attraction was the large number of schools, which employed cooks and bearers. But the schools were full when Prem arrived. He'd been to the recruiting centre at Roorkee, hoping to get into the army; but they'd found a deformity in his right foot, the result of a bone broken when a landslip carried him away one dark monsoon night; he was lucky, he said, that it was only his foot and not his head that had been broken.

He came to the house to inform his uncle about the job and to say goodbye. I thought: another nice person I probably won't see again; another ship passing in the night, the friendly twinkle of its lights soon vanishing in the darkness. I said 'Come again,' held his smile with mine so that I could remember him better, and returned to my study and my typewriter.

Prem disappeared into the vast faceless cities of the plains, and a year slipped by, and then there he was again, thinner and darker and still smiling and still looking for a job. I should have known that hill men don't disappear forever. The spirit-haunted rocks don't let their people wander too far, lest they lose them forever.

I was able to get him a job in a school. The headmaster's wife needed a cook, and Prem assured me he could cook. And he hadn't lied, because the headmaster's wife was delighted with 'the lovely Pahari boy', and he seemed satisfied too, sleeping in their veranda and getting fifty rupees a month, which was a little more than what most other households paid.

But after barely two months 'the lovely Pahari boy' had become 'the insolent Pahari boy', who answered back, was not sufficiently grateful for the 'baksheesh' he was given and laughed so loudly it was an assault on the memsahib's ears.

It was the end of his job. 'I'll have to go home now,' he told me. 'I won't get another job in this area. The Mem will see to that.'

'Stay a few days,' I said.

'I have only enough money with which to get home.'

'Keep it for going home. Your uncle won't mind sharing his food with you.'

His uncle did mind. He did not like the idea of working for his nephew as well; it seemed to him no part of his duties. And he was apprehensive lest Prem might get his job.

So Prem stayed no longer than a week.

After he had returned to his village, it was several months before I saw him again. His uncle told me he had taken a job in Delhi.

And then the uncle gave me notice. He'd found a better-paid job in Dehradun and was anxious to be off. I didn't try to stop him.

For the next six months I lived in the cottage without any help. I did not find this difficult. I was used to living alone. It wasn't service that I needed but companionship. It was very quiet in the cottage; sometimes I imagined I heard Miss Bean pottering about in the garden, but it was usually the old vagrant woman who came to raid the walnut tree and who sometimes grinned at me by way of apology for the theft, but more often didn't seem to notice me. The song of the whistling thrush was still beautiful, but on some days I wished he would speak words, and address them to me. Up the valley, some evenings, came the sound of a flute, but I never saw the flute player.

One November afternoon, having typed the last sentence of a story, I decided to celebrate and took a long walk up the Tehri road. It was a good day for walking, and it was dark by the time I returned to Maplewood. Someone stood waiting for me on the road above the cottage.

'Prem?' I said. 'Why are you sitting out here in the cold? Why didn't you go to the house?'

'I went, sir, but there was a lock on the door. I thought you had gone away.'

'And you were going to stay here, on the road?'

'Only for tonight. I would have gone down to Dehra in the morning.'

'Come, let's go home. I tried to find you. Your uncle told me you were working for someone in Delhi, but he didn't have the address.'

'I've left them now.'

'And your uncle has left me. So will you work for me now?'

'For as long as you wish.'

'For as long as the gods wish.'

We did not go straight home, but returned to the bazaar and took our meal in the Sindhi Sweet Shop; hot puris with chhole, and strong sweet tea.

Then we walked home together in the moonlight.

It was the beginning of a long association, which continues

to this day, as his family has grown, and become mine. Of course there were times when he could be infuriating, stubborn, deliberately pig-headed, sending me little notes of resignation—but I never found it difficult to overlook these little acts of self-indulgence. He had brought much love and laughter into my life, and what more could a lonely man ask for?

Two years after he made Maplewood his home, Prem went to his village near Rudraparayg to get married and returned with his tiny wife, Chandra, who was sixteen then. They took over all the household duties, leaving me to concentrate on my writing. And I was doing a fair amount of writing during those Maplewood years—producing stories and essays for anyone who would publish me.

In 1973, Prem became a father. It was a cold, wet and windy March evening when Prem came back from the village with his wife and first-born child, then barely four months old. In those days they had to walk to the house from the bus stand; it was a half-hour walk in the late winter rain, and the baby was all wrapped up when they entered the front room. Finally, I got a glimpse of him, and he of me, and it was friendship at first sight. Little Rakesh (as he was to be called) grabbed my nose and held on, and I played with his little dimpled chin until he smiled.

Little Rakesh is now in his forties, and I am in my eighties—'Da', or grandfather, to him and his wife Beena; to his three children—Siddharth, Shrishti and Gautam; to his brother Mukesh and sister Dolly, and to *their* children!

But those Maplewood years don't seem that distant. Time, in the hills, moves at its own sweet pace, the seasons follow each other in a reassuringly predictable manner, the walnuts and horse-chestnuts ripen and fall; we ripen too, in our own way, and get a little older and not much wiser, blundering along but surviving somehow.

While Rakesh was still only a few months old I would carry him around the steep paths above the cottage, much to the amusement of the teachers and others who lived in the area. When he was old enough to manage the paths on his own, he would hold my hand and accompany me up to the 'big bend' of the motor road, to watch the cars and buses coming up from Dehradun. He helped me in the garden, planting fruit trees and waiting patiently for them to come up. So that we could take him further afield, we bought a pram (the first time I owned any sort of vehicle), and one day we set out on the Tehri road, then still a stony path suitable only for mules. After two hours of trundling along, we reached the village of Suakholi, where we subsided on to a grassy knoll, the pram and I greatly in need of rest and repair. It was almost dark by the time we got home. After that, our excursions were limited to less remote destinations, and I would let Prem do all the pushing.

~

Somewhere around this time I was approached by the editor-owner of a magazine called *Imprint*, published from Bombay, who asked me if I'd be interested in joining his editorial staff. I had been writing for *Imprint* for a year or two, publishing some of my longer stories in it; stories such as 'Panther's Moon' and 'A Flight of Pigeons'. R.V. Pandit, *Imprint*'s owner, liked my work and wrote to me, offering me a job either in Hong Kong with *The Asia Magazine* (of which he was a part owner) or with *Imprint* in Bombay. I had no intention of leaving Mussoorie (which would have meant abandoning Prem and his growing family, and a lifestyle to which I had grown accustomed), so I turned down the job offer but agreed to write for both magazines on a regular basis. A compromise of sorts was reached when Pandit agreed to my being his managing editor, getting people to write for the magazine and putting it together every month; I could do this from Mussoorie, visiting Bombay just three or four times in the year.

This arrangement worked quite well. The first time I met Pandit he was recovering from a heart attack which he had suffered on a flight from Hong Kong to Bombay. I had come to Bombay to finalize our arrangement, and I found him in bed, recovering in the flat of his friend and business partner, Nusli Wadia of Bombay Dyeing, a grandson of Muhammad Ali Jinnah, the founder of Pakistan.

I spent an hour at Pandit's bedside, nodding sagely at all his instructions, which were many. He was an unusual man, Goan by birth and Catholic by religion, who had 'converted' to Hinduism and had become a staunch nationalist and supporter of the Bharatiya Jan Sangh, the precursor of the Bharatiya Janata Party. He was out of favour with Prime Minister Indira Gandhi, having attacked her policies and style of functioning in a number of hard-hitting editorials. However, my apolitical attitude seemed to suit him, and although we met only occasionally during the next two or three years, we got on quite well. I was told that this was unusual. Not many people got on with Pandit.

He was to be an absentee editor-publisher, because when Indira Gandhi declared Emergency in 1975, Pandit very wisely stationed himself in Hong Kong, otherwise he would surely have been arrested along with the hundreds of scribes and political opponents of the regime who were effectively silenced for a couple of years. So while Pandit cooled his heels in Hong Kong, I ran the magazine for him, my editorials concentrating largely on environmental issues!

Even so, I was to find myself under arrest, although for very different reasons.

I was in our small garden, playing with two-year-old Rakesh and his baby brother Suresh, when an unfamiliar policeman turned up at the gate; unfamiliar, in that he was dressed a little differently from the local Uttar Pradesh police. He carried with him a non-bailable warrant for my arrest; the warrant described me as an editor of *Time* magazine, and an absconder wanted on an obscenity charge, the said 'obscenity' having been committed by my writing and publishing an obscene short story in a Bombay magazine.

I had indeed published a story called 'The Sensualist' in *Debonair*, a risqué magazine edited by Vinod Mehta, who was trying to enliven it with some literary inputs to counter the semi-nude full-page blow-ups of local beauties. 'The Sensualist' was a mildly erotic story about a recluse who reminisces about his misspent youth; but it was no *Lady Chatterley's Lover*. Anyway, I had no option but to accompany the friendly policeman to the Mussoorie police station, while Prem went scurrying off to find someone to come to the aid of the 'wanted' author. Professors Ganesh Saili (a good friend and drinking and travelling partner) and Sudhakar Misra readily did so, and with the help of a local lawyer, Mr Jain, and a friendly station house officer, the warrant was changed into a bailable offence after I had undertaken to appear in a Bombay court the following month.

When invited to Bombay by R.V. Pandit, I had been put up at the Taj. Now I was on my own, and the Taj was well beyond my means. Instead I found sanctuary in the YMCA on Wodehouse Road, and stayed there for over a week, consulting with *Debonair's* lawyers, owners and editors, and appearing in court on the given date.

The case dragged on for two years, but I was given exemption from all but two appearances before the judge—a stern and somewhat irritable old gentleman who was, nevertheless, fair and impartial in his dealings. The complaint had been made by a local legislator, so the police had no option but to pursue the matter; but the prosecution did not appear to be very enthusiastic, and after several hearings I was given an honourable acquittal. Only two writers had appeared on my behalf—Nissim Ezekiel, the poet, and Vijay Tendulkar, the Marathi playwright. Khushwant Singh, then the editor of *The Illustrated Weekly*, declined to do so, although he had known me from my Delhi days; possibly because he did not hit it off with the *Debonair* people.

Pandit always felt that the case had been brought against me as an indirect way of getting at him, and he may have been right. I shall never know. The Emergency also ended about the time the case wound up.

~

It was always good to return to Maplewood after these trips to Bombay, and I was more than ever determined not to move to that fine city. On this last trip, freed from the spectre of spending time in a Bombay jail, I was in a happy state of mind as I took the path down through the oaks and maples to the little cottage. The petunias Miss Bean had planted still flourished on the cottage steps, and we had taken good care of them; and the lightning-scarred maple tree was still being visited by woodpeckers, finches and bulbuls. Prem was putting a mattress out in the sun; Chandra was sweeping the landing with a broom of twigs; Rakesh and Suresh were asleep in a corner of the small garden. I was home.

But all was not well at home. Little Suresh was seriously ill, suffering from high fever and frequent convulsions. The set of his jaw and the rigidity of his limbs made me think of tetanus; but the doctors at the Community Hospital pooh-poohed the idea and sent us home with a course of antibiotics. There was no improvement. We sent for a local physician who diagnosed meningitis. We then took Suresh to the Civil Hospital, where they said it was tetanus. I had been right in the first place. But it was too late to do much for little Suresh, who passed away after much suffering. It is terrible to see a little child suffer and be unable to do anything to relieve the agony. We were all quite heartbroken. It was almost as though the cottage, the hillside, had turned against us.

And even the hillside was being ravaged. The powers that be had decided to build a highway past the cottage, to link up the road to Tehri and the upcoming dam there. Soon trees were being felled, and rocks blasted by dynamite. Stones clattered down on the roof. Birds and small creatures fled. Oaks, maples and walnut trees came crashing down. Miss Bean's flower-beds disappeared, as the road was being taken right through the property.

We fled too—up the hill, to a flat just below the Mall Road. It was all we could find at the time.

~

Pandit was urging me to come to Bombay, and after we'd lost Suresh to inadequate health care, I was almost tempted to go. But there was no accommodation in Bombay for all of us. And much as I enjoy the sea breeze, I was unwilling to give up the deodars. Pandit, now back from exile (Mrs Gandhi having been voted out of power), wanted an editor who could be seen as well as heard or read. This seemed natural enough. We parted amicably.

Follow the dictates of the heart—that had always been my way. It had often left me in some financial loss or difficulty, but I had overcome this by spending more time at the typewriter, and to my typewriter I now returned, full-time again.

There was now no regular income, just the odd cheque from a magazine or newspaper. Ismat Chughtai, the famous Urdu writer whom I had never met, must have been informed by a migrating bird or the wind about a fellow writer in distress up in the mountains, for she recommended my 1857 story, 'A Flight of Pigeons', to the film director Shyam Benegal. He liked it too, and decided to make a movie of it (which he called *Junoon*). He and Shashi Kapoor, who produced and acted in the movie, gave me ten thousand rupees for the film rights.

This did not go very far, even in 1978, and by the time the film was released, I was an indigent writer again. Financial security would come to me only in the late 1990s—when I was in my sixties—about a decade after international publishers like Penguin had set up shop in the country and discovered that I was still alive and writing; and after Indian publishers like Rupa and Ratna Sagar had come into their own.

Before Indian book publishers found me, I was commissioned by a couple of institutions to write books for them. The only one I can now remember is a biography of Jawaharlal Nehru for children, and the reason I remember it is because I enjoyed researching Nehru's life, and meeting the charming Padmaja Naidu on several occasions.

The idea was Karan Singh's, and as he knew me, and thought well of my writing, he recommended my name to the Nehru Memorial Fund. Padmaja Naidu, daughter of Sarojini Naidu, was the chairman of the Nehru Memorial Fund, and it was she who commissioned me. She was a very friendly, pleasant lady, in her mid seventies then and living on the Teen Murti estate, where I would meet her for tea. At that time I had only published two or three books—many stories, but only a few books. *Grandfather's Private Zoo* had just been published by India Book House and I gave her a copy, which she liked very much. She was a child at heart—and I had never really grown up! I think our mutual fondness had a lot to do with that.

Indira Gandhi had been shown the manuscript of the biography, and she said there were some episodes and people from Nehru's life which could be added, so I asked for an appointment with her. I met her for about half an hour in her office; she was sitting behind an oval table, dressed in a cotton sari and looking smaller than I'd thought she would be. She told me mainly about her father's family life—their trips to Kashmir and Mussoorie, his love of nature, and how much he liked to walk, especially in the hills

At the end of the interview, I asked, 'Do you really have caviar for breakfast?' There was a rumour going around that she did.

She laughed and said, 'No, I don't. But when I was in Russia recently, they used to give me caviar for breakfast. So people now probably think I have caviar for breakfast every day! I can't get it, actually. It isn't available.'

She was quite relaxed and shook my hand when I left. It had been quite a pleasant interaction; you wouldn't have guessed she was the prime minister who had imposed a state of emergency in the country, and politicians and journalists were being arrested even as we spoke.

A SAGA OF OLD TIN ROOFS

As I write, hail-stones are rattling on the old tin roof of Ivy Cottage. The roof and the old stone walls have been through hundreds of hail-storms, snow-storms, monsoon downpours, gale-force winds, and hot summer sunshine. I like the sunshine most of all—but best after a shower, when the earth gives out a scent of its own, dusty leaves and grass are washed clean, and the cloud shapes keep changing, so that the light from my window arrives on my writing-pad in various shades—bright marigold yellow to pale nasturtium and balsam tints. The raindrops settle on the window panes, and the sun striking through them converts them into beads of bright topaz, effervescent jewels meant only for a few moments of reverie.

We came to this old building in the autumn of 1980, after some wandering about in search of a suitable home. The flat near the Mall, where we moved after leaving Maplewood, was too public. The house we moved to next, on the summit of Landour—Prospect Point—was a good 1,000 feet higher. The views were magnificent—a chain of Himalayan peaks etched against a sharp blue sky. At night the heavens brimmed with stars, and the Valley below with the twinkling lights of Dehra.

And here, at the top of the mountain, I acquired (for the second time in my life) something like writer's block. Maybe it was too pretty up there, too relaxing; and those Himalayan peaks made one feel rather inadequate.

There was certainly no incentive to write, though there was enough reason to. The family was growing. Rakesh had started going to school, Mukesh, his new infant brother, was a few months old. Money was in short supply and royalties practically non-existent. Our landlord was a rapacious old man who kept thinking up new ways of extracting money from us. And the neighbours were not exactly friendly. These consisted mostly of Australian or European hippies, most of them on drugs; they had taken the place of the more sedate American missionaries who had once proliferated in Landour. There were also a few Brown Sahibs, retired brigadiers, air-marshals and their memsahibs, who looked on us with some disapproval. What was a bachelor-writer doing, living with a Pahari family who would normally be working as domestics for the high and mighty on the hillside?

There was only one walk, around the 'chakkar', encircling the higher reaches of the mountain. The view was splendid, provided the weather was clear. On misty monsoon days all you could see were crosses rising from a gloomy old cemetery. No one seemed interested in rising from the dead.

At one time the area had been a convalescent station for sick and weary British soldiers stationed in India and Burma, but even before Independence the British had stopped using it for this purpose. In the 1950s the Indian government had taken over the hospital and other buildings for 'the defence institute of study work', and the area had been revived a little.

There were a number of residences, most of them old houses, but they were at some distance from each other, separated by clumps of oak or stands of deodar. After sundown, flying-foxes swooped across the roads, and the nightjar set up its 'tonk-tonk' chant, and leopards circled the houses with dogs—one night, walking home, I saw a mother leopard jump over a parapet, with two cubs scurrying after her.

We shared a large building with several other tenants, one of whom, a French girl in her thirties, was learning to play the sitar and played it badly. She and her tabla-playing boyfriend would sleep by day, but practice all through the night, making sleep impossible for our household. Even a raging forest fire, which forced everyone else to evacuate the building for a night, did not keep her from her sitar. Mercifully, her stay there was brief. The hippies who came and went, sometimes laughing through the night, high on marijuana, were far less trouble; many of them were gentle people.

The friends I had were all a thousand feet below Prospect

Point—Bill Aitken, the Maharani of Jind, Ganesh Saili and his wife Abha (who once shepherded me home after I'd had a few bhang pakoras at a party!), and Nandu Jauhar, who owned the iconic Savoy Hotel. The Savoy, where ancient bearers and sundry ghosts outnumbered the guests, became my favourite watering hole for some years.

But most of my time was spent with the family. Early morning, I would accompany Rakesh down to the little convent school, St Clare's, at the end of Landour Bazaar, about two miles distant. I would take a light breakfast before setting out; but by the time I returned, struggling up that steep mountain, I was ready for a second breakfast. Despite all the walking, I began to put on weight, and I haven't stopped since.

On the way to school, Rakesh would often ask me to tell him a story, preferably one about animals. So I made up a man-eating leopard, and every day it would snap up and devour one of the residents of Landour, much to Rakesh's amusement and my own satisfaction. Brigadiers, naval commanders, the odd missionary, and our greedy old landlord, all fell victim to the marauding leopard. Finally, when we left Prospect Point, the leopard had to die, presumably of acute indigestion.

~

Our fortunes changed when we moved into Ivy Cottage. In spite of rumours that the ground floor had once been used as the morgue of a local hospital, the building brought no ill-luck. On the contrary, I found myself writing regularly again, and stories, essays, poems and novellas rained down upon my desk.

It may have had something to do with the little room.

A 'real' writer should be able to write anywhere—on board a ship, in a moving train, in a prison cell, in a hospital bed, in a five-star hotel room, or in a dingy attic—and I have written a few things in several of these places; but over a period of time, it helps to have a permanent abode, a familiar room, and above all, a window from which to look out upon the world. It gives me the sky, clouds of every description, mountain ranges, several roads, red tin roofs in masses of green trees, and a garbage dump as a reality check. I have no garden outside the window, and no walnut and maple trees, but the window-sill affords just enough space to grow geraniums in old tins and small plastic buckets.

I have lived and worked and loved and grown old in this room over thirty-six years, and I now wear it like an old suit, a little frayed but still comfortable.

The house has more rooms now, and has been repaired and reinforced piecemeal, but in the early days, the walls were weak and the windows rattled, and on one occasion the roof blew away.

Built at the very edge of a spur by missionaries in the late nineteenth century, the house had received the brunt of wind and rain that swept across the hills from the east. We'd lived on the top floor of the building for over ten years without any untoward happening. It had even taken the shock of an earthquake without sustaining any major damage.

The roof consisted of corrugated tin sheets, the ceiling, of wooden boards—the traditional hill-station roof. It had held fast in many a storm, but one night the wind was stronger than we'd ever known it. It was cyclonic in its intensity, and it came rushing at us with a high-pitched eerie wail. The old roof groaned and protested at the unrelieved pressure. It took this battering for several hours while the rain lashed against the windows, and the lights kept coming and going.

There was no question of sleeping, but we remained in bed for warmth and comfort. The fire had long since gone out, the chimney stack having collapsed, bringing down a shower of sooty rain water.

After about four hours of buffeting, the roof could take it no longer. My bedroom faces east, so my portion of the roof was the first to go. The wind got under it and kept pushing, until, with a ripping, groaning sound, the metal sheets shifted from their moorings, some of them dropping with claps like thunder onto the road below.

So that's it, I thought, nothing worse can happen. As long as the ceiling stays on, I'm not getting out of my bed. We'll pick up the roof in the morning.

Icy water cascading down on my face made me change my mind in a hurry. Leaping from my bed, I found that much of the ceiling had gone too. Water was pouring onto my open typewriter—my trusty companion for almost thirty years!—and onto the bedside radio, bedcovers, and clothes cupboard.

Picking up my precious typewriter and abandoning the rest, I stumbled into the front sitting-room (cum library), only to find that a similar situation had developed there. Water was pouring through the wooden slats, raining down on the bookshelves.

By now I had been joined by the children—Rakesh, Mukesh and Dolly (born the year we moved into Ivy Cottage). They had come to rescue me; their section of the roof hadn't gone as yet. Their parents were struggling to close a window that had burst open, letting in lashings of wind and rain.

'Save the books!' shouted Dolly, and that became our rallying cry for the next hour or two.

I have open shelves, vulnerable to borrowers as well as to floods. Dolly and her brothers picked up armfuls of books and carried them into their room. But the floor was now awash all over the apartment, so the books had to be piled on the beds. Dolly was helping me gather up some of my manuscripts when a large field rat leapt onto the desk in front of her. Dolly squealed and ran for the door.

'It's all right,' said Mukesh, whose love of animals extends even to field rats. 'He's only sheltering from the storm.'

Big brother Rakesh whistled for our mongrel, Toby, but Toby wasn't interested in rats just then. He had taken shelter in the kitchen, the only dry spot in the house.

At this point, two rooms were practically roofless, and the sky was frequently lighted up for us by flashes of lightning. There were fireworks inside too, as water sputtered and crackled along a damaged electric wire. Then the lights went out altogether, which in some ways made the house a safer place.

Prem, always at his best in an emergency, had already located and lit two kerosene lamps; so we continued to transfer books, papers, and clothes to the children's room.

We noticed that the water on the floor was beginning to subside a little.

'Where is it going?' asked Dolly, for we could see no outlet.

'Through the floor,' said Mukesh. 'Down to the rooms below.'

He was right, too. Cries of consternation from our neighbours told us that they were now having their share of the flood.

Our feet were freezing because there hadn't been time to put on enough protective footwear, and in any case, shoes and slippers were awash. Tables and chairs were also piled high with books. I hadn't realized the considerable size of my library until that night.

The available beds were pushed into the driest corner of the children's room and there, huddled in blankets and quilts, we spent the remaining hours of the night, while the storm continued to threaten further mayhem.

But then the wind fell, and it began to snow. Through the door to the sitting-room I could see snowflakes drifting through the gaps in the ceiling, settling on picture frames, statuettes and miscellaneous ornaments. Mundane things like a glue-bottle and a plastic doll took on a certain beauty when covered with soft snow. The clock on the wall had stopped and with its covering of snow reminded me of a painting by Salvador Dali.

Most of us dozed off.

I sensed that the direction of the wind had changed, and that it was now blowing from the west; it was making a rushing sound in the trees rather than in what remained of our roof. The clouds were scurrying away.

When the dawn broke, we found the window-panes encrusted with snow and icicles. Then the rising sun struck through the gaps in the ceiling and turned everything to gold. Snow crystals glinted like diamonds on the empty bookshelves. I crept into my abandoned bedroom to find the philodendron in the corner by the bed looking like a Christmas tree.

Prem went out to find a carpenter and a tin-smith, while the rest of us started putting things in the sun to dry them out. And by evening, we'd put much of the roof on again. Vacant houses are impossible to find in Mussoorie, so there was no question of moving.

But it was a much improved roof after that, and we looked forward to approaching storms with some confidence. And now, as I give the final touches to this autobiography, Rakesh and his wife Beena are having the roof raised and reinforced, so another generation can live here, safe from storms and ill winds of every description.

In 2002, as my financial condition had improved somewhat, I was finally persuaded by my family, and Ram Chander, our landlord, to buy Ivy Cottage. Fortunately, it only cost a couple of lakh of rupees, and for the first time in my life I became the owner of a piece of property.

~

I became old and found myself in demand. People started recognizing me and asking for my autograph (sometimes on books written by Mark Twain, Mark Tully and Rudyard Kipling). I suppose if you keep at something for fifty or sixty years, you will have produced so much material—pictures or cuckoo clocks or monkey-caps or books—that people will begin to take notice. Perseverance does pay. Men who work steadily for money get rich; men and women who work day and night for fame or power reach their goal. And those who work for deeper, more artistic or spiritual achievements will find them too. What we seek may come to us when we no longer have any use for it, but if we have been willing it long enough, it will come!

I have never desired fame, and I have never wanted to be the lone, loud man on the summit. I no longer scorn money, but wealth doesn't interest me very much once my needs and the needs of those who depend on me have been met. I'm happiest just putting pen to paper—writing about a dandelion flowering on a patch of wasteland, and a stunted deaf and mute child I fell in love with; writing about the joys and sorrows and strivings of ordinary folk, and the ridiculous situations in which we sometimes find ourselves. I'm lucky that many readers, both children and adults, have enjoyed what I've written.

Some of them come up to Mussoorie to see me. They expect to find a recluse living in a cottage full of eccentric birds and animals and surrounded by trees, and they are surprised by this little flat right at the edge of the road. Sometimes they find a grumpy old man in pyjamas whose sleep has been interrupted; more often someone from the family will meet them at the door to explain why a family needs privacy and a writer needs time alone to write.

Not everyone is easily dissuaded, especially people who come with manuscripts they want me to read—they don't want a frank assessment; they want an endorsement and a letter of recommendation to my publishers. I remember this very persistent lady who wouldn't go away even when I told her I had the 'flu, of a very contagious variety.

'I have to talk to you,' she said, standing at the door, one foot inside. 'I've written a novel. I think it's better than Arundhati Roy's but I don't have her connections and publishers won't see me. I want you to read it and write a foreword.'

'Well, why don't you leave the manuscript with me and I'll write you a letter when I've read it,' I said.

'I haven't finished it yet, I want to tell you the story.'

'That might take a long time, and I'm expecting an important phone call. Why not come back when the book is finished?' And I encouraged her down the stairs.

'You are very rude, Ruskin Bond,' she said. 'You did not even ask me in. I'll report you to Khushwant Singh. He's a friend of mine. He'll put you in his column.'

'If Khushwant Singh is your friend,' I said, 'why are you bothering with me? He knows all the big publishers and he's very famous. Ask him for a foreword.'

She went off in a huff, and fortunately I never saw her again. And I never got into Khushwant Singh's column.

Oddly enough, some of the most frequent visitors to my humble flat are honeymooners. Why, I don't know, but they always ask for my 'blessings', even though I am hardly an advertisement for marital bliss, and have never written a steamy novel that might prove useful in their fertile season. Maybe they are under the impression that I've been a celibate man, and the blessings of sexually innocent adults are believed to be potent.

It is seldom that these honeymooners happen to be readers or book-lovers; and they are too much in love to make interesting conversation. I should really send them to more suitable elders, or at least to someone who goes to places of worship. However, since the young couples are attractive, and full of high hopes for their future and the future of mankind, I'm happy to talk to them and wish them well. And if it's a blessing they want, I bless them—my hands are far from being saintly, but at least they are well-intentioned.

Even Bollywood has come calling. Vishal Bhardwaj made a film based on one of my stories, 'Susanna's Seven Husbands' (the film is called *Saat Khoon Maaf*), and gave me a small role in it. I played a padre and was required to exchange a few pleasantries with the beautiful Priyanka Chopra and give her a fatherly peck on the cheek. But I must have been very bad, because I was never offered another role!

My friend Shubhadarshini Singh, however, has a high opinion of my acting skills, and keeps threatening to put me in her television productions. She produced a very nice TV series of my Rusty stories—called *Ek tha Rusty*—which was shown on Doordarshan in the mid-1990s and got my books some attention. She and her director had put together an excellent cast, bringing in the old-timers Nadira, Zohra Sehgal, Pearl Padamsee and Begum Para. Most of the episodes were shot in Mussoorie, and they were all staying at the Savoy Hotel, where I would meet them. Begum Para was lively and flamboyant even at that age, and you could see what had made her a star. She was the glamour girl of Bombay back in the 1940s and '50s, and I remember seeing her pictures in the papers when I was a boy. *Life* magazine had published a photo feature on her, which had made her popular with American GIs in Korea.

My experience with Begum Para was less heady, limited to mutton curry. She loved cooking and displaced the hotel chef to cook us a meal. But she was defeated by the hardy Mussoorie goat, which resisted all her endeavours to turn it into an edible rogan josh. She gave up some two hours later, and we chomped our way through stringy meat.

~

If you live in one place for a long time, the years slip by almost unnoticed, the seasons bring much the same, and the trees and houses on the hillside appear practically unchanged.

Of course children grow up, and middle-aged authors become ageing authors. Today, Rakesh, Mukesh and Dolly are all married, with children. Dolly lives in Punjab with her husband's family, and Mukesh and his wife and children live with Prem and Chandra in a second house half a kilometre below Ivy Cottage.

Rakesh and Beena, and their three children, live with me and take good care to see that I wash and shave and bathe and change my pyjamas regularly. The papers, manuscripts and correspondence pile up on my desk, but I manage to handle most of it, and my literary production is on a par with what it used to be forty or fifty years ago. But I have abandoned the old typewriter and gone back to writing by hand. I write books and letters by hand, and in the age of email and mobile phones, I send postcards. I'm a very backward person, stubbornly refusing to use a computer or cell-phone. New tricks don't suit an old fox.

Fifty years in the hills has made a great change from all those comings and goings during my boyhood and youth. It's good to be in one place for a certain length of time, in order to savour the passing seasons, the changes in the foliage of the hillside, the comings and goings of people, and above all, to watch the children grow up.

I haven't tired of the two windows in my room. The view hasn't changed, but the cloud patterns are never the same, the birdsong varies, so does the blue dome of the sky, which at night is like a tent of deep purple spangled all over. Some nights are dark, lit up only by fireflies. Other nights are bright with the full moon coming up over the crest of the mountain and sending a moonbeam in at my window, over my bed and then across my desk to light up the face of the Laughing Buddha who sits there. He seems more amused than ever in the light of the moon; laughing tolerantly at the foibles of the human race and mine in particular. But he encourages me to blunder on, and to keep writing, building up a store of stories and sketches and random tales.

I'm like a shopkeeper hoarding bags full of grain, only, I hoard words. There are still people who buy words, and I hope I can keep bringing a little sunshine and pleasure into their lives to the end of my days.

EPILOGUE: A SON OF INDIA

LAST YEAR RAKESH AND BEENA ACCOMPANIED ME TO Bhubaneshwar, and from there we went on to Konarak and Puri. In Puri they visited the Jaganath temple. I was not allowed inside. So I sat in the car for almost three hours, reading a fascinating book on Oriya history by J.P. Das.

At Konarak I was told I was a 'foreigner' and had to pay the extra entry fee. Standing behind me was a Sikh gentleman with a British passport, who was allowed in as an 'Indian'. Rakesh and Beena protested, saying I was as Indian as the banyan tree outside, but the gatekeeper was not convinced. 'Nothing to fuss about,' I said, and I paid the foreigners' enhanced fee.

The Sikh gentleman asked me where I'd been born and I told him Kasauli, which at the time was part of the Sikh State of Patiala, later amalgamated with East Punjab and now Himachal Pradesh.

'And where were you born?' I asked.

'Birmingham,' he said.

~

Being Indian, and feeling Indian, has little to do with one's place of birth or one's religion. While I was still at school I wasn't particularly conscious of being anything in particular. It was only after I had left India, in 1951, at the age of seventeen, that I realized that I was Indian to the core and could be nothing else.

It wasn't family that brought me back, it was the country, the land itself, and all that lived and grew upon it. It is India that has made me. I have loved it, and for the most part, it has loved me back.

And in a small flat on a small hill in the vastness of India, I'm writing the last lines of my autobiography. In the still of the afternoon, the deodars stand like sentinels on the northern slopes of Landour. It is late April and the oaks and horse-chestnuts are in new leaf. There is a certain tenderness in the air, and in today's world that is something to be valued.

EPILOGUE: A SON OF INDIA

Rakesh and Beena sit beside me on the parapet. Friend and publisher Ravi hovers protectively over us. Gautam, Rakesh's youngest, is busy with a camera, pretending to be Raghu Rai or Cartier-Bresson. His elder brother Siddharth is in Bombay, working with a film costume designer; his sister Shrishti is in Bhubaneshwar, at KIIT University. Friends and familiars come and go, the earth still revolves around the sun, the world is once again in crisis, but the cricket chirping on my window-sill sounds optimistic about it all.

The lone fox still dances occasionally, but at eighty-three he is not as agile as he used to be. 'When you are old and grey and full of sleep', it is good to have someone to lean on from time to time, and in that respect this agnostic has been blessed by the gods. I still value my solitude, but it is also nice to have someone tucking me into bed at night.

As for my writing life, it is a running stream, for there is no limit to the field of my remembrance. Even as this book comes to an end, I am conscious of not having written about important people, important events; but it is a personal history, and it is the 'unimportant' people who have made my life worthwhile, as an individual and as a writer.

And both as individual and writer, I have known my limitations, and I think I have done my best with the talents I possess. Sometimes it is good to fail; to lose what you most desire; to come second. And the future is too unpredictable for anxiety.

This is the evening of a long and fairly fulfilling life. And it is late evening in Landour. A misty, apricot light suffuses the horizon. Down in the villages the apricots are ripening. A small boy brought me the fresh fruit this morning—still very sour, very tangy, but full of promise. And if apricots could take precedence over missiles, the world would be full of promise too.

I'm afraid science and politics have let us down.

But the cricket still sings on the window-sill.